CW00971320

The Words and Music of Dolly Parton

The Words and Music of Dolly Parton

Getting to Know Country's "Iron Butterfly"

Nancy Cardwell

James E. Perone, Series Editor

 PRAEGER

AN IMPRINT OF ABC-CLIO, LLC
Santa Barbara, California • Denver, Colorado • Oxford, England

Copyright 2011 by Nancy Cardwell

All rights reserved. No part of this publication may be reproduced, stored in a retrieval system, or transmitted, in any form or by any means, electronic, mechanical, photocopying, recording, or otherwise, except for the inclusion of brief quotations in a review, without prior permission in writing from the publisher.

Library of Congress Cataloging-in-Publication Data

Cardwell, Nancy, 1958–
    The words and music of Dolly Parton : getting to know country's "Iron Butterfly" / Nancy Cardwell.
        p. cm. — (Praeger singer-songwriter collection)
    Includes bibliographical references and index.
    ISBN 978-0-313-37803-4 (hardcopy : alk. paper) —
ISBN 978-0-313-37804-1 (ebook)
    1. Parton, Dolly.   2. Singers—United States—Biography.   3. Country musicians—United States—Biography.   I. Title.
    ML420.P28C39 2011
    782.421642092—dc22   2011011133
    [B]

ISBN: 978-0-313-37803-4
EISBN: 978-0-313-37804-1

15 14 13 12 11   1 2 3 4 5

This book is also available on the World Wide Web as an eBook.
Visit www.abc-clio.com for details.

Praeger
An Imprint of ABC-CLIO, LLC

ABC-CLIO, LLC
130 Cremona Drive, P.O. Box 1911
Santa Barbara, California 93116-1911

This book is printed on acid-free paper ∞

Manufactured in the United States of America

Dedicated to the memory of my little sister, Susan Cardwell Houlihan (1960–1990), who admired Dolly Parton's music and also had a bit of her over-the-top blonde glamour, spirited sense of fun, and steely perseverance. And to Erin Faith, Molly, Kate, Haley, and Jane, who have a bit of that same spark, too.
(It must come from Grandma!)

A percentage of the author's proceeds from this book will be donated to Dolly Parton's Imagination Library and the Foundation for Bluegrass Music's "Bluegrass in the Schools Program," in memory of Marvin Allen Cardwell, my father. Dad is the one who taught me the magic of words, and also how to play music. He used to read us bedtime stories like "Ali Baba and the Forty Thieves" and *Gulliver's Travels,* and he could recite long poems like "Casey at the Bat" that he had memorized as a schoolboy. I think Dad would be pleased to have his name associated with programs that help teach kids to read and enjoy good books, and also introduce them to the joy of bluegrass music.

For more info, please go to www.imaginationlibrary.org and www.bluegrassfoundation.org

"And the night shall be filled with music, and the cares that infest the day
Shall fold their tents like the Arabs, and as silently steal away."
—from "The Day Is Done," by Henry Wadsworth Longfellow (one of Dad's favorites)

Contents

A photo essay follows page 87

Series Foreword

Although the term *singer-songwriter* might most frequently be associated with a cadre of musicians of the early 1970s such as Paul Simon, James Taylor, Carly Simon, Joni Mitchell, Cat Stevens, and Carole King, the Praeger Singer-Songwriter Collection defines singer-songwriters more broadly, both in terms of style and time period. The series includes volumes on musicians who have been active from approximately the 1960s through the present. Musicians who write and record in folk, rock, soul, hip-hop, country, and various hybrids of these styles are represented. Therefore, some of the early 1970s introspective singer-songwriters named here will be included, but not exclusively.

What do the individuals included in this series have in common? Some have never collaborated as writers, whereas others have, but all have written and recorded commercially successful and/or historically important music and lyrics at some point in their careers.

The authors who contribute to the series also exhibit diversity. Some are scholars who are trained primarily as musicians, whereas others have such areas of specialization as American studies, history, sociology, popular culture studies, literature, and rhetoric. The authors share a high level of scholarship, accessibility in their writing, and a true insight into the work of the artists they study. The authors are also focused on the output of their subjects and how it relates to their subject's biography and the society around them; however, biography in and of itself is not a major focus of the books in this series.

Given the diversity of the musicians who are the subject of books in this series, and given the diversity of viewpoint of the authors, volumes in the series differ from book to book. All, however, are organized chronologically

around the compositions and recorded performances of their subjects. All of
the books in the series should also serve as listeners' guides to the music of
their subjects, making them companions to the artists' recorded output.

—James E. Perone
Series Editor

Acknowledgments

THANKS to my darling diamond daughter, the brilliant and talented Erin Faith Erdos; my musical genius brother, Ray Cardwell (and Lynda, Andy, Haley, and Jane); my mom and stepfather, Wanda and Frank Mashburn; Greg, Helen, Molly, and Kate Houlihan; Craig and Cynthia and families; the folks who generously agreed to be interviewed for this book; Les Leverett, Dan Loftin, and Becky Johnson for the great photos; Tom T. and Dixie Hall, Hazel Smith, and Ed Morris for the kind words; John Rumble, Michael Gray, Michael McCall, and Jay Orr at the Country Music Hall of Fame and Museum; my editor, Dan Harmon; my coworkers at the International Bluegrass Music Association; my friends at the International Bluegrass Music Museum; my third-grade teacher, Miss Walker, who taught our entire class to write poetry; Mr. Tommy Hall, the best seventh-grade grammar and composition teacher at Cherokee Junior High; Ms. Sarah Alice Liggett, who taught me English grammar by teaching me Spanish grammar; Dr. John Mercer, for encouragement and the great Shakespeare class at Southwest Baptist University; Pete Kuykendall, for publishing the first college class article I wrote in *Bluegrass Unlimited* magazine—and for all the support through the years since then; Wayne and Deb Bledsoe, for the voice they gave me at *Bluegrass Now*; the alumni of Leadership Bluegrass and Leadership Music; the members of IBMA for giving me a bluegrass day job; Terry Smith, The Grascals, and the entire Smith clan; The Persimmon Sisters; The Coventry Carolers; Midnight Flight; Homegrown; Mountain Aire, The Wildwood Girls; the kind souls in Nashville who hire me to play the bass fiddle with them occasionally; my former students and Girl Scout friends; C. S. Lewis, J.R.R. Tolkien, Laurie R. King, and Mitch Jayne, who keep me reading and inspired; Nancy Drew; Ed

Morris, for passing my name along; my Sunday School "Women at the Well" friends at The Donelson Fellowship; Temple Baptist Church; Ronald McDonald Houses (St. Louis, Springfield, and Nashville); to my family and friends who have put up with me researching and writing nights and weekends and lunch hours the past year or so (including familia Cardwell, Erdos, Phillips, Houlihan, Barese, Saalborn, Sandstrom, James, Fairchild, Snyder, Justus, Webster, and Jacobsmeyer); to God for the most awesome gifts of music and words . . . and of course, to Ms. Dolly Rebecca Parton!

—Nancy Cardwell

Introduction

Strikingly beautiful with a mind-boggling figure, sparkling wit, and the brain of one of the most savvy entertainment business professionals around, Dolly Parton has always had a mystique centering on her unique voice, combined with a natural ability to write great songs—scores of them, in fact—in a variety of styles branching off from her (platinum blonde) country music roots. Those who know Dolly well will tell you: What you see is what you get. Her warm personality; quick wit; and disarming, sometimes flirtatious sense of humor are the same onstage and off. She's confident about her talent but self-deprecating in manner—the kind of celebrity whom fans think of as a friend because she's just so real.

After a career that has spanned more than four decades and more than an estimated 3,000 original songs, Parton has found success in nearly every direction she has set her eyes and mind upon: country music, pop music, movies, television, bluegrass, and Celtic-edged folk music—which she calls "blue mountain music" in reference to her Smoky Mountain home in east Tennessee. She's a brilliant songwriter, music publisher, and producer, with 26 gold and platinum records and 113 charting singles (including 25 number 1 songs) to her credit. She founded an international charity that helps children to read by giving them a book every month through the age of five. She owns a theme park empire in conjunction with the Herschend family in Branson, Missouri—including most notably Dollywood, in Pigeon Forge, Tennessee, and also the Dixie Stampede chain, which presents live music and spectacular horsemanship with fried chicken on the side to thousands of tourists every year. In recent years she's written the music for a touring Broadway show based on the *9 to 5* movie she starred in back in 1980; she received an honorary doctorate from the University of Tennessee (that's "Dr. Dolly" to you, now); and she also wrote and published *I Am a Rainbow,* a children's book that gently preaches tolerance and patience as we recognize the colorful moods we all find ourselves in at times.

Standing five feet tall (without her spike heels), Dolly was given an appropriate name. Her almost childlike speaking voice is disarmingly cute. But pound for pound and inch for inch—even considering the generous bustline she's so famous for and has joked about endlessly—there are few human beings on the planet so full of creativity, hope, talent, perseverance, and generosity. Dolly Parton lives life with that rare combination of confidence (a confidence that's necessary to dream big dreams) and the determination necessary to make her dreams happen, come hell or high water.

THE CHAPTERS

This book will focus on the gift Parton has said she treasures most: her work as a songwriter. After a look at her east Tennessee beginnings as a songwriter and performer, we'll examine the music she recorded first under the influence of Monument Records' Fred Foster and then for RCA, produced by the late Porter Wagoner. Parton's gift for characterization in songwriting will be examined, along with religious, spiritual, and patriotic beliefs woven into the tapestry of her original music. We'll follow the years of stylistic experimentation as Parton's music led her to Hollywood and crossover pop radio success. On a personal level Dolly is loyal to a fault, and her music has also taken a turn toward home in recent years with acoustic-based, bluegrass-tinged albums. Her current forays into writing for Broadway, penning children's books, and delving further into philanthropic projects will be discussed, along with a close look at the "Dolly-ized" brand of country music she is currently writing and recording.

THE MUSIC

In the world of country music writers and singers, it can be argued that there are few, if any, who have had a more profound influence than Dolly Parton. The work she did with Porter Wagoner while she was still in her 20s defined duet singing for the genre. But there's more to Dolly Parton than country music. Lyrically, there is no other writer of any genre who does a better job of portraying the human condition through simple, yet compelling lyrics and melodies. The characters and stories in her songs—which range from romance to tragedy, from deeply spiritual to inspired exaltations of the natural world—are unparalleled. And from her perspective as a woman, we see every shade of emotion experienced in every imaginable predicament a girl can find herself in. Men who want to understand women better (as well as the human heart) would do well to study the lyrics of Dolly Parton. It's all there.

The Criticism

The purpose of this book is to provide an honest analysis of Parton's music and writing through a close examination of the lyrics and music she's recorded to date in a very long, prolific career. This analytical work is supplemented with input from Parton's friends and business associates, and since Dolly Parton charms pretty much everyone she comes in contact with, there is more praise than condemnation in the course of this book.

That being said, Dolly Parton has the kind of voice that a listener either loves or hates. As with most singers, her singing has acquired more depth and improved over the years. (Listen to Alison Krauss at 14 on her first Rounder record, compared to what she is doing now, for a similar example.) Some say Parton's sentimental songs are corny and just a bit much. Dolly revels in her sad songs, wringing every drop of emotion out of them. Songs about poor, dying children and the like are tragic, but then again, so is everyday life. Missouri philosopher Jane Stone once said that it's amazing the world can keep turning, for sadness. Parton's songs—some of them admittedly maudlin, simple, and even corny—reflect the pathos of real life: the thrill and excitement of new love, the heartbreak of a failed love affair, the death of a loved one, the tender hearts of children, the exquisite natural beauty in Creation, the overwhelming love of God, the laughter found in unexpected places. Parton doesn't shy away from any of life when looking for song topics. It's all there, from the ridiculous to the sublime and everything in between.

Some criticize Parton for her artificial and exaggerated physical appearance. But the plain truth, according to anyone who knows her, is that the songwriter's heart under the surface is absolutely authentic and real. Parton herself has admitted from the beginning that she uses her appearance to draw attention to herself, and then proceeds to blow her audience away with her talent and heart and witty sense of humor. It's worked. Plus, who has the right to tell any woman how she should dress or wear her hair—or wig, as the case may be? It's certainly not a criticism heard nearly as often when it comes to men in the entertainment world.

Another criticism that sometimes comes up about Parton's career is that she's scattered. The woman must wake up with 20 new ideas every morning! Not content to be pigeonholed, Dolly has let her imagination and fearless attitude lead her from country music records to retail stores; theme parks; a charity designed to help the children of the world learn to read; Barbie-style action figures; pink rocking chairs; Broadway scores; and, most recently, a movie with Queen Latifah! But then again, it's hard to criticize a bird because it sings, a fish because it swims, or a wild horse because it runs. Dolly is just being Dolly.

On one of her award-winning album covers, *Bubbling Over* (photographed by Les Leverett *before* the age of computer graphics, mind you), Dolly Parton's giggling image is superimposed over a bubbling water fountain. This design is probably the closest any photographer has come to capturing Parton's boundless imagination—the essence of who she really is. Ideas pour out of her like a fountain or a mountain stream, and she is driven to share as many of them as possible with the world. It's her calling. Like the proverbial spaghetti on the wall, some ideas stick and some fall. But the creative thrill is in having the dreams and working to make them come true. Whether they eventually fly or not is secondary.

Dolly Parton was not available for an interview for this book, but in some ways that's probably a good thing. She's one of those stars who have been interviewed so often over the years, the quotes tend to repeat themselves. She enjoys the mystique she's created with her image, and sometimes she appears to make up things on the spot during interviews. Thanks to dozens of books and articles and sets of liner notes and good libraries and the Internet, plenty of her comments are available from past interviews. Besides, the real focus of this book is getting to know Parton through the words of her songs. She has said herself that this is the best way to get acquainted with her.

THE SCOPE

Because of the sheer volume of Dolly Parton–penned songs that are out there now (and she has no intention to stop any time soon), it's impossible to fathom the complete depth of her original music. Consider the chapters here as a guide—but a necessarily limited one—of Dolly Parton, the songwriter, with a focus on a few of the songs and albums that this writer thinks are among the most important and impressive. If you were piecing the quilt you might choose different squares and patterns, and I encourage you to do so! It's a big quilt.

If we were standing in front of the glass case at the Dolly Parton candy store, these are a few of the truffles and confections I'd pick out for you to sample. But you definitely should come back and check out the rest of the menu.

DOLLY DATA[1]

- 25 number 1 country singles (55 top 10 country hits)
- 8 top 40 pop hits
- 26 gold and platinum record awards
- 8 Grammy Awards (and 45 nominations), including a Grammy Lifetime Achievement Award in 2011
- 11 Country Music Association Awards
- 9 Academy of Country Music Awards
- 2 Oscar nominations (Best Song, 1980, 2005)
- 5 Golden Globe nominations (Best Actress, 1981, 1983; Best Song, 1981, 2005; Best New Film Star, 1981)

- 1 Emmy nomination (Best Supporting Actress, Variety or Music Program, 1978)
- 1 Tony nomination (Best Score, 2009)
- Member: Country Music Hall of Fame, National Academy of Popular Music/Songwriters Hall of Fame, Grand Ole Opry
- Kennedy Center Honors, National Medal of Arts and U.S. Library of Congress Living Legend Award recipient
- 77 records on the country album charts (1967–2010), 43 pop (1968–2009)
- 42 top 10 country albums (more than any other artist)
- 113 chart singles (79 country only, 1967–2008; 29 country and pop and/or adult contemporary, 1971–2006; 2 pop only, 1965–1997, 3 adult contemporary only, 1988–2005)
- Composer of thousands of songs (estimated 3,000–5,000) recorded by dozens of artists
- Number 1 female country artist of all time as ranked by *Billboard* for albums chart and singles chart performance
- Number 4 "Greatest Woman in Country Music" as ranked by CMT
- Number 34 "Greatest Woman in Rock and Roll" as ranked by VH1
- More than 100 million records sold
- Her own theme park, Dollywood (http://www.dollywood.com/)
- Her Imagination Library distributes more than 6.5 million free books per year to children across the United States, Canada, and United Kingdom (http://www.imaginationlibrary.com/)

My Tennessee Mountain Home

Albums and singles in this chapter: *Dolly Parton and Friends at Gold-band*, "Puppy Love," "Girl Left Alone," "It's Sure Gonna Hurt" b/w "The Love You Gave," "Gonna Hurry (as Slow as I Can)," "Happy, Happy Birthday Baby" b/w "Old Enough to Know Better (Too Young to Resist)," *Hello, I'm Dolly*, "The Company You Keep," "Dumb Blonde," "Something Fishy," "Put It Off until Tomorrow (You've Hurt Me Enough Today)"

YOU CAN TAKE THE GIRL OUT OF EAST TENNESSEE, BUT YOU CAN'T TAKE EAST TENNESSEE OUT OF THE GIRL

It's been said that where you're from has a lot to do with who you are. This is certainly the case with Dolly Parton, who grew up in the shadow of the towering Smoky Mountains of east Tennessee near Sevierville—the setting for many of her early songs, and a place she still occasionally returns to today, to write songs.

There's a Flatt & Scruggs standard called "Little Cabin Home on the Hill," and country music fans sometimes joke about a whole subgenre of "cabin songs." Dolly Rebecca Parton is one artist who comes by her country roots honestly because she actually *was* born in a little cabin home on the hill—on a farm near Locust Ridge, Tennessee. When Dolly Rebecca Parton, the 4th of 12 children born to Avie Lee and Robert Lee Parton, was born on

January 19, 1946, her delivery was paid for with a sack of cornmeal given to the local doctor, Robert F. Thomas.

Avie Lee Parton was a singer and played the guitar, and her whole family was musical—including Dolly's maternal grandmother, known as "the prayingest, singinest, shoutingest resident of Tater Ridge, Tennessee";[1] an aunt who wrote songs; and a string of uncles who played musical instruments. Her grandfather Reverend Jake Owens, portrayed in "Daddy Was an Old-Time Preacher Man," a song Parton wrote with her Aunt Dorothy Jo Hope, was a fiddler and songwriter. In fact, his song "Singing His Praise" was recorded by the Queen of Country Music, Kitty Wells.

Dolly rejoiced in the beauty of her natural surroundings as a child, as she recalls in her song "Tennessee Mountain Home," where "life [was] peaceful as a baby's sigh." Robert Parton worked as a farmer and construction worker and times were hard for the family, but the children felt loved and secure. "If there's one thing positive about being poor," Dolly noted in her autobiography, *My Life and Other Unfinished Business*, "it's that it makes a person more creative."[2]

In an interactive video exhibit titled "The Songwriter's Craft" at The Country Music Hall of Fame and Museum in Nashville, Tennessee, an interviewer asks Parton about the "mixed meaning" in songs like "In the Good Ole Days (When Times Were Bad)."

"I write a lot of songs like [that one]; I have mixed emotions about those times," Parton says. "I wouldn't take nothin' for it. One of my favorite lines is, 'No amount of money could buy from me the memories that I have of them, but no amount of money could pay me to go back and live through it again.' I meant that with all my heart. The only thing I regret about being poor—of my childhood—was seeing Mom and Daddy suffer, for them to be without, to see them work like that . . . to see my Daddy's hands break open and bleed. And I've seen Mama lay in suffering, for need of a doctor we couldn't afford. I wouldn't take nothin' for it. It made me into a person who can feel for other people and appreciate other people, [a person who could] appreciate the value of a dollar and everything else. I want to treasure that. I *do*, but I wouldn't want to have to live that way again."[3]

Dolly was singing before she could talk, and she made up clever songs that rhymed perfectly before she could write them down herself. Her first song, written before she was old enough to go to school (perhaps around three), was written about "Tasseltop," a homemade corncob doll her father had made for her. "There were 12 kids and no store-bought toys," Parton recalls. "She had tassels for her hair—they were corn silk—and Mama dressed her up in a shuck dress. 'Little, tiny Tasseltop, I love you an awful lot. Corn silk hair and big brown eyes; how you make me smile!'"[4]

At five the precocious child penned a surprisingly serious and mature song titled "Life Doesn't Mean That Much to Me," and Avie Lee kept tucking her daughter's lyrics into an old trunk.

"I've always been a writer," Parton says. "My songs are the door to every dream I've ever had and every success I've ever achieved."[5]

At nearly every concert to date, Parton dedicates her favorite original song "to all the good mamas out there"—the "Coat of Many Colors," based on a true story that took place when she was in elementary school. "Of all the songs I have written, the 'Coat of Many Colors' is my favorite because it's more about an attitude, a philosophy of life," Parton explains. "It talks about your parents and your family, and the things they try to teach you. We was as poor as anybody could be, but Mama still had time to try to tell me a story from the Bible and give me some sort of pride, to wear a ragged little coat made out of scraps. I'm sure she knew I'd get laughed at, at school. She wanted to give me something; she read me the story of Joseph and his coat of many colors. I never sing that song, that I don't see my whole life pass before me as a child . . . see my Mama and Daddy . . . see my Mama sewing . . . see Daddy out working . . . see them loving us, trying to teach us all they could with nothing but their love to give us, really. It just matters a whole lot to me, so that's why 'The Coat' will always be my favorite."[6]

Dolly was a nine-year-old student at the Caton's Chapel School, a two-room schoolhouse heated by a potbellied stove, when the "Coat of Many Colors" incident happened. Her mother pieced scraps of material together to make her a corduroy coat to wear on the day they were to take student pictures. Dolly identified with Joseph and his coat of many colors in the Bible story, and she dashed off excitedly to school. Children can be cruel, and Dolly's classmates were no exception. They ridiculed her homemade coat made of mismatched colors, and when her photograph was taken she was smiling through tears. She later told Chet Flippo of *Rolling Stone* magazine the rest of the story.

The other children taunted Dolly and accused her of not wearing a blouse under the jacket. With the number of children and the lack of resources in her family at the time, she was doing well to have one layer of clothing. Embarrassed, she lied and said she *did* have a blouse on underneath. The children pulled at her coat and broke some buttons, and then they shoved her in a closet and held the door closed. The frightened girl dissolved into a screaming frenzy, terrified of the darkness. When she got home and told her mother what happened, Avie Parton said, "I wouldn't worry about it. They're only looking with their eyes, and you're looking with your heart."[7]

In an interview with Alanna Nash, the author of the critically acclaimed *Dolly, The Biography*, Parton's former teacher, T. A. Robertson at the Mountain View School in Locust Ridge, remembered his former pupil. Dolly wasn't a show-off and she wasn't exceptionally loud, but she did things that made her stand out in Robertson's memory. Once she took the red crayons out of her box and smeared them on her cheeks and lips, like makeup. Robertson recalled the unique quality of Parton's voice and that she had a gift for singing, obvious even at that early age. "Her mother told me her tonsils bealed [swelled] and bursted and affected her voice," he said. "I don't know if that had anything to do with it, but she was a good singer. . . . Every time you wanted a group to sing, she was ready."[8]

When Dolly was 7, her uncle Bill Owens taught her some guitar chords, which she took to like a fish to a crystal-clear Smoky Mountain stream. She recalls writing a song to go with each new chord she learned to play. When Parton was 10, Owens took his talented niece to Knoxville to meet local radio and television celebrity Cas Walker. Backed by her uncle on the electric guitar, Dolly became a regular on *The Cas Walker Farm and Home Hour*, starting out at $20 a week. "I sang on the television before my family ever owned one," Parton quipped in 1956.[9]

After eight years Parton was making $30 a night and $25 a night for tour dates. Cas Walker said the young Parton was "as independent as a hog on ice. She stood her ground and didn't let nobody push her around. . . . She'll stand up like a bantam, if she has to." Walker thought better of the comments he wanted to make about Parton's short skirts because he didn't want to antagonize her, but he credited Parton's success in country music to her "independent ways" and "unusual voice"—both of which were evident in the young schoolgirl who starred on his television show.[10]

In 1960 Dolly rode the bus with her Grandma Rena down to her uncle Henry Owens's studio in Lake Charles, Louisiana, to cut her first 45 record. Parton sang "Puppy Love," which she had cowritten with her uncle Bill Owens, and another original, "Girl Left Alone." The record, released on the Goldband label, got quite a bit of local airplay.

HER FIRST RECORDINGS

On the cover of *Dolly Parton and Friends at Goldband* is an autographed publicity photo of Parton at age 13, sporting short, wavy, light-colored hair in the black-and-white picture. She has a friendly, amused look in her eyes, and the trademark wide grin and dimples are there, making her scrappy personality pop off the cardboard album cover. She's wearing a conservative striped blouse with a little pointed collar and a wristwatch with a thin black band. She has small hands and she looks tiny for her age, although there's something in her expression that is rather grown-up and connects directly through the photograph, as if she were looking straight at the viewer. Dolly at 13 doesn't look one speck shy, at an age when most girls are at their most insecure and awkward. She already seems comfortable in her chosen world of music and confident that she will go places.

In the liner notes Goldband Records' Eddie Shuler talks about the "nature and character" of Dolly Parton, as well as her singing talent. "She never forgets a friendship or a kindly deed," he writes. "Here at Goldband, we thought it fitting to compile this album of songs of Dolly and others who have strived and achieved through the doors of our little down home studio. In looking back," he continues, "it seems almost impossible to believe the little girl named Dolly Parton who used to have to sit on the tall stool so the microphone could fit and we could get the fullest capabilities of the song she was recording, that this same Dolly Parton would, in later years, become the great she has in the entertainment field."[11]

"Puppy Love," Dolly's first single on the Goldband label, is a rockabilly ditty, and her clear soprano voice cuts through the layers of electric and acoustic guitars topped with a chorus of harmony singers like a silver dagger through churned butter. "Pu-puppy love, pu-puppy love," she cheerfully croons. "I'm old enough now to kiss and hug, and I like it—it's puppy love!"

On the flip side is "Girl Left Alone," also penned by Parton with her uncle Bill Owens and her aunt Dorothy Jo Owens. The narrator is a desolately lonesome girl who mourns the fact that she no longer has a home. She ominously notes, "I can't tell my story, for whom it would hurt," and she's left alone, without hope. She's made some sort of mistake, and now she's convinced that she must pay for it—for the sake of the ones who still love her. Perhaps she's an unwed mother leaving home to avoid disgracing her family. Maybe the child's father is a married man. She thinks longingly of heaven, where she dreams of being free from sin and happy forever. She is resigned to suffer on earth, but her trembling voice wonders if there's any real hope for her in the hereafter.

PURSUING HER DREAM TO WRITE SONGS AND PERFORM

Even as a teenager, Dolly's goals included being a professional songwriter. In a 2008 interview with Edd Hurt for *American Songwriter* magazine, she said, "I started taking my songwriting very, very, very seriously when I was in high school. . . . I wanted to be a singer, of course, but there was something about the songwriting, then and now, that is the most important thing. It's how I express myself—how I see things. When I see people struggling with emotions and feelings and (they) don't know how to put it down (in words), I'm able to do that. It's really like a therapy, and it's like a buddy and a friend. It's a way out of a lot of things."[12]

In 1959 at the age of 13, Dolly came to Nashville with her equally positive-thinking Uncle Bill. They knocked on doors up and down Music Row, and some old friends from the *Cas Walker Show* in Knoxville, Carl and Pearl Butler, introduced Dolly to the performers backstage at the Grand Ole Opry. Country Cajun star Jimmy C. Newman was sufficiently taken with Parton's initiative and persistence to invite her onstage to sing on his portion of the Opry. Johnny Cash introduced her as the "little girl from up here in east Tennessee," and she proceeded to win three encores from the enthusiastic crowd. (Encores are as rare as hen's teeth at the Grand Ole Opry, where staying on schedule is crucial—at a live radio show divided into 15-minute segments.)

Publisher/musician Buddy Killen signed the engaging young Parton to Tree Publishing, and he set up a studio session for her at Mercury Records at Nashville's historic Bradley Recording Studios. Accompanied by some of the best session players in town, Dolly recorded an original, "It's Sure Gonna Hurt" b/w "The Love You Gave"—the latter written by Marle Jones and Robert Stanley Riley Sr.

Recorded in 1962, "It's Sure Gonna Hurt" features Parton backed by a popular group of studio background vocalists known as the Merry Melody Singers. The song has a "Teenager in Love" vibe with a 1950s "Happy Days"–era chord progression, and Dolly's young, high-pitched voice buoyantly bops along. It's "sure gonna hurt" her to lose the young man described in the song—particularly to some annoying "little flirt." She's painting the town blue tonight, instead of red, and Parton continues: "It may not kill me, but it's sure gonna hurt," to a fade-out.

Dolly Parton possesses a totally unique voice that is difficult to pigeon-hole into a particular genre. At the very beginning of her career producers like Jerry Kennedy, Fred Foster, and Ray Stevens heard her and thought, "Ah, a Brenda Lee–style pop crossover success!" Parton herself preferred to sing stone-cold country music at the time, but her producers weren't entirely wrong, as it turns out. As her career progressed, Dolly would eventually prove that she could sing nearly every type of music.

"Gonna Hurry (as Slow as I Can)" is a demo that came out of the same 1962 sessions at Bradley Recording Studios, previously unreleased until the RCA Nashville/Legacy boxed set in 2009. In addition to this first demo for Fred Foster's Combine Publishing company, Ray Stevens also produced Parton's 1965 singles for Monument, including "Busy Signal," "Don't Drop Out," and "I've Known You All My Life."

Parton's young voice is recorded perfectly here, her soprano vibrato shimmering with emotion. The tone is a bit reminiscent of a young Brenda Lee but at the same time shows the obvious influence Parton's singing has had on later artists like the Grammy Award–winning Alison Krauss, Emmylou Harris, Claire Lynch, Becky Schlegel, Elizabeth Cook, and The Stevens Sisters, among others.

Laden with emotion beyond her years, the young woman narrating this song is having a hard time accepting the end of a relationship. "I'm gonna leave, and I'm gonna hurry just as slow as I can," she promises honestly, playing on the phrase.

The songs didn't generate enough radio airplay and Parton was dropped by Mercury, so she focused on finishing high school and performing on the *Cas Walker Show*. She continued to record songs, she played drums in the high school marching band, and in 1964 Dolly Rebecca Parton was the first person in her family to graduate from high school. Her mother had married when she was in the seventh grade and her father—who Dolly describes as one of the most intelligent men she ever knew—never had the opportunity to learn to read. Parton says this is one of the reasons she started the Imagination Library project years later, beginning in east Tennessee where she could help children from her home area learn to read by simply giving them a book every month until they reached the age of five.

On the Saturday morning after high school graduation Parton excitedly gathered up her clothes, not even taking time to wash them first, and boarded a Greyhound Bus bound for Nashville, where her uncle Bill Owens and his family had already moved. Dolly met her future husband, Carl Dean, her first afternoon in town, outside the Wishy Washy Laundromat. She was so thrilled to be in Nashville, where she planned to make her music dreams come true, she popped her clothes into the washer, grabbed an RC Cola, and started walking down the sidewalk to see what she could see. Naturally friendly, she waved at Dean when he drove by. He circled around, and she waved again. They ended up talking in the laundry for hours and have been an item ever since.

The owner of an asphalt paving business with his father, Dean has been supportive of his wife's dreams since the beginning of their relationship, although he has very little interest in or patience with the glamour associated with her career. Dean's image appears on one of Dolly's early albums (*My Blue Ridge Mountain Boy*), and he once surprised his wife onstage by playing the part of one of her background singers, singing purposefully a bit off-key to get her attention. Carl Dean prefers to stay out of the limelight and enjoys being anonymous enough to walk into a local Nashville hardware store or "meat and three" diner without being recognized by his wife's legion of fans. Married on May 30, 1966, the Deans never had any children, but they did end up practically raising five of Dolly's younger brothers and sisters in their Brentwood, Tennessee, home.

Parton and Bill Owens sang and played on demos in Nashville and worked odd jobs. Dolly appeared on *The Ralph Emery Show* and *The Eddie Hill Show* a number of times, again thanks to a recommendation from Carl and Pearl Butler. Then in 1965 she came to the attention of Fred Foster, founder of Monument Records and Combine Publishing.

FRED FOSTER AND MONUMENT RECORDS: A STAR IS DISCOVERED

In a 2010 interview in Nashville, producer/label head Fred Foster warms up to his memory of meeting Parton for the first time with a little background information. "I had started Monument Records when I lived in Washington, DC. [I got the name for the label because] I used to go out traveling all the time through the week, and when we'd come in we'd bank around, coming over the 14th Street Bridge, and right there was the Washington Monument on the left. Every time I'd see that I'd think, 'Home again. Thank goodness,'" he recalls.

"My first artist was Billy Grammer, and he was on *The Jimmy Dean Show*," Foster continues. "There was a telecast out of Washington for a long time, and then it moved to New York. And when he moved to New York, he left the whole cast behind and hired another band and everything. Billy was the lead guitarist. I'd seen him working nightclubs and things, and he was a communicator. There was a duet on the show called 'The Country Lads—Billy Graves and Dick Flood.' When 'Gotta Travel On,' the first hit by Billy Grammer, became such a huge hit, the kids started doing a dance [to it] called 'The Shag.' A DJ in Baltimore called me and said, 'Man, you ought to do a thing called The Shag.' I said, 'Well, I never write.' So I went over and watched the kids dancing. Then I called Dick Flood and said, 'Let's write a song called "The Shag."' He said 'OK,' so we wrote a song called 'The Shag.' I had intended for him to record it. Now that the TV show was gone, they [Graves and Flood] were thinking about going with their separate careers. But it was a little too edgy for him. He was kind of a crooner. So I called Billy Graves and said, 'Do you want to do 'The Shag'? He said, 'Yeah,' so we did it and it became a hit. Dick Clark booked him on one of his package tours that went everywhere. Billy came off of that tour and he said, 'I'm sorry if you wasted money on me, or if you're making money on me. I'm sorry to cut it off, but man, I can't do it. I hate it. I just can't do this kind of business. I love music, but I can't get out there and do this every night.' So I said, 'Well, OK.'

"Billy moved to Nashville and went to work for Capitol, and Marvin Hughes was head of the office here," Foster said. "Then I moved here not too terribly long after that, in 1960. So one day I get a call from Billy Graves. He said, 'Would you do me a favor?' I said, 'I'm not going to put you back on the label, if that's what you mean,' and he laughed and he said, 'There's a girl singer I want you to hear. Everybody's turned her down here at the label. I don't know why they don't like her, because I think she's great.' I said, 'Does she write?' and he said, 'Yes.' So I said, 'Send her out!' Billy said, 'Her uncle will probably come with her.'

"Bill Owens called me, and we set up an appointment for the next day," Foster recalled. "Now when I'm auditioning someone that writes, I never ask them to sing me one song—because anyone might luck out and fall into one. I said, 'Sing me four songs that you've written, that you consider representative of what you do.' So she did, and I said, 'OK.' She was 18. I said, 'You're looking for a record deal?' And she said, 'Yes, but I don't even know why you even saw me, because everyone in town has turned me down.' I said, 'That's not my problem. If you'll come back tomorrow, I'll have your contract. But I also want you to sign with Combine Music, which is my publishing wing.' And she said, 'OK.' She said, 'But you're serious?' And I said, 'Yeah, I wouldn't tell you to come back otherwise.'"

When Parton and her uncle came back the following day, "I handed her the contracts," Foster said, "and I said, 'Take them to a lawyer. Make sure you understand everything and you agree. If everything is fine, sign them. But I have to ask you a question,' and she said, 'What is it?' I said, 'As different as you are, in the beginning at least half of the people [who hear you] are not going to like you,' and she said, 'Oh.' She said, 'I don't care who doesn't like me, as long as *somebody* likes me—because I'm gonna make it.' So I said, 'Good. Go see your lawyer and we'll get this done.' As she was starting to leave I said, 'You're a very determined young lady,' and she said, 'Yes, I am.' I said, 'I'd hate to be standing between you and something you really wanted.' 'Oh, I'd run over you,' she said. 'But I'd run over you easy, because you're so nice.'

"Ray Stevens was on the label [Monument], and he came to me just screaming and hollering, 'Oh, man, let me produce her.' So I said, 'OK,' and he started producing her pop," Foster said. Parton debuted on the Pop Music Chart October 2, 1965, with a cover of "Happy, Happy Birthday Baby" b/w "Old Enough to Know Better (Too Young to Resist)." The A side was later re-issued as a duet with Willie Nelson on the album *The Winning Hand* (Monument Records, 1982).

"I knew she could do anything," Foster said. "There was no doubt. When I told her that, she said, 'You're the craziest thing I've ever been around. You scare me, you're so crazy.' I said, 'Dolly, there's no limit to you.' [The liner notes I wrote for her album, *Hello, I'm Dolly*] she has framed, hanging in her house in L.A. That's what I predicted. I knew she could do anything she wanted to do—be a movie star or whatever. I compared her to [Jean] Harlow and [Marilyn] Monroe, two other fabulous blondes, and I never doubted her for a second."

Parton drew $50 a week from Combine Publishing in the 1960s, while also working as a receptionist and a waitress. She wrote more than 100 songs during her three years at Foster's publishing house.

"One day she called me and said, 'I need to see you,'" Foster continued. "She came in and said, 'Look, I'm tired of trying to do this pop stuff. I know what I am and who I am.' She said, 'I want you to produce me country, and if you don't want to do that, then let me go.' Well I said, 'I don't want to let you go,' so I listened to all the songs she had, and unfortunately she'd given her best one away, 'Put It Off until Tomorrow.' She was writing, and she had two or three that were real close, but I didn't think [any of them was] the record to introduce her as country. I was just calling around, as I always did do and still do occasionally to see what's new around the publishers. Tree had one called 'Dumb Blonde,' a Curley Putnam song. So he came out and played it for me and I said, 'I love it. Let me play it for Dolly Parton.' And he said, 'Who's that?' And I said, 'You'll see.' So she said, 'Yeah, I like it.' We cut it and it was a hit. And we followed it with 'Something Fishy,' which was a pretty big hit (making it into the Top 20 in 1967).

"Now because we wasted all that time with the pop stuff with Stevens, our contract was ending," Foster said, "so I sent her a new contract and gave her a raise and all sorts of stuff . . . made it more beneficial to her. She called me and said, 'I love it. I'll bring it over in a day or two.' So then Porter (Wagoner) called me and he said, 'If I can get her to come on the TV show, when we go into a major market do you have any promotion people that could meet us?' And he said, 'Could I buy x number of copies (of her records) for promotion?' And I said, 'Sure.' I thought we had it all worked out. He seemed agreeable. I confronted him about this much later, and he just kind of grinned. I said, 'You never intended for her to stay on Monument.' He told her that RCA wouldn't let her do duets with him if she wasn't on RCA, and I asked Chet [Atkins, the head of RCA at the time] about it later, and he said. 'No, I never said that.'"

Porter Wagoner, the country star whose syndicated television show was already being aired in around 100 markets nationwide, had heard Parton on the radio and asked her to come and see him. His enormously popular "girl singer," Pretty Miss Norma Jean, was getting married and planned to move to Oklahoma, and she'd given her notice to Wagoner. After auditioning with an original, "Everything Is Beautiful (in Its Own Way)," Wagoner promptly offered Parton a $60,000 salary to replace Norma Jean and join his television show.

"I was doing a session with Billy Walker, I believe, in my old studio up on 7th Avenue," Foster continues, "and Dolly called me and said she needed to have lunch with me, and I said, 'Fine.' She said Porter was insisting that she be on RCA or they couldn't do duets, and she hated to, but she was going to have to leave. I said, 'I'd sure hate that, because we were just really getting started,' and she said, 'I understand.' That was sort of a blue day for me," Foster said, the sting of disappointment still apparent in his voice 43 years later. "My attorney was in town from New York and he said, 'What's the matter?' I said, 'Dolly is moving over to RCA.' He said, 'What did she say about the contract?' I said, 'She called me and said she loved it and she was going to bring it in, and stay.' He said, 'Well, you've got her. Her intent was to stay, and something has come between her intent and now, and you can hold her.' I said, 'No, I'd rather have her as a friend. She's a great talent, and I know what I'm missing, but no, I'm not going to sue her.' And I didn't, and sure enough we've been friends ever since. She—I think—regretted the move, but I'm just guessing, even though it worked out for her."

Looking back, Foster says there was just something about the teenage Dolly Parton that convinced him she would be a star and literally go as far as she wanted to go.

She was different," Foster states simply. "Look at all the people I signed on Monument. This goes back to when I was a farm boy back in North Carolina, and you may think this is ridiculous. Everybody I ever told it to said I was crazy as a loon," Foster admits, laughing. "We had a 300-acre farm about six miles out of Rutherfordton, North Carolina, the county seat of Rutherford County. About a mile and a quarter from our farm was a service station, up on this hill on Highway 108. Rob Simms was the owner, and he and his wife had 26 children. She was the mother of all of them. He had put in a juke-box, which was one of those Wurlitzers. I could hear it playing, when people would play it and I'd be out working in the fields. I could recognize the song, but I couldn't understand the words except one: Ernest Tubb. I said, 'Now, that's the way to do it! He's so different and unique that whenever he sings, everybody knows immediately who he is.' I said, 'When I get me a record company, that's all the kind of people I'm going to have.' And so if you'll look and see—well, let's think of the bigger ones: Roy Orbison, Willie Nelson, Dolly Parton, Kris Kristofferson, The Gatlins, Ray Stevens, Tony Joe White, people like that. You *instantly* know who they are. Dolly had a unique voice, and Chet denied this for a while, until I confronted him about this one day," Foster said, chuckling at the memory. "When he [Chet Atkins, at RCA] had turned her down, he had told somebody he thought she sounded like a screech owl. Then one day at the golf course I said, 'You *know* you said that.' And he said, 'Well, I might have. I don't remember.'"

Admittedly, Parton does have a sharp edge on her penetrating, quick vibrato-embroidered soprano voice, and it was even more pronounced when she was younger.

"Well, Grandpa Jones was the same thing," Foster said, mentioning another one of his Monument stars. "We had hits with Grandpa. Her writing, though, is the foundation," he says about Parton. "I love songwriters. As a group, they're my favorite people. A songwriter is a dreamer, and I was too."

It's obvious Foster was—and still is—a dreamer, but he's also a songwriter. "Yeah, more or less," he qualifies, "but I don't say much about that in the presence of real writers. I said to Kristofferson when he was getting into the movies and everybody was freaking out, saying, 'Well, there goes his record career.' I said, 'Well, let me find out.' So I went to Kris and said, 'If you were suddenly in a foreign land—like in a jungle somewhere—if your plane crashed and you survived and a native asked you what you did for a living, what would you say?' He said, 'I'd tell him I was a songwriter.' I said, 'Good. Fine. You got it.'"

Despite Parton's young age, Foster (the producer who invented the sound isolation chamber for vocalists by pulling a coat rack between Roy Orbison and the band so the singer could be heard over the instruments one day in the studio), said Dollly was "great" to work with when they were recording. Although Parton has always had production and arrangement ideas of her own, Foster said, "She wasn't hard to work with. I don't remember us ever disagreeing much in the studio. If you pointed out how it could be maybe not exactly her way and it made sense, she said, 'OK.' She was flexible with arrangements. She is a miracle. Four songs she sang me, at first. I'll never forget it," Foster said, shaking his head.

Parton's audition songs for Monument included an original called "The Company You Keep."

"It's where she's talking to a sister or a relative," Foster says. "You're known 'by the company you keep.' One was a novelty song called 'I Will Oil Wells Love You,'" he grins, "and I thought that was the cleverest thing I'd ever heard. It was about finding a rich guy. She was always very, very smart. She has created the Dolly persona, and it works for her—kind of like Diamond Lil or a modern-day Mae West. She created that image. If you ever get serious with Dolly and sit down and talk to her, she's slightly different. She's the salt of the earth. Dolly is a very spiritual girl. I saw her not too terribly long ago, and she's so clever. Rightly or wrongly, I was just inducted into the

Musician's Hall of Fame in October [2009], and she made a video. 'Sorry I can't be there,' she said, 'but it's your own damn fault! You're the one that made me famous. You got me busy.' It was right off the top of her head; it was great.

"She's a great writer," Foster affirms—"not just a good writer, but a *great* writer. 'Coat of Many Colors' is a classic. The first time I heard that (driving in my car), I nearly had a wreck. . . . That was autobiographical. But there's no 'Jolene' in my mind who could take a man away from Dolly," Foster smiles. "If that's so, I'd like to meet her."

Foster and Parton decided together which songs would be on her 1967 album released on Monument Records, *Hello, I'm Dolly*. There were a number of backup musicians. "It would have been Buddy Harman on drums, Ray Eddington on acoustic (guitar), Harold Bradley on electric and acoustic (guitar), probably Hank Garland on electric, and Floyd Cramer on keyboards. And we used a harpsichord on 'Dumb Blond,' and I'm sure that was Floyd," Foster says. "I guess the Anita Kerr's [background singers] were on there, too. It's been so long, I can't really remember. Bob Moore was on bass, and that's basically the band I was using."

Commenting on her career during the past four decades and her influence on country music as a genre, Foster said, "When she went on her own totally and went into the movies, she made country glamorous, so to speak, and took it across a lot of borders it hadn't crossed much. And she wrote and recorded that 'Here You Come Again' that had some elements of country, but had enough elements of other genres that it could cross all the lines—which it did. And '9 to 5,' what a great rhythm she created with that. She's very smart, I told you. Very. She may have been one of the first country singers to show she could be a complete entertainer—the movies, television, and even Broadway. She could be at the Grand Ole Opry, or she could sing for 20,000 at an arena."

After predicting the scope of Parton's career accurately four decades in advance in his liner notes for *Hello, I'm Dolly,* one wonders what Foster thinks she'll do next. "I have no idea, but whatever she decides to do, she will do it successfully," he said. "I don't know that she will continue to be. . . . I'm just guessing, and I don't like to do that. It may be that she'll cut back a little bit on front line entertaining—on touring all the time. But I know she's interested in young people's education. She's got that book thing. I think she'll take that farther. I don't know what she might do next, but I have complete confidence that she'll make the right decision, which she does uncannily well, seems to me."

Foster turned 80 in 2011, but he's not one to rest on his laurels. "I've just finished doing four sides for the [Country Music] Hall of Fame," he says. "The great writer, Cindy Walker, left all her writer royalties to the Hall of Fame when she died, so they wanted to do an album of Cindy's songs with different artists, and they're going to send it to motion pictures and television people and record labels and artists, trying to get some more activity with her songs. They asked me if I would do four sides, Tony Brown did four, and Vince Gill did four. So that's done. I'm also working with a girl who is 20 or 21 years old, a graduate student at Belmont [University]," Foster continues. "Her mother's from Venezuela and her father's deceased—he was an Indiana redneck. She's, of course, bilingual, and I think she's really good. She's a beautiful girl. Her name is Kristina Ellis. I'm starting to work again with Tony Joe White [of "Poke Salad Annie" and "Rainy Night in Georgia" fame] and he's, of course, an incredible artist and writer." Foster describes Ellis's music as "modern, progressive country. We're working toward getting a couple of songs out with Spanish lyrics, too," he adds.[13]

In a ceremony held May 20, 2010, Foster, along with two of his protégés, Kris Kristofferson and Willie Nelson, were honored as the latest recipients of the Leadership Music Dale Franklin Award in Nashville. The award, named for the first executive director of Leadership Music, was created in 2004 to recognize a music industry leader who exemplifies the highest quality of leadership, and leading by example. "Individually and collectively Fred Foster, Kris Kristofferson, and Willie Nelson have been and continue to be iconic leaders in the industry by influencing popular music in countless ways over the past six decades," said Pat Collins, president of the Leadership Bluegrass Board of Directors on August 29, 2010. "Their contributions to the art of music are immeasurable."

PARTON'S FIRST ALBUM: *HELLO, I'M DOLLY*

Parton's first full-length album for the Monument label starts out with her first song to debut on the Country Music Chart (January 21, 1967), "Dumb Blonde," written by Curly Putman. The feel is more country than Dolly's pop singles previously produced by Ray Stevens, but this song still has a bit of a Brenda Lee vibe to it, with the unexpected addition of a harpsichord in the mix. The blonde narrator demands that her two-timing man not try to lie his way out of this situation. "I've found new thread for my old spool," she sings. The color of her tinted hair has nothing to do with the brains underneath the hairspray, and this blonde "ain't nobody's fool." Both "Dumb Blonde" and the Parton-penned "Something Fishy" on this album landed at number 24 and number 17, respectively, on the *Billboard* Country Chart.

"Your Ole Handy Man," written by Parton, challenges the traditional role of women—a gutsy thing to do in 1967. "I have to mow the lawn and I have to wash the car, and I'd like to know just who you think you are!" the narrator rants at her lazy husband. Her man has two hands of his own, but he never lifts a finger to help out with the chores. At this point the missus has had enough and she's ready to fly the coop—no more of being "Your Ole Handy Man." Parton, along with her contemporary Loretta Lynn, blazed the trail for independent-minded women willing to stand up for themselves in country music songs. Although young women in big cities across the United States were burning their bras and aggressively participating in the feminist revolution of the 1960s, the rural, more conservative country music audiences were not out picketing. The ladies did enjoy hearing Loretta and Dolly speak up for them on country radio, though.

In "I Don't Wanna Throw Rice," written by Parton and Bill Owens, the jilted narrator considers violence. Standing by and watching her love marry someone else, she admits, "I don't want to throw rice; I want to throw rocks at her." In a takeoff on the post-wedding tradition of decorating the couple's car with shaving cream and tin cans tied to the bumper, the piqued singer proclaims that she would prefer to plant a few sticks of dynamite in the happy couple's car.

"Put It Off Until Tomorrow (You've Hurt Me Enough Today)" foreshadows the stone country duet style Parton crystallized later with Porter Wagoner. The song, which had been a hit for Bill Phillips in 1966, reaching number 6 on the *Billboard* Country Chart b/w "The Company You Keep," was Parton's first cut as a cowriter with her uncle, and she was also the uncredited harmony singer on Phillips's version. The song, later cut by a number of artists including Loretta Lynn, brought Parton her first country music award from BMI as a songwriter. In this song the narrator is numb with shock after hearing that his love plans to leave, and he begs her to wait one more day . . . to "put it off until tomorrow. You've hurt me enough today." One can assume Parton wrote the song from a woman's perspective, but it's interesting to note that the lyrics work either way.

"I Wasted My Tears" is a Parton/Owens cowrite, and Dolly wrote "Something Fishy" by herself. The latter has a bit of the same spirit Loretta Lynn revealed in songs like "Don't Come Home A-Drinkin' (With Lovin' on Your Mind)"—only with a school of fishing metaphors. It's 10:00 p.m. and the narrator is fuming because her husband's still not at home. She's not so sure she believes his story about going on a fishing trip. Perhaps she's like a sucker (a species of fish) that's swallowing his line. Then she nails him with the memorable comment: "I guess some largemouth bass left that lipstick on your shirt." Her man has not been fishing. He's a two-timing, good-for-nothing flirt.

On the B side of her first full country album, Parton presents "Fuel to the Flame" and "The Giving and the Taking," both cowritten with her uncle, followed by "I'm in No Condition," written solo. In a devastated, weary tone older than her years at the time, she laments the fact that she's simply not in any condition to fall in love again. "The man I love just broke my heart, and it must have time to mend." Parton utilizes the one to seven chord progression early in the song, creating an introspective, lonesome-edged effect that she uses in a number of her later songs. (Hum "Me and Joshua" to hear this pattern.)

As Foster noted previously, in the Parton/Owens song "The Company You Keep" the singer is warning a younger sister or some other family member to guard her reputation. The album ends with another Parton/Owens song, "The Little Things." In the lyrics Dolly is saddened by the little things her love doesn't think of—like remembering her birthday. Her lead vocals are doubled (two unison tracks), and then they split into perfect two-part harmony. It's a combination of little things that matter in a woman's heart—something men would do well to take note of.

Foster took the photos for the *Hello, I'm Dolly* album under a willow tree in his yard in Hendersonville, Tennessee, and Dolly's natural, at this point subdued beauty shines off the LP cover. The platinum blonde Dolly displays a quiet, almost Mona Lisa smile on the front cover. She looks pleasant but gives the impression that she knows exactly what the viewer is up to. Her eyebrows are carefully arched and her hair swoops up and curves down, to about collar length. Her light lipstick matches her coral dress. On the back she's sporting more of a grin. Tiny flowers dot a homemade yellow blouse with a modestly high V-neckline and a tiny golden chain. There's a hopeful, quietly excited, yet assured look on her face.

Foster's prophetic liner notes are duplicated here, with his permission:

Sometimes you just know . . . sometimes. And that makes up for all the times you had to guess. Rightly sometimes; wrongly sometimes. You work the whole hot summer with hot breezes blowin' on your neck and dust flyin' up between your toes, and you never see a drop of rain or think of fall at all. Then a different breeze starts playin' with your neck and the dust don't rise so high from your big toe, and then you know. And then you're glad you kept on walkin' for what's ahead is worth the wait' and the wantin' and the workin' . . . sometimes.

Then there's the mountains of recorded tapes and demonstration acetates. They can make you weary too . . . sometimes. The road that leads to fame is hot and dusty too, and some find the spotlight shines on stages set too high, and microphones hang deaf in studios with no doors. And sometimes it's not worth the waitin' and the waitin' and the workin'. For a Name is nigh impossible to claim . . . sometimes. And you wonder where and why some find the way to try, 'cause some never were and some never are, and sometimes you just know.

It's when you feel a different breeze a-blowin' on your neck and findin' no dust between your toes, that you know you've found One. You feel the whole scene changin' . . . and the people who knew her before you act indifferent sometimes and blasé sometimes, like she isn't important at all, and secretive too, like they really don't want to share what they knew . . . sometimes. And then you really know. All the same things put together made something different this time. For in the shadows playin' 'round her eyes you see the Harlows and Monroes and all the deepening shades of tragedy . . . too much for one young life. And you start to read up on reincarnation and wonder if it is so, and if it is which life's experience inspired this one or that one.

And through it all she remains untouched somehow by all this new around-ness . . . not quite aloof, not quite yielding . . . just observing, just enjoying. And she greets the new members of her legion with, "Hello, I'm Dolly."

On January 19, 1946 Robert and Avie Lee Parton gave the world a babe it would turn to in twenty-one years. Sometimes you just know, don't you?

—Fred Foster[14]

Butterflies and Therapists and Hank Williams

It's appropriate that Dolly's first album photo shoot was outdoors under a willow tree, since she finds so much comfort and joy in the beauty of nature. Parton has said she respects and draws strength from simply being in the presence of creation; in fact, one of her career symbols is the butterfly. "Butterflies are colorful and bright and gentle," Parton says. "They go about their business and bring others pleasure while doing it, because just seeing one flying around makes people happy." Parton's hope is that her music brings the same kind of delight and enjoyment to her listeners. "I'm content with what I am, and butterflies seem to be content to be just what they are, too," she continues. "They're gentle, but determined."[15]

Like a butterfly, Parton too seems to be guided by nature—an inner voice that brings new inspiration and new ideas and guides her timing and choices. Perhaps it's a spiritual thing. Maybe she knows herself so well, it's obvious what she should do next. Perhaps it's both. "I'm a dreamer," Parton says, "but I'm a doer, too. All of my life, there has been this strange thing about me. A thing that I can feel; it's almost as if it's something within me that says, 'Do this and that.'" What observers call her "career" is what Parton feels has already been divinely ordained and revealed to her, step by step. "Even as a very small, young child, I knew when I should walk in a room," she says. "I knew when I should sit. I knew when I should be somewhere when I was wanted; I knew when I was not. I knew the right things to say and do to get out. See, I don't know what it is. That's why I say it's a God-given thing."[16]

In "The Songwriter's Craft" exhibit at the Country Music Hall of Fame and Museum in Nashville, Parton is asked why she is compelled to write songs. "I have to write songs because it's therapy for me," she says. "I think I'd just blow up and bust if I couldn't get it out. Some people go to a doctor, to a friend, to their pastor, and some go to a counselor if they're having trouble in mind. Me, I go to my notebook and my guitar and my tape recorder. It's my way of expressing myself—getting my feelings out, whether it's sorrowful or joyful . . . just a way in the back of my mind, or something I'm working out. I somehow seem to be able to do better with my life, by being able to write it down and get it out and sing it. I feel like it's not just for me. . . . If it can be therapy for someone else—it brings a feeling of self-satisfaction," she adds. If "someone else was feeling the very same way and couldn't [express] it, they'll hear [one of my songs] and I can be their therapist, too."[17]

Parton looks to writers for inspiration who connect with listeners on an emotional level, who live and breathe the dust and sweat and heartbreak of the human condition and are able to communicate that in their music. When asked what songs or songwriters she admires most, Parton says, "Well, I love Hank Williams because I know a lot about Hank Williams and knew what a hard life he had. One of my favorite songs is 'I'm So Lonesome I Could Cry.' When you talk about hearing the lonesome whippoorwill, Lord, I can hear that whippoorwill singing. And when you hear that lonesome whistle blow . . . I can hear that whistle blow. I feel that come right out of his gut and his heart. Songs like that touch me like you wouldn't believe—songs like 'Mama Tried,' by Merle Haggard. I can see his mama. I see how he screwed up his life and how he felt in that song. [He said,] 'Mama *tried* to raise me better. It wasn't Mama's fault.' I can see a boy like that, how he was ashamed that he hurt his mother. I can see his mother. You want to be able to hear and write songs that touch you in that way."[18]

Hello, I'm Dolly! Porter's "Girl Singer" Finds a National Audience

Albums and singles in this chapter: "Mule Skinner Blues," *Porter Wayne and Dolly Rebecca*, "The Answer Is Love," *Bubbling Over, My Blue Ridge Mountain Boy*, "The Last Thing on My Mind," *Just Between You and Me, Once More, Coat of Many Colors, Joshua, My Tennessee Mountain Home, Love and Music, Love Is Like a Butterfly, The Bargain Store, Jolene*, "I Will Always Love You," *Just Because I'm a Woman*

THE PORTER WAGONER YEARS: A TENNESSEE MOUNTAIN ROSE BLOOMS ON NATIONAL TELEVISION

Landing the gig with Porter Wagner on his weekly, nationally syndicated television show brought Dolly Parton to a national audience. In addition to being her employer and duet partner, Porter produced all of her first RCA albums and personally shaped the next stage of her career after Fred Foster. Dolly jokes that she learned a lot about the music business from Porter during these years—both things to do and things not to do. In particular, Parton says she learned as much about entertaining and connecting with an audience from Wagoner as anything music-related.

Porter Wagoner and Dolly Parton had the best duet in country music from 1967 to 1974, and many say they're still unrivaled. "If such a thing as royalty existed in country music, Porter Wagoner and Dolly Parton would be the choice of millions of record buyers for king and queen," Marvin Kaye said in *Show-Biz Spotlight* in 1970. Their musical and physical chemistry lit up black-and-white television screens across America, and the Country Music Association named them Vocal Duo of the Year in 1970, the first year the award was given, and again in 1971.

Their first single as a duo, "The Last Thing on My Mind," went to the top 10 on the *Billboard* Country Chart in 1968, launching a six-year streak of top 10 singles.

"I left Monument with mixed emotions because they had been very good to me," Parton told Kaye. "I was reluctant to leave, but everybody I talked with urged me to make the change." Her first RCA release, *Just Because I'm a Woman*, sold 150,000 copies in the first few months, Kaye reported. "We teamed up because we find that when we sing, we feel things alike on phrasing, the ingredients of a good song, and how they should be sung," Parton said about Wagoner.[1]

In a 1970 interview with Jack Hurst for *The Tennessean*, she noted honestly, "My voice was [always] real different—not that it's good, because a lot of people just cannot STAND to hear me sing. Anybody with a real different voice, a lot of people don't like to hear them sing, but people who do like them usually like them especially well."[2]

Wagoner wisely chose to feature Dolly's original songs on his television show, so one of the first impressions America got of Dolly Parton was that of a prolific songwriter. "When I'm writing, I can be anywhere and anything that I want to be," she told Hurst. "If I'm writing about a dog or a cat or whatever I'm writing about, I am that thing. And I'm the kind of person that even the ugliest duckling is pretty to me, some way or another. . . . All my Mama's people pick some sort of musical instrument, but none of my people had ventured out of the mountains with it," Parton continued. "I was the first one that wanted to. I knew there was something else. I just believed it. I had some talent and a lot of backbone and a lot of gall and a lot of people helping me."[3]

At her first appointment with Wagoner to be interviewed for the job in his band, Porter asked, just in conversation about the music they both liked, if she knew "many hymns." Dolly thought he said "Minnie Hems"—a woman's name, so she said no, she didn't know her.

Because of the romantic nature of some of their duets, fans sometimes wondered if Parton and Wagoner had a personal relationship as well. They were married, they told reporters, but to different people. When asked once about her husband, Carl Dean, Dolly said, "He's not a show person. He's a quiet and home-loving person. If he comes to a show, he likes to go on his own. Most of the time I don't know when he's coming. It's good that way. I want him to do what makes him happy and if he does, he can make me happy. We don't find fault with each other. When you look for fault, it's not hard to find."[4]

BUCK TRENT: WAGONMASTER, BANJO STYLIST, AND INVENTOR

When she joined Porter Wagoner's television show, Dolly Parton also became a member of his band, The Wagonmasters. Buck Trent, the innovative banjo player and inventor who later went on to appear regularly on the *Hee Haw* television show; play Vegas and tour extensively with Roy Clark; and eventually establish his own morning show in Branson, Missouri, vividly remembered Parton joining The Wagonmasters. "I went with Porter's band in '62, and until '74 I was with Porter. Pretty Miss Norma Jean was there then, and I recorded on all of her hit records. Then Pretty Miss Norma Jean left and Jeanie Seeley worked with us for about a year, and then Dolly came along. She was with us about seven years. Boy, I'm telling you. She's one of the most talented people I've ever seen!

"Well, she impressed me right off the bat," Trent continued. "She could sing any kind of song. She could write any kind of song. She could write a song in no time at all. It would just come to her like crazy. We were riding down the road on the bus and she writes 'Coat of Many Colors' in five or ten minutes . . . just riding down the road, and she writes it! And she wrote it on some laundry tags—some cleaning tags that were off of one of Porter's suits. She wrote it, and then she come over to the house, her and her friend, Judy, and I'd just bought a new recorder, and we put down a few songs. 'Coat of Many Colors' was what it was, and she wrote it on the cleaner tags, and she left them, and I saved them. I gave them to Porter, later on, and he framed them and gave them to her. I think she put them in her museum at Dollywood.

"*The Porter Wagoner Show* was number 1 when I left and went with Roy Clark and the *Hee Haw* show in '74," Trent said. "Then Dolly left about six or seven months later. She wanted to do more. . . . She went on *The Johnny Carson Show*, and Johnny Carson loved her. They clicked like that, and he thought the world of her, so he put her on *The Tonight Show* many times, and then she got *9 to 5*, the first movie she ever made, she wrote the theme song to it and it was number 1. What is that?" Trent exclaimed. "That's talent, isn't it?"

Trent said Parton was easy to work with on the set and on the road. "She never had a cross word, for seven years. The reason—and every time I see her, she is just like she was—it's because she don't have 40 or 50 people around her to tell her what they think she wants to hear. She has the one friend with her, Judy [Ogle], and they went to school together. So that way, she's just like she was when I worked with her. And never once was there a cross word with the band, or anything like that. And everybody thought the world of her. She is a very talented lady. She can do anything."

Because Trent's electric banjo sounds like an electric guitar and his gut-string banjo sounds like an acoustic guitar, fans may not realize it's him taking a lot of the solos on Porter and Dolly's early records and radio hits. "I wasn't on 'Dumb Blonde,'" Trent clarified. "She did that on Monument, with Fred Foster. But from then on when she went with Porter, I was on all of them. I played guitar on some of them, and I played the electric gut-string banjo on some. 'I'll Always Love You'—I played that with her, and 'Jolene,' and 'Muleskinner Blues.' We were on the bus one day and Porter said, 'Dolly, you need to write some up-tempo songs, 'cause most of your songs are sad, slow songs like 'Jeanie's Afraid of the Dark' and stuff like that.' Just off the top of my head I said, 'How about Mule Skinner Blues?' She could yodel, you know. So we went in the studio and recorded 'Mule Skinner Blues,' and Porter cracked the whip, I kicked it off on the electric gut-string banjo, and it wasn't her first number 1, but it was close. It really kicked, too. It really does. . . . I could just go on and on with what she has, and the albums she did. 'The Coat of Many Colors'—I was on that, too. And all of the duets with Porter and Dolly."

Parton's cover of the Jimmie Rodgers song popularized by Bill Monroe and his Blue Grass Boys, "Mule Skinner Blues," was her first solo top 10 hit, debuting on *Billboard*'s Country Chart July 4, 1970, and climbing to number 3. She changed the lyrics slightly to fit her "lady muleskinner" perspective, and she was nominated for a Grammy (Best Country Vocal Performance by a Female) for the song.

Along with it being an incredibly creative time, the band was constantly busy, Trent said. "Oh, yeah," he exclaimed, "it was. It was really something. We did 52 shows a year for Black Draft Soltice and the Chattanooga Medicine Company. Then we did 26 open-end shows for shows around the country, and they'd put their own sponsor to it. So we were busy all the time, and Porter and Dolly got a studio, and they recorded their songs. So it was really tough when Dolly left."

Parton had become nearly irreplaceable in Wagoner's show, so obviously it was a shock to him—and their fans—when she decided to leave. "It was really emotional," Trent remembered. "I had already left and went with Roy Clark and the *Hee Haw* show. We opened in Vegas in '74, and then a few months later Dolly left. And she done it, man!" Trent said, admiration showing clearly in his voice. "She built Dollywood, and she's just a very, very intelligent gal. Usually entertainers ain't good businesspeople. Porter was a good businessman. Don Warden [Wagoner's steel player and road manager], he was a good businessman. He [Warden] went with Dolly when she left Porter. Porter said he was going to slow down with his band, and he said, 'Why don't you go with Dolly and handle her business?'"

Wagoner continued to produce Parton's albums initially, after she left his band. "They had a contract," Trent said, "but boy, there's no limit to what she can do. She's a legend in the business. She really is. Every so often we'll get together, and she's just like she was. . . . She really knows, too. When I did Porter's 50th Opry anniversary and I kicked off 'Jolene,' she turned around and said, 'Oh, I can't believe you remember that!'"

A multi-instrumentalist herself, Parton has always been an artist who appreciates good musicians, and she never seems to forget anyone who has helped her. "When she had her ABC network show," Trent said, "it was in California. Well, she came to Nashville and put everybody on her show that had helped her, for a week. Porter—I mean *everybody*—people who had put her on the Opry when she was just getting started and all. She really helps people. She's got the Imagination Library—the book thing for the kids, and she's got the Dixie Stampede. And she's in with Silver Dollar City. She's a great business gal. Most entertainers aren't, but she is. She's tough," Trent credited. "I'm not much of a songwriter," he continued. "I wrote some instrumentals. But Dolly and I wrote a song together, 'The Answer Is Love.' She's just a great human being. She is," Trent emphasized. "I believe you've got to give it away to keep it, and she does. She helps everybody."[5]

Trent, a natural storyteller, recalled more about his days with Porter and Dolly on a self-produced DVD he sells at his shows in Branson: *Buck Trent, Entertaining You for Over 50 Years*. "I learned a lot from Porter," Trent said. "He did this carnival barking thing: 'Hey, come in, come in! See Spinedula the Spider lady! She walks, she talks, she crawls on her belly like a *rep* tile. Come in, come in! See the monkey climb the pole. The higher he climbs, the better you can see his . . . Hold tight, monkey! Two little nickels, one thin dime, ten little pennies! Come in, come in! See little Leekey. He eats chickens. Hey, he just snapped the head off of another one!'

"Porter was always doing this [vaudeville carnival barker routine], going down the road," Trent said. "We stopped at a café and got some chicken to go. Porter took a bite and said, 'Hey boys, I don't think this chicken is done all the way through.' So I turned around and said, 'Snap the head off another one!' Then Porter rolled the window down and threw the whole thing out," Trent laughed.

"The first song I recorded with Porter was a Bill Anderson song called 'I've Enjoyed As Much of This as I Can Stand,'" Trent continued, rattling off the timeline until, "Then *here comes Dolly Parton* from Sevierville, Tennessee, back in the hills," he shouted. "The day she graduated from school she caught the Greyhound bus to Nashville and she said she had matching luggage because the grocery bags she had her clothes in came from the same grocery store. So the show just got bigger and bigger."

At one date with Porter in Wichita, Kansas, Trent said, "Dolly read where [psychic/astrologer] Jean Dixon said the Holiday Inn is gonna fall that night, the night we were staying there! So she was scared, so she sleeps on the bus. So the next morning when we come out of the hotel, we look up. And if the hotel would've fell, it would've fell right on the bus!" he chuckled.

Trent, who invented the electric banjo he plays, tells a story about how once during this same period Grandpa Jones accidentally picked up Trent's banjo case one night backstage at the Grand Ole Opry. Trent was in the studio with Hank Cochran when he realized the mistake, so went back over to the Opry to find Jones—who had already stashed the banjo in the trunk of his car. Jones insisted he had the right instrument, so they went out to his car and opened up the trunk. "He opens up the case and here's all the stuff on my banjo with knobs and pickups," Trent recalls, laughing. "And Grandpa looked at it and said in his most annoyed voice, 'Well, I'll say. It'd take three German scientists and 12 wise men to tune that thing!'"[6]

DOLLY PARTON THROUGH THE LENS OF LES LEVERETT

Les Leverett, the official photographer of the Grand Ole Opry from 1960 until he retired in 1992, is another industry personality who got to know Dolly Parton when she joined Porter Wagoner's band. Leverett's photographs have appeared on numerous album and CD covers as well as in books, magazines, and TV documentaries. His awards include a Grammy for the cover of Porter Wagoner's 1966 album, *Confessions of a Broken Man*, a 1972 *Billboard* magazine award for Best Country Music Album Cover for Dolly Parton's *Bubbling Over*, a "Walkway of Stars" award in 1994, a Distinguished Achievement Award from the International Bluegrass Music Association in 2001, and the Reunion of Professional Entertainers (ROPE) Media Person Award in 2004.

In a December 2009 interview Leverett recalled, "One hot summer they wanted a picture of Dolly, and Chet Atkins and Bob Ferguson, who produced her, had talked about it with Dolly and Porter and decided what they wanted. They said, 'We want a picture of Dolly leaping up in the air with her arms and legs out.' So I thought, 'How are we going to do that?' I came up with the idea of going over to Centennial Park around the Parthenon, around the outer edge over toward Charlotte Avenue, over toward the hospital now. There were some banks on either side of the road, as they went down to the street. I got Dolly to go and stand on that bank, and I got down real low with that camera. . . . I figured that would give us the height we needed. Dolly had on a real tight pink jumpsuit. I don't know what you call it, but it was stretchy material. I made a good number of shots and they were in a hurry, so I carried them down to the *Nashville Tennessean* to get them to rush develop those things. I could have done them in my studio, but it's a strange technical thing between a two-and-a-quarter film and a 35 millimeter, and we don't need to explain that," he smiles patiently. "But I paid them to do it, and I picked them up the next day. Dot [Leverett's wife] brought the car. She brought me out to RCA and we all went into a little conference room where there was a little projector, and there was Porter and Dolly and Bob Ferguson and Dot and I in that room. And they projected those things. I already knew that they would never work because of the simple reason that this stretchy suit took on [the shape of] every anatomical device Dolly had on her body."

Like a dancer's leotard, the pantsuit "tightened up in the wrong places," Leverett said. "Nowadays they can put it on a computer or airbrush it, like they would in the old days, but they didn't want to do that. Oh, they were complaining and I was thinking, 'Oh, I need this money. I need this cover,' because National Life didn't give me enough to live on. We agreed it needed to be reshot. Now, what are we gonna do? The title of the album was *Bubbling Over*, and Dot's thinking of water. She said, 'Why don't you go over to the fountain at the [Country Music] Hall of Fame?' and everyone thought that was a great idea, and it was. I think I called somebody that I knew at CMA and told them we were going to do that because I was afraid that the tourists were going to see this and crowd around. So they said, 'We'll take care of that. We'll get a policeman to keep the crowds out of your way.'

"Sure enough," Leverett continued, "as soon as people saw her, they started gathering. They notified Channel 5 and they sent someone out and filmed it in 16-millimeter color movie film. We horsed around. Dolly decided she needed to dip her toe in the water, so she kicked her shoes off. And I kicked my shoes off and rolled my britches up and waded across the water and held her hand while she did that, which they got on the movie. Anyway, I had to be out in the thing to shoot the shot I had to have. I wound up taking some close-ups and sandwiching [a photo] of that fountain and Dolly and taped them together, to send to New York. Everybody in Nashville liked it, and they liked it in New York. And so help me, *Billboard* magazine came along and gave me the award for Country Cover of the Year for that picture in 1968. That was a lucky thing, right there."

A permanent fixture behind his lens backstage at the Opry for many years, Leverett said, "I had a lot of good experiences with Dolly. I love her to death, to this very day. When we did that [*My Blue Ridge Mountain Boy*—RCA Victor, 1969, album cover shoot], where she's lying on the couch with a tear running down her cheek, they put a glycerin tear on Dolly. They wanted a picture of Carl [Dean] to go on the top, and Dolly to be on the bottom part, because she's dreaming about her man. So I went out to Channel 4 after one of their shows and in just a matter of a few minutes, we shot that thing. I got the lighting man to light the background really bright, because I had an idea. The next day I arranged to meet Carl at a Shoney's out on Nolensville Road, and we were going to go look for a place with an old house, an old country home. We found one out there somewhere, with a big old dead log that he sat on. He was wearing a plaid shirt, like a country boy. And I took a big, white mounting board to hold in front of the lens so the sun could hit that white and 'whiten out' up the bottom half of the shot. Up close it was out of focus; it was blurry. So I put those two together with a piece of tape, and it turned out beautiful."

What stands out to Leverett when he thinks of Dolly Parton is that "she was just a down-home, down-to-earth country girl," he said. "She's what she says she is. . . . She's got a good heart. That's what I love about her. Dolly was always easy to work with. I've never seen her throw a tantrum or get aggravated. Porter got mad at me, oh yeah. But I've never seen but one side of Dolly, and that's her good side."

For the cover of the album, *Porter Wayne and Dolly Rebecca* (RCA LSP-4305, 1970), Les shot a photo of two pictures of the artists as children, mounted in a worn, leather-bound scrapbook on a crocheted doily, lying on a cherry table. Porter is wearing overalls and a plaid shirt, and he looks to be about 10 years old. Dolly is around the same age, in a rough, homemade-looking jacket with a dark collar (her "Coat of Many Colors"), her wispy curls parted on the left side, and the unmistakable grin and glint in her eyes that's still there. She looks tiny, like a miniature porcelain doll, up to some sort of mischief.

Leverett was given the two photos, and Porter's had been torn across the bottom so he had to repair the picture by hand. "I copied them and printed them the same size and sepia toned them to make them look old," he recalled, "and I borrowed that little book, borrowed the little doily, and that little picture frame from Carl and Pearl Butler and we had the little round-top table, which has gone to ruin now. One Sunday evening I had the four-by-five camera and I went back in the bedroom and got the sunlight coming in from that back bedroom window and got it just where I wanted it and shot that picture, and I thought it turned out well. I loved that one."[7]

A FEW WORDS FROM PORTER

Years after the famous country duo split, Porter Wagoner was interviewed by Rob Simbeck. "Dolly has been a great asset to my whole life, not just in music," Wagoner said. "She's a wonderful lady. When I had problems with the IRS I had to sell off a bunch of things to pay the bills, and she came to my aid. I sold her the songs I'd written while I was with Owepar Music (which combined the names Owens and Parton), the company she and I started [with Bill Owens]. Then last year I wanted to buy the songs back from her. I wanted my family to have them when I go on to that other Grand Ole Opry up in the sky. I wrote Dolly a letter and told her I was prepared to pay exactly what she had paid me for them, and she wrote back and said, 'The songs are on the way, but I'll accept none of your money. I know how you feel about your songs because the ones I write, they're a part of me, part of my inner soul.' Few people would have done that, and I told her what that meant to me. It wasn't a matter of the money. It was the personal feeling I had about it, and it shows the kind of person Dolly is."[8]

In a 2008 interview—a year after Wagoner passed away—Parton said, "Porter and I were always like family, or a husband and wife in a way. We fought all the time but we loved each other deeply and truly. We were both so stubborn and so much alike that we couldn't get along. We had our differences, but there was always that bond, and the last several years we had become really close again."[9]

DOLLY'S RCA YEARS

Wearing matching bright-red turtleneck sweaters, Dolly Parton and Porter Wagoner are hugging each other on the cover of *Just between You and Me,* released by RCA in 1968. Dolly's lipstick is bright red, and Porter's blue eyes match Parton's blue eye shadow. The two photos on the back of the album are black and white—Dolly in the same sweater with a black skirt, looking up at the light. Her bangs are swept to the side and swirled, and her hair is teased sky-high in a popular style of the time, typified in old Doris Day movies. Porter and Dolly are sitting at the mouth of a cave or some type of rock formation. In the bottom photo Dolly is wearing a jacket with plaid lapels that match her blouse and a delicate, diamond-like necklace on a simple chain. Dolly's look is sophisticated but still emphasizes her natural beauty. Porter has the "comb it back and slick it down" Brylcreem pompadour look popular with so many country artists of the era. Actually, this hairstyle is still seen today among male country and bluegrass artists and Nashville session players over the age of 40—though they're probably using mousse now instead of Brylcreem.

Bill Turner, director of *The Porter Wagoner TV Show*, began his liner notes for the album by extolling, "Porter and Dolly—Blended perfection!" It was "inevitable," he said—"matching one of the greatest male singers in the country field with one of the greatest female singers. The result is an A&R man's dream, a fan's delight, a collector's item."

Turner continued: "So there we have the ingredients. . . . The long, tall man from the Missouri Ozarks and the small, attractive blonde from the hills of East Tennessee. Couple these factors with some of the most powerful tunes ever assembled, and they spell pleasure—sheer, unadulterated, unspoiled enjoyment for you." He also brings attention to the fact that Parton wrote 4 of the 12 cuts.

The advertising on the paper sleeve encasing the LP reads, "RCA Stereo Cartridge Tapes—The Exciting NEW way to Enjoy the Music You Want In Your Heart . . . In Your Car . . . Or Wherever You Roam! 8-Track Stereo Cartridge Tape . . . Developed and Introduced by RCA Victor . . . Adopted by All Major U.S. Auto Companies."

Side 1 starts out with a Parton/Owens–penned country shuffle, "Because One of Us Was Wrong," underpinned by a prominent walking electric bass line, drums, and electric guitar (or Buck's banjo? One never knows, with the sketchy credits in early album liner notes.) The two singers switch lead lines in the verses, giving the effect of a real conversation. "I'm sorry I was weak enough to step out on you," Porter says. "Well, I should have been strong enough not to step out on you, too," Dolly replies. They continue to sing, alternately blaming each other and themselves, until they agree at the end to try to work things out and hang on to the love they still feel for each other. There are two sides to the relationship story in Parton's song—a touch of stark realism and also a device that strengthens the traditionally weaker woman's voice in society at the time. The man may be the head of the house, but in this song both partners messed up, both admitted it, and both made a concerted effort to repair the damage and work together to repair their marriage.

"The Last Thing on My Mind," written by folk star Tom Paxton and debuting on December 2, 1967, was Porter and Dolly's first number 10 hit on the *Billboard* Country Chart, eventually going to number 7. The song was originally recorded on October 11, 1967, and the musicians included George McCormick and Wayne Moss, guitar; Roy Huskey Jr., bass; Jerry Carrigan, drums; Hargus "Pig" Robbins, piano; Pete Drake, steel guitar; Buck Trent, banjo; Mack Magaha, fiddle; and Anita Carter (of the renowned Carter Family) and Delores Edgin on vocals.

The song kicks off with a folksy, up-tempo acoustic vibe with well-placed guitar licks between vocal phrases, as Porter croons, "It's a lesson too late for the learnin', made of sand." Equally adept at lead and harmony singing, Parton and Wagoner switch back and forth in the same conversational style as in the previous song—a hallmark of their duet singing. Dolly says, "I could have loved you better; didn't mean to be unkind," with a cry in her voice that rings with true regret. The chorus doubles around at the end, backed by soaring harmonies and building to a strong finish, punctuated by a classic country steel guitar lick—and the template for dozens more classic Porter and Dolly duets has been set.

"Love Is Worth Living" (Parton) is a positive love song set to moderate three-quarter time. "The love in your eyes is so easy to see," Dolly sings. Porter answers her, agreeing how real and good the love he feels in his heart is for her, also. The sentiments presented her echo the collaborative efforts needed to keep a marriage together, presented earlier in "Because One of Us Was Wrong."

The title cut, "Just Between You and Me," written by the infamous "Cowboy Jack" Clement, had been a hit for Charlie Pride, bringing him a Grammy nomination in 1966. In the cleverly written lyrics set to a signature melody Porter wonders if it's true that time will heal all wounds. He's heard this is true. . . . But then they continue: "Just between you and me, I've got my doubts about it. . . . You're too much to forget." The Dolly Parton mystique has officially begun. As music historians, her fellow entertainers, and fans will attest, she definitely is "too much to forget."

In the original "Mommie, Ain't That Daddy," Dolly offers an example of the extremely sentimental songs she loves to write and sing in a story about a young mother walking with her children through the snow to a Goodwill store to buy clothes. The youngest child recognizes a beggar on the street and wonders aloud if it's his father. The child's mother in the song ponders the sad story of her family, unsure if she did something to make her husband end up like this. Wagoner, in his most solemn recitation voice, notes: "No, you didn't fail me. My weakness was too strong." He admits that over the years he has allowed drinking to become more important than his wife, his little children, and their happy home. He feels like he's stooped too low to ask for forgiveness, but he does ask his estranged wife one favor: If his children see him again in passing sometime in the future and ask if he's their father, he wants her to say, "It used to be.'"

The themes found in country music are not, and have never been, for the faint of heart. Train wrecks, murders, unfaithfulness, hard liquor, and violence abound. But the characters who do the foulest deeds usually repent at the end. They regret their actions and show true remorse—like the father in "Mommie, Ain't That Daddy," whose alcoholism has irreparably harmed his family.

Thankfully, the mood lifts for "Four O Thirty Three" (Owens, Montgomery), a song from the perspective of a happily married couple who have "found heaven right here on earth at 4033," their street address. The key modulates up for the third verse and Parton sings about all the children playing in the yard at this particular address. They're hers, she proudly states—"a symbol of our love for all the world to see."

Side 2 of the album shifts back to heartbreak with "Sorrow's Tearing Down the House (that Happiness Once Built)," credited to Tillis/Westberry. The couple's carefully planned future is falling apart, due perhaps to "weekly parties that never seemed to end" and hanging around with the wrong crowd of "so-called friends." Backed by steel guitar, acoustic bass, acoustic guitar, and drums, Parton and Wagoner switch lead and harmony parts every few lines, pulling together like a well-matched team of singing horses.

"This Time Has Gotta Be Our Last Time" (Owens) has Dolly and Porter playing the parts of two lovers who are cheating on their spouses. Accented by agile acoustic guitar fills, they sing about how their consciences are hurting them. "I'm not this kind of woman," Parton insists, followed by Porter: "And I'm not this kind of man." The theme of the album—that marriage is a two-person job—is repeated.

The duo nails the popular "Before I Met You" (Seitz/Lewis/Rader) in Jimmy Martin–speed three-quarter time, followed by "Home Is Where the Hurt Is" (MacRae-Barton), about a married couple who choose to spend their evenings honkytonking rather than staying at home and facing each other in a loveless marriage.

"Two Sides to Every Story" (Owens, Parton) is an example of the lighthearted banter displayed in a number of Parton and Wagoner's "couple" songs. Neither is being completely honest in telling the whole story. The album ends with Wagoner successfully stepping into the duo spot previously filled by Bill Phillips in the earlier Owens/Parton hit for Decca, "Put It Off until Tomorrow."

On the cover of *My Blue Ridge Mountain Boy*, released by RCA in 1969, Dolly is lying on a black leather couch, dressed in an embroidered aqua brocade dress with leaf patterns and sequin trim on slit sleeves. She wears a delicate, diamond-studded wristwatch and a sparkly choker that matches the trim on her dress. Her eye shadow is a smoky blue-gray and her lipstick a delicate spring pink, her eyeliner and mascara heavy. She's wearing one of her more subdued wigs, short, blonde, and wavy in a bouffant style, and her eyebrows are sculpted and dark to match her lashes. She is thinking of a log cabin scene in the hills, pictured on the top half of the album cover. The ruggedly handsome man (actually Parton's husband, Carl Dean) is sitting on the end of a large fallen tree trunk in front of the cabin. Carl is dressed in blue jeans, a red and black plaid shirt, and brown leather work boots, laced up to his ankles. He appears to be lost in thought too, or perhaps he's just taking a break after sawing down the tree. This is the album shot Les Leverett mentions in the interview cited earlier.

Parton starts out with Mac Davis's song "In the Ghetto," the same song Elvis Presley had a hit with. Dolly is one of the few artists in any genre who can cover another artist's material and make it completely her own—she jokingly calls it "Dolly-izing" a song. Her version of the song went to number 50 on the *Billboard* Country Chart.

She continues with another cover, "Games People Play," which Joe South wrote and recorded himself the same year. In fact, South's record by the same name may have been the first multitracked album in country music. A session musician, he sang all the parts and played all the instruments himself, winning a Song of the Year Grammy in 1970. The lyrics are definitely set in the '60s, as Dolly spits out, "Oh, they teach you how to meditate, read your horoscope, and cheat your fate." She later prays that God will somehow give her the serenity and presence of mind to just remember who she is. The instruments are split to one side or the other rather than mixed equally in both speakers.

"'Til Death Do Us Part" (Parton) starts out as a recitation with a weepy steel guitar in the left speaker and trembling electric guitar chords on the right side. In one of her darkest songs, the narrator has found out that her husband is leaving her. He's taken his wedding ring off his hand, and now she's going to carry out her wedding vow, "'til death do us part," by killing herself. The somber song ends with diamonds (whole notes) and a church organ instrumental tag. Parton, who married young and has had many years to contemplate the state of matrimony in her own relationship and others, writes a lot about the institution. She also frequently employs double meanings and plays on words, as in this song: the deadly, precise meaning of the phrase "'Til Death Do Us Part" for the narrator.

"Big Wind" (Walker, Zanetis, McCormick) is an up-tempo song about diving for the cellar when a tornado is coming, with a bluegrassy/traditional country vibe. Parton offers the intriguing rhyme: "All but Dad was in the cellar. By now the sky was yella." Does Dad make it? You'll have to listen to the album to find out.

Parton's original song "Evening Shade" begs to be made into a short story or a *Lifetime* television movie. Mrs. Bailey, the "meanest matron" in the Evening Shade home for orphans, accidentally fell in some water used to scrub the floors. It was a Dickens-like abode of misery, where children were mistreated and beaten for wetting the bed. Little Joe Johnson stole the kerosene, Dolly got the matches, Becky Adams made sure all the kids were outside, and Billy Watson "looked out for the evil eye." By sundown the song ends and the cruel orphanage burns to the ground. The evil children's home matron got what she deserved, and the children escaped her cruelty by doing something truly horrible themselves. Something to ponder.

Side 2 features the title cut, "My Blue Ridge Mountain Boy," written by Parton. With Buck Trent's banjo rolling slowly in the background, Parton sings, "From a shack by a mountain stream to a room in New Orleans . . ." The narrator, who regrets her decision to leave her mountain home in Virginia to find excitement in the big city, now is unhappy with her life as a prostitute and mourns her old love back home, who finally gave up waiting for her and married someone else last October. The song went to number 45 on *Billboard*'s Country Chart.

The disturbing "Daddy" (Parton) is a daughter's plea to her father not to walk out on her mother. At age 23, she sings, "Your new love is even younger than me." No subject appears to be off-limits for Parton as a songwriter. She likes to write about sunshine and butterflies, but she also quite enjoys delving into the darkest corners of the human condition, with graphic story lines and characters in palpable anguish. The song went to number 40 on the *Billboard* Country Chart, b/w "'Til Death Do Us Part."

"We Had All the Good Things Going" (Monday/Shriner) reiterates the theme that money can't buy happiness, and "The Monkey's Tale" (Leona Reese) finds Parton wisecracking to a fiddling Cajun beat, noticing how much her man is like a monkey. "Compared to you, all their chatter sounds so true." Because of the lies he's told her, the man is the one who should be locked up in the zoo. In a clear example of songs written from a woman's perspective, the narrator is the witty, smart one who is not going to let her man get away with lying to her.

"Gypsy, Joe and Me" (Parton) is a sad vignette of a homeless girl driven to suicide. Gypsy is the narrator's little dog, "found in a ditch," and Joe is her man, "the flower of [her] soul." The dog gets hit by a car on the highway and Joe, dressed in rags with winter coming on, catches "the chill" and dies in the singer's arms. The story ends as she stands on the edge of a bridge, ready to jump, and she sees their faces in the water looking up at her. Parton demonstrates her penchant for bone-chilling sad story songs here. We don't know if she jumps or not.

In "Home for Pete's Sake" (Rudy Preston) Dolly is a pregnant runaway, but she writes to her parents to see if she can come home because she heard that Pete, the boy she broke up with, is about to lose his mind over losing her. She's coming home now, the very next morning, "for Pete's sake . . . my baby's and mine,"—demonstrating another clever turn of phrase.

In liner notes, Parton's uncle, Bill Owens, talks about his talented niece's sunny personality and strong character. "Some people who become famous sometimes get a little conceited and impressed with their own importance," he commented, "but not Dolly. I've known her all her life and she hasn't changed one bit. Dolly doesn't forget people who have tried to help her. . . . Dolly was born with an instant smile and I've never seen her without it."

In the packaging fans are urged to visit the Country Music Hall of Fame, and the reader is also informed: "The RCA Record you are holding is a Dynaflex Record. It is thinner than any other record you have ever owned. It is freer of imperfections—ticks, pops, and blisters. It is much less susceptible to warpage. And, its life will be far longer than conventional records. It is the record of tomorrow, yours today."

Side 1 of the 1970 duet release *Porter Wayne and Dolly Rebecca* starts out with "Forty Miles from Poplar Bluff" (Frank Dycus/Larry Kingston), a straight-ahead, three-chord country song about a place in southwest Missouri near Wagoner's hometown of West Plains where "a man thinks of his neighbor, and not his neighbor's wife." Trumpets unexpectedly join the traditional country instrumentation, and the song continues with a memorable line about Daddy's "tobaccer" and Grandma's snuff. These items helped keep the family warm through the wintertime, 40 miles from Popular Bluff, Missouri. Rural themes familiar to Parton's childhood in Tennessee are echoed in an Ozark setting here.

"Tomorrow Is Forever" (Parton), recorded December 2, 1969, went to number 9 on the *Billboard* Country Chart. Kicking off with a "Last Date" Floyd Cramer–style piano intro, the narrator begs her love to "take my hand and run with me out of the past called yesterday." The song includes a string section, and the bridge modulates to a higher key—two devices country music producers and artists were experimenting with in the '70s, as the Nashville Sound progressed.

Another trumpet kicks off Jack Clement's song "Just Someone I Used to Know," a number 5 country charting hit for Parton and Wagoner that showcases their trademark hand-in-glove vocal harmony. In this song recorded April 21, 1969, the narrator describes a picture that she still carries in her wallet that was obviously taken a long time ago. When anyone asks her about the man in the photograph with her, she says it's "just someone I used to know." Like the marriages in the songs Parton sings, the breakups are not so simple either. The singer wants to move on, but she can't bring herself to get rid of that telltale photo in her wallet.

The traditional "Each Season Changes You" (Ruth Talley) notes, "Like the weather your heart changes with each season." Porter and Dolly's voices are so different, it's curious how they blend so well together. His midrange baritone has no vibrato at all, and her high-pitched, quick vibrato–laced soprano contrasts starkly. Visually, he was tall and thin, while Parton is diminutive and curvaceous. On Wagoner's show, Dolly stepped up on a wooden box for duets so their faces would be at the same level on the television screen. Perhaps it was the perfect phrasing and the seamlessly shared emotion that made them a perfect musical duo. Whatever it was, it worked.

"Mendy Never Sleeps" is another Parton tale from the dark side of life, written from the perspective of the parents of a rebellious 16-year-old girl who by the end of the composition is apparently dying in their arms of a drug overdose. Each line of the song begins with Mendy's name, followed by simple observations about her appearance and her recent behavior. Her parents are paralyzed with grief, helpless to do anything but repeat their daughter's name and beg her not to go to sleep. For anyone with teenage children, there's not a more horrifying thought—except maybe a midnight call from the police about a car accident. Parton's probably written that one, too.

Side 2 begins with the poignantly tender Parton-penned "Silver Sandals," about a little disabled girl who "could only watch the children as they played," and eventually ends up wearing silver sandals to walk up the silver stairs to heaven. A recitation is included, in which the girl's parents describe how she always asked for sandals, and how it would break their hearts when she asked them why she couldn't walk. "Silver Sandals" joins a number of songs in the bluegrass music genre about poor, dying, disabled children who someday hope to walk the golden streets of heaven, including "Slippers with Wings," "Put My Little Shoes Away," and "Willy Roy, the Crippled Boy."

Bill Owens's "No Love Left" asks the musical question "Why do we keep trying when there's no love left?" In "It Might as Well Be Me" (Parton/ Hope) the couple flat-out admits that they'll never get along. "There's no use for us to live a lie, when we're wasting the best years of our lives." As in the previously mentioned relationship-gone-wrong songs, marriage is a two-way street. Both partners' voices are heard equally. They both take responsibility— either deciding to give it one more shot or give up.

In a September 2010 interview, legendary country songwriter Tom T. Hall brilliantly observed that the vast majority of songs are written about "this old boy and this old girl. That sums it up," he said. "We write songs and we record songs about human beings. Most of this music, about 98 percent of it, is about 'this old boy and this old girl.' Our source of inspiration for this music is never going to change as long as there are human beings on the planet. So we know what the future of the music is. It's basically about this old boy and this old girl. Now, in bluegrass you have this great liberty to kill off a few of them if you want to, which amuses and entertains people— the way vampire shows do," he smiled, "but we don't have to worry about the music. The music is going to be OK. There will always be something to write a song about."[10]

Parton figured out this concept long ago, and she also has the genius to imagine virtually every fix "this old boy and this old girl" can get themselves into, when it comes to matters of the heart. Then, as Buck Trent points out, she can write a song about it "in no time."

In "Run That By Me One More Time" (Parton) the tone is quirky and impetuous. "I might be crazy, but I'm not dumb," Dolly sings, "and I know a lie when I hear one." Porter insists the wine she smells on him is aftershave, and Parton says she has no idea where the rent money in the cookie jar went to. Neither one believes the other's lies, and the musical banter continues, ending with spoken likes like "Shut yo' mouth"; "I don't have to—you ain't my boss." The album ends with the self-explanatory "I'm Wasting Your Time and You're Wasting Mine" (Parton), set to a melody reminiscent of "Me and Joshua" and ending with twin "chicken picking" electric guitar lines.

In his brief liner notes producer Bob Ferguson calls Wagoner and Parton "the dynamic duo of country music. There is magic in the air when these two brilliant artists perform together. . . . "It's a magic born of their intensity, realism, and projection." Indeed, "realism" is the key here. These are real couples and families and children in very real predicaments. Sometimes the endings are happy; sometimes they're not.

On the cover of *Once More,* released by RCA in 1970, Porter Wagoner is dressed in a black suit and pinstriped vest with a pink shirt. Dolly glistens, standing next to him in an elegant high-necked, white sequined dress with a pink jacket. Her makeup is pink and dewy, with heavy blue eye shadow. In the Parton wig version of a country star mullet, she sports tousled curls on top and long wavy hair on the sides.

The first cut, "Daddy Was an Old Time Preacher Man," written by Parton and her aunt, Dorothy Jo Hope, is a tribute to Dolly's grandfather, the Reverend Jake Robert Owens. The single, which went to number 7 on the Country Chart for Wagoner and Parton, says Owens "preached so plain a child could understand," but also cranked up the oratory in the fire and brimstone department. The song quotes from a couple of old familiar hymns, "In the Sweet By and By" and "I'm on My Way to Canaan's Land." Like much of her material, the song is reminiscent of Parton's real home in the mountains and real characters or family members who lived there. She doesn't shy away from religious themes because they were a very real part of her growing-up days, as well as her current belief system.

Next up is a cheating classic from the repertoire of Reno and Smiley, "I Know You're Married, But I Love You Still," written by banjo stylist Reno and the fiddler on this session (also on Porter's TV show), Mack Magaha. Proving the old adage that sad songs are usually a lot more interesting than happy ones, "Thoughtfulness" (Owens) is an abstract song about the concept that makes the relationship between a man and woman last.

"Fight and Scratch" (Parton) is decidedly lighter, with cat meows heard in the background. The consensus between the two narrators is that "there surely must be more to love than to fight and scratch with you." Porter and Dolly kid each other with light, spoken insults between the lines of the song. Wagoner compares her to a catfish, which evidently has a very large mouth and a very small brain.

"Fight and Scratch" depicts the two partners sparring playfully, but things are serious in "Before Our Weakness Gets Too Strong," written by Louis Owens—a twin-fiddle country shuffle focused on the resolve of two potential cheaters deciding to stop things before it's too late. Nothing portrays potential heartbreak better than two sobbing county fiddles, playing in close harmony.

Side 2 kicks off with the classic title cut, "Once More" (Dusty Owens), which has been cut by 100 artists, according to the songwriter's website. In addition to Dolly and Porter, the list includes Roy Acuff, Don Gibson, The Osborne Brothers, The Desert Rose Band, Hank Locklin, Red Sovine, Floyd Cramer, George Jones, Vince Gill, and Bill Anderson, among others. In the ongoing theme of Parton's albums during this era of the hard work needed to keep a relationship together, the singer goes through a list of things he would do, if only he could see his love "once more."

"One Day at a Time" (Joe Babcock) is a different song than the one Cristy Lane had the megahit with but shares the same advice. Some things are just too overwhelming to think about at once. It's best to face the challenge "one day at a time."

"Ragged Angel" is another one of Parton's pitiful child tearjerkers. The main character in the song, little Cindy, sleeps with her paper dolls on a blanket on the floor, Parton sings sadly, and "she would shiver as the wind blew through the crack beneath the door." The sentimental song brings the audience—at least those whose hearts aren't made of stone!—to tears with the final recitation. Parton tells us that God came for the ragged angel, and that now poor Cindy will never have to worry about not having enough to eat or a warm coat to wear anymore, her voice quavering on the last phrase.

"A Good Understanding" (Parton) sounds like something Parton could have written about her own marriage. The couple in the song agreed when they got married that they would both continue to "do as we pleased," as long as they "done each other right." The album ends with "Let's Live for Tonight," another Don Reno cut rationalizing that what happens between the couple will stay between them, and no one will be the wiser. "What tomorrow brings, nobody ever knows," the singer reasons. Of course tomorrow they each might be alone.

In liner notes Louis Owens, manager of the duo's Owepar Publishing Company, cheerfully notes, "Like a hunter buying a double-barreled shotgun, in this album you get two great artists for the price of one."

Dolly wrote her own liner notes for the album named after her favorite song, *Coat of Many Colors,* released in 1971. She recalls lying at her mother's feet as a child while her mother sewed on an old treadle machine, listening to stories from the Bible as Avie Lee sewed her daughter's now-famous jacket of green, blue, red, and yellow corduroy. Dolly holds the song, the story, and the school picture of herself in the little coat dearly, she says in liner notes, "because it holds a precious memory of my Mama, a mama that loved and raised twelve children with the help of God and a daddy with a strong hand and a gentle heart." She dedicates the album to her parents.

The title cut of this album, "Coat of Many Colors," which went to number 17 on the *Billboard* Country Chart, was recorded April 16, 1971. Underpinned by Buck Trent's gentle rolls on the gut-stringed banjo, Parton tells the autobiographical tale simply and sincerely. The song is too perfect to write much about, in this writer's opinion. Best to put the book down, run to your computer, and buy the single online if you don't already own it. Better yet, Google the lyrics, pick up a guitar, and enjoy singing this classic yourself.

The racy "Traveling Man" (Parton) is a story told about a young girl whose door-to-door salesman lover runs off with her (you guessed it) . . . mother! The song has a Jerry Reed–style electric guitar intro and vibe and accomplishes an impressive rhyme with "courtin'" and "orghta" (as in "ought to.")

Parton sings harmony with herself throughout "My Blue Tears," an original song written in Carter Family style, with Maybelle-influenced guitar work. Singing to a bluebird, Parton says, "Go shed your blue wings, and I'll shed my blue tears"—because the narrator's love has left her. This song wouldn't be out of place on a songbook page following the English ballad "Barbara Allen."

"If I Lose My Mind" (Porter Wagoner) is a bizarre confession from a son to his mother. He says he was afraid of what he might do if he stayed at home, perhaps in reference to an abusive father or stepfather who has a number of perverse issues probably best left unexplained exactly. In "The Mystery of the Mystery" (Wagoner) the narrator ponders ageless questions such as "Where does the wind go," "how does life begin," and what happens after death. His conclusion is that these things must remain unknown, that some things are beyond the comprehension of mere mortals. See the lyrics of the old hymn "Farther Along" for more on this familiar topic.

Side 2 starts with the breezy cover "She Never Met a Man (She Didn't Like)," followed by "Early Morning Breeze" (Parton). The latter invites listeners on an early morning stroll through a mountain meadow with Parton, where the "dew still lingers on the iris leaves." It is here she goes to "have a word" with God in the early morning. The piano kicks off "The Way I See You" (Wagoner), which compares his love to the beauty of dawn, and the way "the sun sets and paints its picture in the blue." Both of these last two songs portray the closeness Parton has to nature, growing up running around and playing in the mountains. She sees God in his creation, and she uses nature-based terminology to describe the man she loves.

The album ends with "A Better Place to Live" (Parton), in which Parton suggests that we could make the world a better place if we take our brothers and sisters' hands and "love each other instead of finding fault." Equally important, we should always forgive each other and ask to be forgiven ourselves, she sings. This Golden Rule–based, "live and let life" philosophy is one that is repeated in a number of Parton's spiritual songs. Just the simple act of loving and respecting each other is the key.

Side 1 of *Joshua*, released in 1971 by RCA, starts with the title track. Parton's first number 1 hit debuted on the *Billboard* Country Chart on December 12, 1970, and peaked at number 1 on February 6, 1971. The song was also nominated for the Grammy for Best Country Vocal Performance by a Female. In it, Parton tells the story of an orphan girl who wanders across the railroad tracks to see if all the stories she's heard about the dangerous hermit who lived down there in a shack were true. They get along famously, and "we just couldn't help falling in love," Parton explains simply, ending with a bluegrassy yodel and a little Dolly scat.

"The Last One to Touch Me" (Parton) is a serious love song with a hard-core country feel in which the narrator wants her "perfect love" to be the last one to physically touch her before she leaves this world, and also the first one who reaches out to greet her in heaven. "Walls of My Mind" (Parton) features smooth, pop-ish background vocals and a dominant electric bass with a piano kick-off. The singer is standing, "lookin' at the memories hanging on the wall of [her] mind." The utilization of photographs to represent over-powering memories is an effective device in country music songwriting. The Flatt and Scruggs hit later popularized by Ricky Skaggs, "Cryin' My Heart Out Over You," as well as the Tim O'Brien–penned "Way the Way the Wind Blows" made famous by Kathy Mattea come to mind—along with the starkly emotional heartbreaker "A Few Old Memories," written by Hazel Dickens, in which the narrator has to keep a framed photo turned upside down on the shelf in her home because she simply can't bear to look upon her love's face.

In "It Ain't Fair that It Ain't Right," (J. U. Eggers and B. Eggers), the narrator is inconsolable because a man had his way with her and then left her because he thinks she's not a "good girl." The double standard prevalent in society at the time is obvious. A boy is simply sowing wild oats, but the girl is a bad person. In this song it's (at least half) the man's fault that the woman made a poor decision—but then he adds insult to injury by saying that's precisely the reason he's leaving her. Go figure.

Another interesting character from Parton's fertile imagination is introduced in "J. J. Sneed" (Parton). In a story song that could've been a John Wayne movie, the singer doggedly hunts down her former outlaw lover and decides to kill him for betraying her—just as the sound of hoofbeats from the sheriff's posse are heard in the distance.

Side 2 starts off with "You Can't Reach Me Anymore" (Parton/ Dorothy Jo Hope), a song about a girl who's been hurt too badly for her repentant lover to win her back. Laden with steel guitar and multiple fiddles, the instrumentation in this country weeper reflects the emotion in the song.

"Daddy's Moonshine Still" (Parton) begins with a trademark Parton vocal hum and rips into a groove reminiscent of Jim Croce's rockin' songs (e.g., "Bad, Bad Leroy Brown," "Roller Derby Queen") Rather than treating the subject lightly ("They call it that good ole mountain dew . . ."), the narrator says moonshine—in her experience—did nothing but tear the family apart, break her mother's heart, and make their lives "a living hell." Two of her brothers lost their lives running shine, the singer left home and took up prostitution in order to send money home to her mother, and her mother and father died from depression and liver damage, respectively. There's nothing quaint about corn liquor at all, in Parton's take—probably based on people she actually knew in the hills.

The mood gets lighter with "Chicken Every Sunday" (Charlie Craig and Betty Craig), in which the singer picks up her tambourine and says she doesn't mind being poor at all, if it means a chicken dinner every Sunday and a trip to town with her dad on Saturday morning, which includes a "picture show" and a "picnic on the ground." Nostalgia is a theme Parton returns to often in her songwriting.

In "The Fire's Still Burning" (Parton/Dorothy Jo Hope), the singer admits that if her unfaithful husband returned, she'd take him back. "I never will stop loving you," she mourns. This unfortunately accurate portrayal of the human condition some women live with points to the reason we still have abuse hotlines and shelters for women and children who find it unsafe to live at home.

In the sentimental "A Letter to Heaven" (arranged by Parton), an old man's little granddaughter climbs up in his lap and asks him to help her write a letter to heaven. She misses her Mommy, and she tells her grandpa, "I'm coming to see her real soon, I hope." On her way out to the mailbox she is hit by a car and dies instantly, and she gets her dearest wish. The arrangement is simple, with a single acoustic guitar and bass accompanying Dolly's voice in three-quarter time. The real stories in life, as portrayed so often in Parton's songs, are usually the most tragic.

Dolly's session bass player, Bobby Dyson, contributed liner notes for the album. A fan, as well as the man in the back with a bass, Dyson compliments Parton on her songwriting, her "strong and exciting" melodies, and the lyrics "full of human emotions and understanding of life." He asks her to "stay the way you are—never change, because the heart and soul that you put into your songs has the power to reach out and touch the lives of so many."

The cover for *My Tennessee Mountain Home,* an all-original album of music released in 1973, depicts Dolly's homeplace in east Tennessee: a weathered gray one-story cabin with a long front porch stretched along the front and a tin roof sloping toward the back of the house. A few old tire rims lie in the front yard, next to some purple flowers cheerfully announcing springtime in the mountains. The illustrations inside appear to be the pages of a family scrapbook, with old-fashioned picture holders in the corners of photos of Dolly's parents, Dolly with her two older brothers and her older sister on the front porch, and Dolly with her Grandma and Grandpa Parton, Bessie and Walter. (Dolly's face is shaped like Bessie's.) There's Dolly in her "Coat of Many Colors" school picture, and also a shot of her with her grandpa, Brother Jake Owens.

In the photo of Dolly on the back of the album shot by Bill Preston, a thin pink ribbon weaves through a long blonde wig piled high on Dolly's head. Her eyes are lined heavily with black eyeliner and shadowed with pinks and grays. She's wearing a flowing pink pastel dress with sleeves gathered loosely at the wrists and rhinestone-edged scallops along the neckline of her jacket.

The first cut is a recitation called "The Letter," with a harmonica playing "Home Sweet Home" softly in the background. Dated June 2, 1964, it's Dolly's first letter to her folks after moving to Nashville at age 18. "I didn't realize how much I loved you and all them noisy kids until I left," she writes, until she and her parents all started crying at the bus station. Parton asks her folks not to worry about sending her money because she's already lined up a singing job on the *Eddie Hill Show*, on early morning television, and she's already gotten some interest in recording her songs. Nashville is not quite what she expected it to be like. She's just a teenager, away from home for the first time, and success doesn't happen overnight—even if your name is Dolly Rebecca Parton. She vows to stick it out and determines she will like Nashville once she gets used to it. "I Remember" continues along the same lines, focusing on memories of her parents.

Dolly talks, more than sings, "Old Black Kettle," another nostalgic piece that compares "the simpler things that are gone" now to her mama's black cooking kettle—which is also gone now. Ah, cast iron. There's nothing better in which to fry a chicken or simmer a homemade soup.

In "Daddy's Working Boots" Parton turns to an image that reminds her of her father and his many sacrifices to keep the family fed and clothed. After a key change she asks God to let her Daddy "walk the golden streets in a new pair of golden boots." Parton sings a tribute to her family's country physician, "Dr. Robert F. Thomas" (the fellow who was paid with a bag of cornmeal for delivering Dolly), followed by "In the Good Old Days (When Times Were Bad)," described in a previous chapter.

The title track, "My Tennessee Mountain Home," which went to number 15 on the *Billboard* Country Chart in 1973, starts with a simple vocal and an acoustic guitar. Dolly describes a typical afternoon, sitting on the front porch at home. She watches one of the younger kids tie a thread to a june bug's leg, and then laugh as it circles his head like a buzzing airplane. Later on the children chase fireflies, catch them, and put them in a Mason jar. "Life is peaceful as a baby's sigh" up there in the hills (unless you happen to be an insect).

In "The Wrong Direction Home" the nostalgia continues and Parton feels homesick, and in "Back Home" she does something about it and happily leaves the "factory smoke and city life" to move back home with her family. In "The Better Part of Life" she chooses to dwell on the memory of their shared dreams rather than the difficult times. In "Down on Music Row" Parton talks about hitting the pavement at 8 a.m., trying to get folks in music business offices to listen to her music. In the obviously autobiographical song she eats a stale sweet roll on the steps of the RCA Records building and washes her face in the fountain at the Country Music Hall of Fame and Museum, where she reads the names carved into the concrete "Walkway of Stars," imagining hers there too, someday.

In the liner notes Dolly's mom, Avie Lee Parton, talks about how her fourth child walked and talked very young and by the age of three was happy to sing for anyone who asked her. Avie's favorite song on the album is the one about her husband's worn work boots. "There was never enough money," Mrs. Parton said about her family during Dolly's growing-up years, "but we tried to make up for that with love and understanding for them all."

Robert Lee Parton, Dolly's father, adds: "It gives me a great pleasure to have a chance to say a few words about my beautiful daughter, Dolly." He goes on to say how proud he is of her and how much he loves her. "Dolly has always been full of love, and her singing helps her show it to the whole world."

Porter and Dolly appear in all their golden blonde splendor on the cover of *Love and Music*, released by RCA in 1973. Their photo is cut in the shape of a heart bordered with gold curlicues, set against a fuchsia pink field.

"If Teardrops Were Pennies," penned by Parton's old friend from east Tennessee Carl Butler, went to number 3 on the Country Chart. In the first verse the singer promises "an acre of diamonds," "a solid gold mansion" and "an airplane or two" to his love, if only his tears and heartaches could be counted in pennies and gold.

Following Wagoner's poetic "Sounds of Night," the duo kicks into "Laugh the Years Away" (Howard Tuck), another song about riches that money can't buy. In "You" (Parton) the narrator wakes with joy in the morning, in love and thanking her husband for the happiness he has brought to her. Wagoner's "Wasting Love" swings in the opposite direction for a couple who have "lost the feeling somewhere along the way." Distance grows, and they're just wasting the most valuable thing on the planet: love.

In "Come to Me" (Parton), the singer offers her heart and her help, saying, "Let me be the one you run to in your time of need." The Wagoner-penned "Love Is Out Tonight" paints images from nature that reflect romantic love—things like "stars that spell out our names as they flicker and shine." Porter is on a romantic roll as he continues with "In the Presence of You" (Wagoner). In a song dripping with emotion-laden steel guitar and strings, the narrator wonders why words fail him when he's near the one he loves. "Searching for how to say I feel about you don't come easy," he says, "in the presence of you."

In a sentimental ballad about a five-year-old child left alone in her apartment to fend for herself, "I Get Lonesome by Myself" (Parton), Dolly delivers a recitation in a high little-girl voice. She looks out the window and tells the man passing below about how her mommy drinks since her daddy left, but she knows she still loves him because she says the girl favors him. Porter, playing the part of the man standing on the sidewalk below, is reminded of the family he left years ago—and is then astounded to realize this is his own daughter. He tells his daughter he'll wait until his wife comes home, "and I'll tell her I still love her and I'm sorry I ever left." In a recurring theme for Parton, there are consequences for doing the wrong thing—and sometimes the most innocent are the ones who pay the highest price.

In "There'll Always Be Music" (Parton) we're told of the important role music plays in the world—in a mother's song for her baby, in nursery rhymes, in work songs sung by field hands, and music in the very sounds of nature— the wind and the rain. "There'll always be music, as long as there's a story to be told," the narrator says. A choir chimes in to proclaim, "Music is the voice of the soul."

Carl and Pearl Butler, the country singers from east Tennessee who introduced Dolly to everyone backstage at the Opry when she was just 13, admit to being "about scared half to death" when someone from RCA Records called to ask them to write liner notes for this album. Carl agrees with the album's theme—that "love and music are very closely related." And with a nod to the "good to the last drop" Maxwell House coffee slogan, the duo promises Dolly and Porter's songs are "good to the last note and word."

In the center of the light yellow-green album cover of *Jolene*, framed by Spyrograph-style black curlicues, sits Dolly Parton, barefoot, on something blue and furry. Her elaborate blonde wig is big on top and long on the sides, and her blue and white pantsuit sports puffy white sleeves with long striped cuffs, a V-necked bodice, and striped pants.

"Jolene," originally recorded June 12 and 14, 1973, went to number 1 on *Billboard*'s Country Chart, number 60 on the Pop Chart, and number 44 on Adult Contemporary. The haunting melody that starts off in a minor chord suggests a sense of urgency, and high, otherworldly vocal harmonies echo "Joleeeeeeene." Musicians on the cut include Fred Carter Jr., Jimmy Colvard, and Dave Kirby, guitar; Bobby Dyson, bass; Kenny Malone, drums; Hargus "Pig" Robbins, piano; Stu Basore, steel guitar; Johnny Gimble and Mack Magaha, fiddle; and June Page and Dolores Edgin on vocals. In the story the singer goes to see the rival for her husband's affections, a woman "with ivory skin and eyes of emerald green." He's talking about her in his sleep already, and the singer begs Jolene not to steal her husband "just because you can."

In "The Songwriter's Craft" exhibit at the Country Music Hall of Fame and Museum in Nashville, Parton is asked about her inspiration for this song. "The title came years ago when I was working with Porter," she says. "When I first started in the late '60s I met a little girl when we were sitting on the edge of the stage, signing autographs for everyone after one of the shows. She was a beautiful little red-headed girl, around seven or eight, with fair skin and tiny little freckles, with green eyes. She was one of the prettiest children I've ever seen. I said, 'Who is this to?' And she said, 'Jolene.' I told her, 'Don't be surprised if you hear a song on the radio called Jolene, and you'll know it's about you!'" Parton said she has never seen the little girl again, although she always kind of hoped she would someday. "I picked a story to write," she says, "but the title was inspired by this beautiful little girl with the red hair and green eyes. I just made up the story to go with it."[11]

"When Someone Wants to Leave" (Parton) begins with a simple finger-picked guitar as the singer ponders the dilemma of an unbalanced love affair, where "one doesn't care at all and one cares too much." In "River of Happiness" (Parton) the narrator, hopelessly in love, "laughs and sings," and dances "to the tune that [her] happiness brings"—again utilizing images in nature to illustrate her emotional euphoria.

"Early Morning Breeze" (Parton) kicks off with a fretless bass intro, echoed by the steel guitar and joined by a descending electric guitar pizzicato. On an early morning walk amid the trees and flowers and butterflies, Parton, "misty eyed," says, "It's there I find the courage to face the day." It's outdoors, surrounded by the natural world that reflects God's majesty, that the singer goes to speak to her Creator in prayer, in the early morning light.

Side 2 reveals Parton's most popular song of all time, "I Will Always Love You," which went to number 1 on the *Billboard* Country Chart the first time in 1974. The song was originally recorded on June 13, 1973, and musicians on the session included Jimmy Colvard and Dave Kirby, guitar; Bobby Dyson, bass; Larrie Londin, drums; Hargus "Pig" Robbins, piano; Stu Basore, steel guitar; Bobby Thompson and Buck Trent, banjo; and Hurshel Wiginton, June Page, Dolores Edgin, and Joe Babcock on vocals.

"If I should stay, I would only be in your way," Parton begins, her voice a little unsteady with emotion in the song she says was inspired by her decision to leave Porter Wagoner's band in 1974. She begs him not to cry, because "we both know that I'm not what you need," ending with a heartfelt wish for his joy, happiness, and love.

Parton has had a hit with the song three times—solo in 1974; then on the soundtrack for the movie *The Best Little Whorehouse in Texas,* in which she starred with Burt Reynolds; and most recently as a duet with Vince Gill. The third version won the CMA Vocal Event of the Year award in 1996, and Parton was nominated for a Grammy for Best Female Country Vocal Performance in 1982 for the second version. Linda Ronstadt recorded the song in 1975 but didn't release it as a single. Whitney Houston's 1992 version stayed at number 1 on the Pop Chart for an amazing 14 weeks, selling more than four million copies. Since then it's been recorded again by more artists, including Leann Rimes and John Tesh, among others.

"Randy" (Parton) is a love song written to an intriguing gentleman by this name, and "Living on Memories of You" (Parton) is a country shuffle underpinned with honkytonk piano and French harp. "Your memory keeps blocking my view," the singer moans. Wagoner's "Lonely Comin' Down" describes a man who wakes up alone and realizes his love is gone. Underlined by descending riffs on piano and cello, the narrator sighs. Perhaps he can still smell his former lover's perfume, her presence is still near, and he sings, "Once again I felt the lonely comin' down." "It Must Be You" (Blaise/Tosti) utilizes a melody that sounds more pop than country, in a style vaguely like the Carpenters' "Top of the World." When her love is alone, the singer suggests, "Just think of me and I'll be there."

In the title cut of *Love Is Like a Butterfly,* Parton demonstrates her agility as a vocalist, hitting every interval perfectly in the uniquely challenging melody that flits around like a butterfly's flight pattern. "Love makes your heart feel strange inside; it flutters like soft wings inside," she croons, making the comparison. The song was recorded on July 16, 1974, and the musicians on the cut include Jimmy Colvard, Dave Kirby, Bruce Osbon, and Bobby Thompson, guitar; Bobby Dyson, bass; Larrie Londin, drums; Jerry Smith, piano; Stu Basore, steel guitar; and the Lea Jane Singers on vocals. The song that gave Dolly her trademark career emblem went to number 1 on the *Billboard* Country Chart, number 38 on Adult Contemporary, and to number 105 on the Pop Chart in 1974. All the songs on this album were written by Parton except for "If I Cross Your Mind" and "Highway Headin' South."

Dolly sings "If I Cross Your Mind" (Wagoner) with a quiet cry in her voice, requesting the listener to "think of only good things if I cross your mind." In her original song "My Eyes Can Only See You," Parton sings at the edgy top end of her vocal range and absolutely nails the high notes. Burning with desire and single-minded love and devotion, she sings, "I can't help myself. I can see no one else . . ."

In "Take Me Back," Parton goes back home again in memory to east Tennessee, remembering her mother washing clothes on a "rub board" on the back porch while the children played in the yard. The song expresses her mother's contentment with being a wife and mother and her father's satisfaction in being "the man my Mama lived for." Things may be different for many women now, but there's a respect for the traditional way things used to be.

"Blackie, Kentucky" is a story told by a girl who left the poor mining town where she grew up to marry an older wealthy man. Alas, things do not turn out well. She is not able to make true friends and can't adjust to high-society living, she sings, regretting her decision to live "in a mansion with a husband who never loved me." The song ends with a recitation—her suicide letter, requesting that she be buried back home in Blackie, Kentucky. Money can't buy love—a theme echoed in several of Parton's songs.

Side 2 starts with the exuberant "Gettin' Happy," featuring a rocked-out drum solo intro, joined by electric bass and steel guitar. "You're the One That Taught me How to Swing" blames the singer's husband for planting her high-heeled shoes on the wild side of life—which includes taking up smoking and drinking. "I used to blush at dirty jokes," she sings, "but you're the one who taught me how."

In "Highway Headin' South" (Wagoner) the narrator is "on a highway headed south somewhere to Dixie," where the white on the horizon is cotton rather than snow. She evidently prefers warm weather and resolutely plans to "rest these weary bones in the southern sunshine."

"Sacred Memories" starts with a bluesy intro on electric guitar, bass, and drums. Although her love was almost celestial in the beginning, Parton sings, the "heaven in his eyes" eventually turned into "a cold and distant stare." Although the lyrics are not Parton's most profound, she absolutely wails on the vocals.

All the cuts on *The Bargain Store,* released by RCA in 1975, were written by Dolly Parton except "Live to Remember," written by Porter Wagoner, and "You'll Always Be Special to Me," written by Merle Haggard.

On the cover of her 1975 solo release, a slightly out-of-focus, blonde-bewigged young Dolly looks thoughtful, her lips parted slightly, as she stands in front of a department store window display. On the back cover the double glass store doors open onto the sidewalk from a brick building. The songs are listed inside the store on a display board. A man stands at the counter on the left, and a woman is visible on the right—both with stars scattered above their heads.

In "The Bargain Store," Parton compares her love to a thrift-store item. If the buyer doesn't mind the merchandise being used, she sings in a haunting minor key, "with a little mending it can be as good as new." She continues the metaphor, inviting the listener to come in the bargain store, which is open for business. The song went to number 1 on *Billboard*'s Country Chart and number 35 on the Adult Contemporary Chart in 1975.

"Kentucky Gambler" begins with a Travis-style guitar lick, quickly diving into the story of a Kentucky coal miner whose dreams were bigger than a family at home with four children. He left his family and got lucky in Reno, winning everything. But he couldn't stop while he was ahead and ended up losing it all. When he comes back to Kentucky, he finds no one waiting for him. Another man has quickly taken his place, and Parton muses, "Seems to me a gambler loses much more than he wins."

"You say that you're bored with life and that you're bored with me," Parton sings on "When I'm Gone," a song that warns her lover that he'll miss her when she's gone. In "The Only Hand You'll Need to Hold" Parton finds herself in a happier, although damper situation; she offers to "be your umbrella when it rains."

In "On My Mind Again," the singer tries to move on, but little things keep reminding her of the one whose memory she's trying to leave behind, a recurring theme for Parton. "I Want to be What You Need" sounds like a woman who wants to shape herself into what her man is looking for, but the message is a little deeper than that. She's actually offering him her strength—a shoulder to lean on when he needs love and comfort.

"Love to Remember" is a steamy song with the details to be filled in by the listener's imagination. "Your love's as fresh in my memory as this morning sunrise," Dolly sings. In "He Would Know," the singer admits she's imagined having an affair, but she stops because "there's someone who's countin' on me." If she came home to her husband after cheating, he would know somehow because they've loved each other for so long they could see deception in the other's eyes. Although she's definitely tempted, the pleasure is not worth the emotional pain it would create for her husband or the guilt she herself would feel.

In "I'll Never Forget" Dolly remembers eyes that said more than his lips did and a lingering kiss "as soft as a sigh, gentle as snowflakes, but warm as July"—an appropriate song for an album focused on passion and romantic love, which, as in true life, sometimes ends well and sometimes doesn't.

Another important Dolly Parton song should be mentioned in conjunction with her RCA era. "I wrote 'To Daddy' for myself, but I freely gave it away to Emmylou Harris," Parton recalls. "We were gonna put it out as a single, and Porter and I got in a fight over it. That is when I realized how seriously I took myself as a writer, and how much more important my songwriting was, even more than my singing. Emmy was in town and came over to the studio and we were playing the songs, and she begged for that song, and Porter said, 'No, that's Dolly's next single.' Emmy said, 'That is the greatest song. I just have to have that song.' She said, 'You write all the time. You can write other songs.' I told her, 'You can have it.' I thought, "If I'm gonna ever get songs recorded by other artists, then this is the time to do it. She asked for it, I'm a writer and I'm gonna let her have it.'

"Porter was real mad and thought it was the stupidest thing in the world to do," Parton smiled. "It was a good move, though. She recorded other songs of mine, and other people got interested in me and my songs because she promoted me as a writer to other people. You just have to take yourself seriously, and I let her have it. It was years later that I recorded it myself."[12]

"To Daddy" starts out from a child's perspective. The narrator sings about how her mother never really noticed the material things the family didn't have: "If she did, she never did say so to Daddy." In addition, Mom never wanted to be more than a wife and a mother. She didn't mind being left alone at times, and she didn't miss the flowers and gifts her husband failed to bring her. In fact, Mama was completely used to the feeling of being taken for granted. It was a normal way of life, the daughter sings matter-of-factly. Then one morning the family finds a note on the table from Mom. The kids are grown up and don't need her much anymore, she reasons. In so many words, Mama writes that she's been starved for love for so long, she cannot stay there any longer. She is leaving for good—or at least that's the impression she gives to Daddy.

By the mid-'70s Dolly Parton had become the country music artist and songwriter she dreamed of being as a little girl, but her progress was fully fueled by hard work and faith. "I never dreamed anything except that things would go well and I'd be what I wanted to be—a star," she said in a 1975 interview. "I wouldn't accept anything else. I've been disappointed a lot of times but I've never been discouraged. I never once thought about giving it up. I didn't believe I ever did."[13]

Story Songs and
Mountain Characters

Songs in this chapter: "Apple Jack," "Daddy, Come and Get Me," "Down from Dover," "Jeannie's Afraid of the Dark," "Joshua," "Marry Me," "Me and Little Andy," "Mountain Angel," "These Old Bones," "Romeo," "Single Women"

DOLLY PARTON: THE CHARLES DICKENS OF COUNTRY MUSIC

Parton has always been a master at telling sometimes sentimental but always compelling stories about intriguing, clearly defined characters. In fact, her songwriting is full of enough fascinating individuals to populate a small planet.

In a review of *Best of Dolly Parton*, a compilation album released in 1975, rock critic Robert Christgau noted, "In her productivity and devotion to writing, Parton is like a 19th century woman novelist—a hillbilly Louisa Mae Alcott."[1]

As with the characters in a good book, the problem with the (mostly fictional) people in Parton's songs is that once you've met them, you keep wondering from time to time what they're up to now. Whatever happened to Jolene? Did she decide to take the narrator's man just because she could do it, or not? And what about J. J. Sneed's lover? Was she hanged for killing her double-crossing outlaw husband? And the poor homeless girl in "Gypsy, Joe, and Me"—did she jump off the bridge, or change her mind and head for a shelter for the night and a better life?

A number of characters from classic as well as contemporary movies spring to life as a result of the combined talents of a gifted writer, an actor, and a producer. Who wouldn't enjoy sitting down on Forrest Gump's front porch for a conversation about life and the box of chocolates we are all individually dealt? Coffee and some girl talk with Bridget Jones sounds delightful. The quirky yet bizarrely real characters the Coen brothers create are recalled like weird uncles in our own families or odd neighbors.

Classic films offer several examples of well-developed and profound characters who are quite realistic—for instance, Jimmy Stewart's portrayal of George Bailey in *It's a Wonderful Life* and Gregory Peck's reading of Atticus Finch in *To Kill a Mockingbird,* directed by Robert Mulligan.

More contemporary examples across the gamut of style include the hysterical, bumbling, but brilliant Chief Inspector Jacques Clouseau in the Pink Panther detective series; Robin Williams's comedy-tinged-with-pathos roles in *Dead Poets Society, Good Will Hunting, Good Morning Vietnam,* and even *Mrs. Doubtfire;* and the memorable Dustin Hoffman in movies such as *Tootsie* and *Rain Man.*

Although fictitious, each one of the roles referenced here is remembered as fondly as a real character in history or everyday life. Dolly Parton has always been able to do the same thing. She has a talent for creating interesting, believable, very deep characters . . . and she does it within the confines of just a few rhyming lines in a three-minute song.

Southern Settings and Characters

Parton's song characters and stories have a sense of place. As with well-known novelists Flannery O'Connor, William Faulkner, and Harper Lee, the setting for a large percentage of Parton's songs is in the South, and the characters who emerge are country people. These are the people she grew up with and the kind of person she still feels like inside—despite her material wealth and fame.

One example is "Applejack," originally released in 1977 on the album *New Harvest . . . First Gathering.* The main character was inspired by a real person from Parton's childhood who really did play clawhammer banjo, according to bluegrass/country artist Pam Gadd, who recorded the song on her recent album, *Benefit of Doubt,* with Dolly guesting on vocals and tambourine.

The good-natured Jackson Taylor, who speaks in a soft Southern drawl and probably wears overalls every day of his life, lives in an old shack on the outskirts of town near an apple orchard where he does occasional day work as a farm laborer—that is, when he's not brewing up a barrel of applejack whiskey or picking the banjo in the old-time frailing style. Parton, in the role of a little neighbor girl, comes over to sing and play a little tambourine with the old man she calls "Applejack." Flashing to the present by the end of the song, Parton tells us that Taylor left his banjo to her when he passed away, and she still remembers the kind old man fondly every time she picks up his five-string.

THE DARK SIDE

Many of Parton's song characters explore the dark side of human nature and the stark cruelty of life. Two examples are the emotionally deranged narrator in the little-known "Daddy, Come and Get Me," released in 1970 on the album *The Fairest of Them All* on RCA Victor, and the mournful, unmarried teen mother in "Down from Dover," released on *Little Sparrow* by Sugar Hill Records in 2001.

Most songwriters say it's easier to write a sad song than a cheerful one. If the writer has had her heart broken—either firsthand or secondhand through an imagined story or idea culled from someone else's experience—writing a song can be a healthy, cathartic experience. On the other hand, if a writer is head over heels in love and in a splendid mood, then he will more likely be courting his true love or having fun at the beach or riding bicycles. It's not the time to mope about in dark rooms with guitars, writing sad songs. Alison Krauss, whose early hits included several songs written by her bass player, John Pennell, has said she always looked forward to hearing that John, a college student at the time, had his heart broken again because she knew he would write a good song for her. Check out the title cut of Krauss's breakout album, *Every Time You Say Goodbye*, for evidence.

In the melancholy "Daddy, Come and Get Me," written by Parton with her aunt, Dorothy Jo Hope, the narrator is a young woman who has been committed to a mental asylum by her ex-husband. She narrates the song, nearly drained of all hope, as she gazes through the iron bars of her hospital window. She admits to being "crazy with jealousy" and crying for days on end after her unfaithful spouse told her he'd fallen in love with another woman. Unable to deal with her traumatic reaction, the louse checked her into an asylum, to get her out of the way as much as anything else.

Betrayed by her unfaithful husband, the narrator turns to her father, who always promised her that she could come to him if she was ever in need. This time, however, she'll be writing a letter to her father, asking him to come rescue her and take her home.

"Down from Dover," set in Europe possibly around the turn of the century, explores the age-old theme of a young girl fooled by a lover with no serious intentions. When she becomes pregnant, he heads off in the direction of Dover, a ferry port in the southeast region of Great Britain, facing France across the English Channel. The singer continues to watch the horizon, hoping anxiously for her lover's return, while her parents are overcome with shame over the girl's condition, beyond hiding at this point. In the last verse as she bears the child, she realizes something is terribly wrong. The baby doesn't cry, "and dying was her way of telling me he wasn't coming down from Dover," the young mother realizes, sobbing.

"Mountain Angel," also from *Little Sparrow*, is another "driven insane and died of a broken heart" tale set in the hills. Characters have been dying of broken hearts for hundreds of years, in traditional songs like "Barbara Allen," a Child Ballad (#84) collected in England, and the raucous "Tavern in the Town"—both of which Parton likely heard as a child. The ballad of Barbara (or "Barbry") Allen was first published in England in 1750 but had existed in oral form for at least 100 years before. In the story, sweet William is dying of unrequited love for Barbara Allen, but when she finally comes slowly to his deathbed she is rather unsympathetic. "Young man, I think you're dyin'," she observes, cool as a cucumber. After William dies, she has a change of heart and ends up dying of grief over what she did to him. They are buried in "the old church yard," and the rose that grows from William's grave twines with the briar that sprouts out of Barbara's final resting place. The lovers with the rotten emotional timing are finally united in death.

In "Tavern in the Town," a favorite in Irish and British pubs alike that dates back to the late 1800s, the narrator sings: "Oh, dig my grave both wide and deep, with a tombstone at my head and feet. And on my stone [or "breast" in some versions] carve a turtle dove, to signify I died of love."

Parton's "*Little Sparrow*" starts with a warning to young women that is similar to the message found in "Fair and Tender Ladies" and "The Water Is Wide." Maidens in listening range are urged to "heed my warning" and "never trust the hearts of men" who will leave them for other women and crush their hearts like little sparrows. The heartbroken singer wishes she could fly above the pain she feels, and maybe even fly straight into her false lover's face and demand an explanation for the deceitful way he has treated her.

PITIFUL, SICK, AND DYING CHILDREN

Sick and dying children are a popular theme for sentimental ballads. Popular traditional songs like "Willie Roy, the Crippled Boy," "Slippers with Wings," "The Little Girl and the Dreadful Snake," along with the more recent "Teddy Bear" by Red Sovine and Harley Allen's "The Little Girl," recorded by John Michael Montgomery, allow listeners to shed a tear and be drawn into a touching story about a child in some horrible situation.

In "The Little Girl" the protagonist is orphaned and set free from the hellish world her drug-addicted parents brought her into. When her new foster parents, who give her "kisses and hugs" she has never had before take her to Sunday School, she sees a picture of Jesus on the wall and recognizes him as the man who held her as she was crying, hiding behind the couch at home when her parents fought and her father shot her mother.

In "Scarlet Ribbons," which The Browns had a hit with in 1959, a sad story ends with another miracle. A little girl prays at her bedside for God to bring her some "scarlet ribbons for [her] hair." Her father overhears her and walks the streets of his city all night long, looking for a shop open with red hair ribbons for sale. Alas, there are none. But when he finally comes home and peeks in her room at daybreak, he is startled to see "the scarlet ribbons, in gay profusion lying there" on her bedspread. If he lives to be 100, he'll never know where they came from.

Parton embraces these kinds of story lines wholeheartedly in her early writing, perhaps because of the traditional ballads she was raised on, combined with her tender, charitable heart. Two examples are "Jeannie's Afraid of the Dark," from the 1968 RCA album *Just the Two of Us*, with Porter Wagoner, and also "Me and Little Andy," an unlikely original song Parton included on her pop crossover album, *Here You Come Again*, in 1977.

In "Jeannie's Afraid of the Dark," a song fans will remember Parton performing on *The Porter Wagoner Show* in the 1960s, the couple narrating the story remembers how their little daughter would wake in tears nearly every night, begging to come to bed with them because she was so afraid of the dark. Then one summer day when they were laying flowers on family graves at a nearby cemetery, Jeannie became terrified at the thought of being buried after she died. She pleaded with her parents, "When I die, please don't bury me 'cause Jeannie's afraid of the dark."

They never could understand the child's seemingly irrational fear. She received the best of care and all the love her parents could give her. Sometimes parents know things in their guts that are beyond rational thought, and these two admitted later that they somehow knew they would never see their daughter grow up. They simply couldn't imagine her married with a family of her own, or working in a career of her choice. She died of unknown causes one night, just as they had all unconsciously feared. There was nothing they could do but remember the promise they had made to their little girl. They placed an eternal flame on her grave that never went out, because "Jeannie's afraid of the dark."

In the sentimental "Me and Little Andy" the narrator hears a dog barking and a small knocking on her door. On the doorstep that cold, stormy night stands a little girl named Sandy, who introduces her puppy as "Little Andy." Parton raises the pitch of her speaking voice to sound like a child, as "Sandy" asks for something to eat and a place to sleep for the night. Combining nursery rhyme–style verses with the sordid reality of her young life, she reveals that her father is out drinking again in town and her mom has run off somewhere, too. "If you don't love us, nobody will," she says in her plaintive little voice. They both die in their sleep—maybe from pneumonia, after wandering the streets in the cold rain. The little girl who clings to her little puppy is accompanied by him still as both are escorted by angels down the streets of heaven.

ROMANCE!

With her striking appearance and quick wit, Parton is a natural flirt. She explores young love to steamy passion—and everything in between—in her song lyrics. In "Marry Me," another cut from *Little Sparrow* on the Sugar

Hill label, the narrator of the song is a love-struck teenage girl from the hills who has met the young man of her dreams at a square dance. He has "sky-blue eyes, a big wide smile" and he's as "tall as a sycamore tree."

She's convinced this boy from Grassy Branch, Kentucky, is going to marry her because he's "done kissed her on the mouth"—a sign of commitment, in her eyes. After marrying, she dreams of buying a new car and driving around town. Maybe they'll cruise the square or hit the Dairy Queen. He'll buy her a ring, build her a "pretty little house," and then they'll have "a baby or three." Her beloved is a bit of a mama's boy. The narrator mentions the necessity of cutting some apron strings and says her future mother-in-law is "mad as an old wet hen" about their pending marriage.

Parton ends the song with a signature yodel-scat device that always indicates a mood in her songs simply too joyous for actual words.

In "Romeo," an original that Parton sings with Billy Ray Cyrus, Tanya Tucker, Mary Chapin Carpenter, Kathy Mattea, and Pam Tillis on the album *Slow Dancing with the Moon*, the narrator and her posse are hanging out in a nightclub waiting for a good-looking man they've nicknamed "Romeo" to come in and hit the dance floor. The narrator is not shy at all about announcing she "plan[s] to be his Juliet." She and her girlfriends call Romeo, played by Cyrus on the track and in the video, "a cross between a movie star and a hero in a book."

The song breaks into a country line dance, with the step directions spelled out in the lyrics. The narrator notices how good old Romeo looks in his jeans, warns the other ladies away, and goes off in hot pursuit of her crush. A fun music video was produced of this song, in which Cyrus looks to be having as much fun as his growling and flirting admirers.

"Joshua," one of the original songs Parton performed on *The Porter Wagoner Show* while she was still in her 20s, was released in 1970 on the RCA Victor album by the same name. In this hillbilly-style romance novel told in a Tom T. Hall style and set to music, the protagonist is a young woman raised in an orphanage who has always heard stories about the hermit who lived "a good ways down the railroad track." Spurred on by curiosity, she takes a walk and ends up on the tall bearded man's porch, facing his large, rather unfriendly-looking black dog.

They hit it off, of course, and end up staying up all night talking. They say every jar has a lid, and in this story two lonely souls have found each other. Their love grows out of companionship, and eventually the little shack down by the railroad tracks becomes a happy home for "me and Joshua," the narrator sings—and the dog, of course.

With the flip of a coin the yearning (bordering on despair) side of romance and love is realistically explored in "Single Women," a song written by Michael O'Donaghue and interpreted with exquisite loneliness by Parton on her 1982 album *Heartbreak Express*. "Single bars and single women with a single thought in mind," she laments. The pickup lines and the age-old "dance" reminiscent of other varieties of strutting mammals trying to stand out in the herd and attract a mate are set in a neon-lit Amarillo night club. Woven between the smiles and cigarette smoke and perfume and flirtatious remarks is a single strand of hope, waiting to be dashed by the reality of morning. The young woman in the story calls a telephone number that her new acquaintance wrote down on a matchbook and gave her the night before, and a woman answers the phone. She hangs up, realizing he's married. (The song was evidently written before caller ID.) Yet the woman shows up again next weekend at the same place, a twenty tucked into her billfold next to her toothbrush, just in case. Hope springs eternal, sometimes in the worst places—or in the only place it can find.

The Spiritual—Faith and Mystery

Parton has written scores of gospel, Christian-based songs, but she's also drawn to mysterious spiritual characters and topics. In "Me and Little Andy" she alters her voice to sound like a child. In "These Old Bones," released on the *Halos and Horns* album in 2002 by Sugar Hill Records, she drifts into a very old woman's voice to tell the story of her character's life. In fact, Dolly's younger sister, Stella Parton, has said the voice sounds exactly like their own mother, the late Avie Parton.

The old woman in the song (with Avie's voice) lives alone on the mountain, and she's known to be clairvoyant. She keeps a burlap bag of small animal bones tied with a piece of twine, which she tosses like dice on a table to tell fortunes for the folks who seek her out. She can tell someone who they should marry or what financial decision they should make. Some things she sees are better left unsaid.

The narrator goes to see the old woman when she is near death and finds out that she is her biological mother. The county had taken the girl away as a baby because they thought the mountain woman was not right mentally. "Just because a body's different, that don't make them mad," the narrator reasons. In fact, some have been crucified for "the special gifts they had," she adds, with a quick allusion to Jesus.

Her mother gives her the little bag of bones and shares their secret with her: they are just "for show." The real magic is inside her. After she passed, the daughter walked the 11 miles back to her mother's home one last time to get Wink, the one-eyed cat, Billy the goat, and a blue tick hound appropriately named "Blue." Along with the old bones, her mother passes along a desire to help others with her gifts and also the wisdom to tell some things and keep other things to herself.

The Seeker

Albums and songs in this chapter: "The Seeker," *The Golden Streets of Glory, Letter to Heaven: Songs of Faith and Inspiration, For God and Country*

DOLLY'S RELIGIOUS BACKGROUND AND FAITH

During an interview in the 1970s Dolly Parton said she doesn't claim to be a Christian, but it's not out of a sense of irreverence or because she doesn't believe in God. Rather, it's because Parton holds such a high standard of what it truly means to follow Christ, and she knows good and well that she's not perfect. Dolly said she does believe and has been baptized. But even though she's in the habit of praying and talking to God regularly and she's personably responsible for countless acts of charity, Parton said she doesn't deserve to claim the title of "Christian" until she comes to the point in her life when she devotes as much time and energy to the Lord as she does to her career.[1]

Religion was a natural part of her growing-up years. "I was brought up in the Church of God, which is the church where they shout and sing and everything, which I love," Parton said in a 1970 interview. "When you get to singing those old gospel songs and get that good spiritual feeling—well, there's nothing like it."[2]

Church services, prayer meetings, and revivals were social events in the hills—one of the few forms of recreation available. Folks didn't feel required to dress up to come to church. If they didn't own shoes, they didn't wear them. Parton said that just going to the mailbox was a four-mile hike from the house she grew up in. Some families walked to church. Some husbands drove their wives and children to church in a car, and then sat outside waiting for the service to be over. Young boys would sometimes watch through the windows and try to get a pretty girl's attention while she was sitting in a pew. The services were mostly music, so after a prayer, "The preacher would say, 'Does anybody have any special songs?'" Parton recalled. "'Course everybody did, so we took turns. People'd bring tambourines, guitars, banjos, fiddles. And we would *sing*."[3]

According to journalist/webmaster Duane Gordon, "While Parton says she's not a real 'religious' person (involved in organized religion), she says she is a very 'spiritual' person who enjoys a strong, personal relationship with God, on whom she relies for strength and from whom she says all of her gifts, talents, and successes come. She also builds small, private chapels in each of her homes and offices where she goes to pray."[4]

Parton said she has always felt God's direct presence in her life. She's very aware and appreciative of his love and guidance on a daily basis. "I talk to him just like I talk to anyone," she said. "If something's goin' wrong, I'll talk to him about it. I feel that God protects me; I feel he's with me even though he knows what I am. And I feel that he appreciates me bein' honest about it, because he's gonna know anyway. I feel he helps me even though I am a sinner. I know that he's never left me. I know that I can count on him."[5]

DOLLY PARTON: A SEEKER

"Daddy Was an Old Time Preacher Man" is a song written about Parton's grandfather and her religious upbringing, and the contemporary Christian faith anthem, "He Is Alive" on the *White Limozeen* album (1989), reflects Dolly's personal passion for the resurrection story of Christ. *For God and Country*, released in 2003 by the Welk Music Group/Blue Eye Records, explores patriotism and faith in a traditional sense. However, it's probably her original song "The Seeker" that comes closest to describing how Dolly defines herself spiritually.

"The Seeker" was released as a single, debuting on the *Billboard* Country Chart June 7, 1975, and moving to number 2. On the Pop Chart it debuted August 23, 1975, and rose to number 105. In the lyrics Parton identifies herself as a "seeker"—someone who has the same human frailties and weaknesses as anyone else, but her desire is to love God and follow him. She's always looking for God's presence and guidance in everyday life. In the song she portrays God as a "reacher" and a "teacher." She asks him to lead her in the decisions she makes and to protect and shelter her from harm.

Metaphorically she sees God as a fountain flowing down from a mountain, and those waters can wash our sins away. Christianity comes across as first having the faith and desire to follow Jesus, but it's also the daily journey involved in following . . . and falling down, getting back up, and choosing to follow again, with God's grace giving us the strength that we could never have on our own. "You are a leader," Parton sings faithfully. "Won't you show me the way?"

Parton told author Alanna Nash that when she wrote the song, she was at a point in her life when she was trying to reestablish a closer relationship with God. There were more and more people around her who depended on her, and she felt that she was failing them. Perhaps because of her success, those around her were looking to Parton for advice, guidance, and help and as a role model—rather than placing their faith in God. "I got it on my mind that there were too many people bein' led astray by tryin' to do as I do," she said. "Religion is such a touchy thing to me. I take it so serious. . . . It's so sacred to me that I won't mess with it to try to present a big image for myself. I am God-loving, and I'm also God-fearing."[6]

In the same interview Parton went on to admit, "I've never been able to allow God to use me the way I've always used Him, but I know that someday that will come." She doesn't know when or how the time will come when she will be led to focus totally on God's work, but it will become apparent to her and those around her when the time is right. In the meantime, she said, "I feel like He is allowin' me to touch people, to reach out, in my own way."[7]

Interestingly enough, Parton chose to include "The Seeker" on an album that she describes in liner notes as a collection of "some of my favorite love songs." The rest of the songs are all concerned with romantic love. Parton evidently values the spiritual variety of love enough to include "The Seeker" prominently in the mix.

DOLLY'S LETTER TO HEAVEN

A great place to start listening to Dolly Parton's gospel music is *Letter to Heaven: Songs of Faith and Inspiration* (RCA Nashville/Legacy), a compilation of songs originally recorded in 1970 and 1971 and reissued in 2010.

The collection, which includes several cuts from Parton's 1971 album *The Golden Streets of Glory*, starts with Dolly's rendering of the old favorite "I Believe," written by Ervin Drake, Jimmy Shirl, Irvin Graham, and Al Stillman.

In "Yes, I See God," a powerful devotional song written by her Aunt Dorothy Jo Hope, Dolly sings about the different places she sees God's love—in nature at the point where the mountains touch the sky, in the flight of eagles, and in the smile of a baby. After a key modulation she continues, seeing God "when the bridegroom meets his bride, in the eyes of her father, in the tears of her mother," and in "a love that never dies."

"Heaven's Just a Prayer Away," written by Tommy Tomlinson, is followed by Parton's original "The Golden Streets of Glory." Starting out with lines from the old hymn "Glory to His Name," this is a song about heaven. "None will enter there except the pure and holy," Parton sings, and she hopes that her "feet are clean enough" to walk on Heaven's streets some day.

Next comes "How Great Thou Art," probably America's favorite gospel song, along with "Amazing Grace" and "I'll Fly Away," the other two top favorites. Once again, Parton pulls off signature covers of well-worn standards, presenting original interpretations of the three songs that hundreds of artists have recorded over the years.

"I'll Keep Climbing" is another number written by Parton's aunt, and "Book of Life" is from her grandfather, Jake Robert Owens, the "Old Time Preacher Man" in Dolly's song.

Parton presents a moving version of "Wings of a Dove," written by her longtime producer, Bob Ferguson, and popularized by Ferlin Husky in 1960, followed by "Lord, Hold My Hand," which Parton cowrote with Ginny Dean. Set to a catchy melody, "Lord, Hold My Hand" is a prayer, punctuated with a sincere "Amen" at the end. Parton sings, "Let the path I walk be straight," and asks that everything she does be guided by kindness. She never wants to hesitate to help a brother in need, and she prays that even the words she speaks will have the right meaning.

"Would You Know Him (if You Saw Him)," written by Parton and Dorothy Jo Hope, was recorded at the 1970s sessions for *The Golden Streets of Glory* album but was not released until the 2009 RCA Nashville/Legacy boxed set collection, *Dolly*. In the lyrics she wonders if we would recognize Christ if we saw him in the form of a poor man in rags or a hungry man in the street begging for his next meal. The stranger we meet—perhaps a lonely neighbor, a barefoot newsboy, a hungry little girl, a little orphan, or a crippled man—any of these might be "an angel in disguise," she sings.

"Comin' for to Carry Me Home," recorded in 1971, is Parton's version of the old spiritual "Swing Low, Sweet Chariot." Released as a single by RCA, it debuted on the Country Chart April 18, 1971, moving up to number 23. In Parton's arrangement she features a cappella verses, with her lead vocals accompanied by background vocals from Joseph Babcock, Delores Edgin, June Page, and Hurshel Wiginton. Then she kicks into an up-tempo chorus, backed by percussion, resophonic guitar, and electric bass high in the mix. The splendors of heaven are easy to imagine as the instrumental and production intensity in the song build to the finish.

The classic "Daddy Was an Old Time Preacher Man," performed by Porter Wagoner and Dolly Parton (written by Parton and Hope), debuted August 1, 1970, on the *Billboard* Country Chart, moving up to number 7, and it appeared on the album *Once More*. "Daddy worked for God, but asked no pay," Porter and Dolly sing, because he believed God would always provide for him and his family in some way.

Parton's spiritual feelings about nature come to the forefront in her original song "God's Coloring Book," which she included on the album *Here You Come Again* (RCA 1977). Though she doesn't hear audible words from God, she sees him everywhere in creation—in fact, everywhere she looks. Every day "is just a new page in God's coloring book." The clouds are white, the dew is silver, the sun is golden, and the sky is baby blue. She mentions evergreen trees, red and orange flowers, a purple hazy sunset, a rainbow, and even a stormy black sky and the brown leaves of autumn crunching underfoot.

"Letter to Heaven" (Parton), previously described in the album *Joshua,* follows, in which a little child climbs into her grandpa's lap to ask him if he'll help her write a letter to her mother in heaven.

The compilation wraps up with "Sacred Memories," another Parton original, recorded in 1972. Released originally on the album *Love Is Like a Butterfly,* this is a song about memories of her grandfather's church from when she was growing up. Throughout the song, Parton quotes from gospel favorites like "I Can't Feel at Home in This World Any More," "Lord, I'm Coming Home," "Amazing Grace," "Power in the Blood," and "Precious Memories (How They Linger)." These are, indeed, sacred memories for Dolly.

In liner notes Nashville journalist Deborah Evans Price writes, "A seven-time Grammy Award winner, the Tennessee-born singer/songwriter has enjoyed hits in the pop, country, and bluegrass genres, but no musical art form better reflects the soul of Dolly Parton than gospel music.

"Throughout this project," Price continues, "[Parton] imbues each track with an extra measure of passion that can only come from singing about the things that matter most. The final track, 'The Seeker,' is a song Parton has described as her 'talk with God.' . . . Her deep faith has always infused Parton's life and been reflected in her art. 'I act on faith all the time,' Parton has been quoted as saying. 'I feel like this is my ministry, not just my job, and I have to be able to touch and reach the people. I'm always asking God to show me ways and give me avenues to do that so I can uplift people, so I can be a blessing.'"

PATRIOTISM AND SPIRITUALITY

Like many artists after the indescribable horror of watching the twin towers of the World Trade Center in New York collapse on television on September 11, 2001, Parton was inspired to write and record.

On the cover of *For God and Country,* released by the Welk Music Group in conjunction with Parton's Blue Eye Records in 2003, Dolly is dressed in a red and white vertical-striped top and miniskirt with a slit up her left thigh. White stars sparkle on her navy blue pillbox hat, her blue pointed collars, and the blue cuffs on her sleeves. To top off the effect, she's wearing extremely high-heeled red shoes with little white bows on the toes and the straps.

Parton begins by reciting the 23rd Psalm in "The Lord Is My Shepherd," with an original arrangement and melody. "The Lord is my Shepherd, my friend and my helper," she sings.

"The Star-Spangled Banner," arranged by Parton, is accompanied by a string section and a grand piano. "God Bless the USA," the Lee Greenwood classic, starts with a fife and drum and a personal message from Parton.

"Hello America," she says. "I'm Dolly, and I want to welcome you to this special project. It came to me in such a special way, I believe it to be inspired.

And I truly always ask God to lead and guide me in everything I do, and allow me to do things that praise and glorify him, to uplift people, and to allow me to have some fun. 'For God and Country,' well, that just seemed to be the perfect title for it because I love God and I love my country. I also wanted to do something to honor all the brave men and women who have sacrificed so much to keep us free. And may God continue to bless the USA."

She goes on to narrate the remaining tracks, continuing with "Light of a Clear Blue Morning."

"This is a song I wrote years ago when I was going through a very hard time personally in my life," Parton says. "We all have those moments. But it seemed to fit the hard times that we've been through lately in America. But you know what? I can see the light of a clear blue morning." She sings about looking for sunshine, after being in darkness for too long. "Everything's gonna be all right that's been all wrong," she affirms. With images of eagles that are born to fly, the song ends in glorious banjo-propelled double-time rhythm.

After a unique arrangement of "When Johnny Comes Marching Home," Parton presents "Welcome Home," an original song. In the first verse a re-lieved father waits at the door to greet his son. He's come home from war and the father tells him, "I've been praying and been hoping and I never did give up." Now the boy is at home and he can rest. In the second verse, the mother of a soldier wakes up in the night, knowing her son has "passed into the light," and in the third verse we hear God, the Father's voice welcom-ing the young soldier home to heaven. Backed by an acoustic arrangement (fiddle, mandolin, guitar, Dobro, and light percussion), Parton ends with a recitation, comparing the sacrifice God made to send his son to die for our sins to the families who have lost a son or daughter to war.

"Gee, Ma, I Wanna Go Home" follows, with a lighter arrangement. Par-ton improvises a bit with the lyrics, joking that the reason she couldn't join the army was because her feet were flat. "And since I cannot see them, I'll take their word for that," she sings in a chipper voice, joking again about her famous voluptuous bustline. Later in the song she sings, "Oh, the generals in the army don't fight like all the rest. But you shoulda seen 'em fight to pin this medal on my chest. . . . These are my two secret weapons: shock and awe!" she laughs.

Serious again, Parton sings the old favorite "Whispering Hope." The cut starts with the tolling of a church bell, and she whispers, "No matter how big our problems are, God stands right there next to us, whispering hope." This simple statement of faith is the crux of the album, and of Dolly's spiritual outlook.

Backed by gospel piano and background vocalists powered on the bottoms end by a gifted bass singer, Parton sings the Thomas A. Dorsey song "There Will Be Peace in the Valley for Me."

A bluegrass original follows: "Red, White and Bluegrass." In the second verse Dolly asks, "Where else but in America can people live so free? And I'm proud of every soldier that has stood and fought for me. And I'm proud of every bluegrass band that's ever picked a lick. And I'm proud to be American. That's why I'm a singing' this!"

While she has the bluegrass band cranked up, Parton sings "My Country 'Tis of Thee," followed by another original, "I'm Gonna Miss You," speaking to the dedicated servicemen and servicewomen who will not be coming home. She's proud of their service and bravery, but mostly she just wishes they will all come home again safely. "I can't accept the fact that you're gone," she sings, the emotion obvious behind her vocals.

In the rip-roaring, Pentecostal-flavored original "Go to Hell," Parton sings about how she loves and fears God, but like most of us she has always struggled with knowing what's right and doing it consistently. Personally, she says she's always been "a little too good to be really bad" and "a little too bad to be really good."

She reminds listeners that good will always win out, and then shouts, "Get thee behind me, Satan. Just leave me the hell alone!" Then she suggests (strongly) that the devil take his wars, political corruption, lust, and avarice, pack them all in a handbasket, and take them back home to hell—because heaven is waiting for Miss Dolly Rebecca Parton!

In a manner that would have done her preaching grandfather proud, Parton hauls into a cadenced recitation punctuated with several "ahs" at the end of each phrase. "My God can do anything (ah!) My God can heal the sick (ah!) mend broken hearts and take our souls to heaven (ah!)" She stands on God's name, looks the devil in the eye, and laughs in his face, rebuking him with a final "Ha! Ha! Ha!"

Parton wrote a new verse to the Barry A. Sadler/Robert L. Moore Jr. song "Ballad of the Green Beret" that mentions Delta Force, the CIA, the marines, covert missions, and special ops. "Brave Little Soldier" (Parton) is written in the style of a children's song, with a choir of young singers joining in on the chorus. "The enemy is stalking me, just waiting for the kill," she sings, but like young David, the shepherd boy in the Bible story who would later become king of Israel, the singer claims the battlefield he's looking at—a modern-day Goliath.

Charging ahead with "Tie a Yellow Ribbon" (Russell Brown and Irwin Levine), the song made popular by Tony Orlando, Parton next presents "Color Me America," an original that uses red, white, and blue imagery to encourage her fellow Americans. Red is the color she sees when she hears someone speaking evil, and red is the color of bloodshed in the street. Blue represents the sorrow of dealing with war—the injuries, broken spirits, and lives lost. The light of God's loving spirit is white, and the Lord "lifts us up and hands to us an olive branch," she sings, symbolizing a fervent desire for peace.

The last cut, "The Glory Forever," is simply the Lord's Prayer set to an ancient-sounding, Celtic-flavored melody that Parton wrote herself.

Although probably not for the faint of heart, *For God and Country* is one of the most powerful musical and spiritual statements Parton has ever made on a recording. But then again, difficult times call for strong measures. Whether you agree with Parton's spiritual and political views or not, it's clear that she is singing sincerely from the heart, with hope for peace. The message may be too simple for some to accept, but sometimes the most profound messages are honest, short, and to the point—something a child could understand, as Dolly wrote in the song about her grandpa.

Perhaps Deborah Evans Price sums up Parton's gift for gospel music best in her liner notes for *Dolly Parton, Letter to Heaven: Songs of Faith and Inspiration*: Parton "has the ability to write and perform songs that come from a deeply personal well, yet strike a universal chord with audiences all over the world," she notes. "Always honest and never afraid to be vulnerable, Dolly Parton shares her faith in these inspiring tunes and never has this Smoky Mountain songbird sounded more compelling."

Freedom!

Albums and singles in this chapter: "Light of a Clear Blue Morning,"
*New Harvest . . . First Gathering, Here You Come Again, Heartbreaker,
Great Balls of Fire, The Great Pretender, White Limozeen, Slow Dancing
with the Moon*

PARTON, POST-PORTER

The late, great songwriter John Hartford ("Gentle on my Mind") once said
that a musician's style is defined by his limitations. When an artist has very few
limitations—as in the case of Dolly Parton—it can be quite fascinating (and
entertaining) to see what transpires next.

Dolly's parting with bandleader and producer Porter Wagoner was a bittersweet but necessary career decision. Even as a child, Parton had big dreams
along with the personal confidence that she could make them all come true.

The 1970s took Dolly Parton, country singer, down the first left turn on a
genre-bending rocket ride that has led her to become one of the most loved
and admired pop icons of our time.

Albums like *New Harvest . . . First Gathering* with her family in 1977; the
platinum-selling *Here You Come Again* (1977); 1978's rocking gold record
Heartbreaker; Great Balls of Fire, released in 1979; *The Great Pretender* in
1984; the gold-selling *White Limozeen* (1989) with the number 1 hit "Why'd
You Come in Here Lookin' Like That;" and the platinum-selling 1993 release

Slow Dancing with the Moon, gave Dolly the chance to write and record pop, rock, and even disco music on a career path that led her to more widespread national television exposure—including her own TV show, a number of movies, and a Broadway play.

Artistically, Parton spread her wings like the eagles she's fond of mentioning in her songs and took off after leaving Porter Wagoner. She's living proof of the adage "What the mind can conceive and the heart can believe, one can achieve," and there's no limit to this woman's imagination.

Keith Herrell, press staff reporter with *The Evansville Press* in Indiana, caught up with Dolly Parton backstage after a concert at Roberts Stadium in 1975. She split the bill with Johnny Rodriguez and Billy "Crash" Craddock that night for an enthusiastic crowd of 3,500, and when Herrell asked her how she was getting along without Porter Wagoner, she said, "Just fine." She thought of the Wagonmasters often and missed them, she said, "but I'm really proud that I'm at the point in my career where I can head my own show."[1]

Parton was still collaborating with Wagoner in Nashville, since they jointly owned the Owepar publishing company and a recording studio. She was performing that night with the Travelin' Family Band, comprised of her 21-year-old brother, Randy; two cousins; and one non–family member. She talked about feeling more pressure as a bandleader and emcee than as a featured singer in Porter's show. More than anything, though, she was excited about her songwriting.

"I love to write," she said. "That's my favorite thing in the whole world. I love to sing and entertain, but writing is so personal to me." When the reporter alluded to the fact that some critics attributed her current popularity largely to her appearance, she answered, "I want people to know me. I'm like any woman. I try to look as good as I can. I love makeup, but I'm not made up on the inside. I want people to appreciate me for what I can really do."[2]

DOLLY'S APPEARANCE

When asked about the wigs and over-the-top fashion preferences, Parton always said it stemmed from her idea of what beauty looked like to her as a little girl in east Tennessee, growing up in a family too poor to buy nice clothes. In a 1992 interview with VH1 she explained, "There was a woman in our hometown, and everybody said that she was the trash, you know, the town tramp. But I thought she was beautiful 'cause she had this yellow hair, and she had bright red lipstick, and she wore makeup and tight clothes and bright colors and red fingernails and high-heel shoes. And I thought, 'That's how I want to look!' I thought she was beautiful. . . . My look came from a very serious place. It was a country girl's idea of what glamour really was. The more people tried to get me to change my look, the more I realized people were looking at me. And I thought that if I can hold their attention long enough for them to see that I am a talented person and that I am sincere about my work and that there is a brain underneath all of this hair and there is a heart underneath these boobs. . . . If people can really see beyond that, then I can get past that. Overcoming my own image has been a challenge to myself."[3]

"Light of a Clear Blue Morning" appears on the *New Harvest . . . First Gathering* album released in 1977, which Dolly produced herself. The single went to number 11 on the *Billboard* Country Chart and number 87 on the Pop Chart. In the song Parton exuberantly sings about making it through a "long, dark night" to "the light of a clear, blue morning." She's thrilled with her freedom, as she talks about getting rid of "clinging vines" she doesn't need anymore and moving mountains with pure, unadulterated faith in her dreams. The instrumentation starts with a piano behind a simple vocal line and builds to a tambourine-shaking, cartwheel-turning finish.

The message of the song is symbolic of Dolly's creative attitude at this stage of her career: the sky's the limit. Daisy Mae is in Hollywood and the locals are turning around to stare, as she wrote a few years later in a song for the *White Limozeen* album. Most writers occasionally write songs that fall stylistically outside the genre boundaries of their own bands. Dolly was already writing these songs, but at this point she had the freedom to experiment with instrumentation and production to make them happen. Nothing was holding her back, a new audience was discovering her, and she was having *fun*.

DOLLY'S MUSIC CROSSES OVER

Looking 30 and voluptuous on the cover of *Here You Come Again* (1977), Parton is wearing a bright-red long-sleeved blouse covered with tiny white polka dots, tied at the waist. Cuffed jeans with high-heeled, open-toed off-white shoes complete the subdued (for her) outfit that accentuates her hourglass figure. This is the image of Dolly that comes to most fans' minds, with a full platinum-blonde wig and a wide smile. "Dolly" is written in silver neon-style script, with "Parton" in smaller font underneath. Already one of those artists known by her first name alone, Dolly is striking a series of dance poses across the front cover of the album and halfway across the back cover. On the back is a close-up version of Parton in the same outfit, and she's leaning against a stone wall wearing a quieter smile. The background in the four dancing shots is black, with white horizontal light lines here and there. It could be more neon, or perhaps the headlight trail of moving traffic.

Inside the graphic design shifts to an almost Victorian-style portrait of Parton's face and shoulders in a large double-album panel design. The painting style is pointillism, in which the viewer's eye mixes individual points of paint to form an image. Parton is holding an enormous bouquet of pink and white flowers in her right hand. She's the demure image of a floral femininity in spring. The stark contrast of "disco Dolly" on the cover and "demure Dolly" on the inside of the album packaging is no accident. Which one is she, really? The answer is a multifaceted butterfly-wing "yes."

The title track, "Here You Come Again," debuted on the *Billboard* Country Chart October 15, 1977, and went to number 1, where it stayed for five weeks. It appeared on the Pop Chart the same day, moving to number 3, and on October 22 the song landed on the Adult Contemporary Chart, rising to the number 2 spot. The album was certified gold on December 27, 1977, for sales in excess of 500,000 units and platinum on April 28, 1978, for more than a million units sold. "Here You Come Again" brought Parton her first pop Grammy nomination for Best Pop Performance by a Female, and the album won the Grammy for Best Country Performance by a Female.

Written by Barry Mann and Cynthia Weil, a man "lookin' better than a body has a right to" comes waltzing back into the narrator's life (well, maybe disco dancing) just when she's managed to get her life back together without him. All he has to do is smile, and her defenses evaporate into the same old powerful attraction she's always felt for him. Here he comes . . . and there she goes. The production on this cut, and throughout the album, is decidedly more complex than her earlier efforts and definitely pop oriented, leaning heavily on the then new novelty of synthesized keyboards. She went to Hollywood to do this record, after all. When in Rome . . .

"Baby Come Out Tonight" (McCord) finds Parton begging her love to meet her for one last tryst and "dance in the moonlight" before he's gone for good, back to his wife and family. She regrets they'll have no more Tuesday night sleepovers or episodes in the shower (yes, she really said that). Her voice sounds resigned to the prospect of his leaving, but she's still powerless to resist one last night together. "Let me gaze into your eyes until we both go blind," she sings, in a vibe reminiscent of Maria Muldaur's in "Midnight at the Oasis."

In her original "It's All Wrong, But It's All Right," Parton is still in a frisky mood. Aggressively, she purrs, "I like your looks; I love your smile," and follows that with, "Can I use you for a while?" The single debuted on *Billboard*'s Country Chart on March 18, 1978, and went to number 1 for two weeks.

You can take the girl out of east Tennessee, but you can't completely take east Tennessee out of the girl, as is evidenced by Parton's "Me and Little Andy," one of the pitiful, dying-child story songs she seems to really enjoy writing. In interviews Dolly has noted that she never intended to leave country music. She just wanted to take it with her to new places it had never been before. The desperately sad story of little Sandy and her dog, Andy, starts out with an acoustic guitar and the sound of wind howling in the background, building in intensity with the help of the inevitable synthesizers. The last time through the chorus Parton, raising her voice in pitch to sound like a child's, is treated with reverb and ends with a ghostly whisper. It's interesting to note that megastar Alison Krauss, who loves Parton's music and has the same acoustic/bluegrass roots, has stated that she has a penchant for sad songs over any other type. The more a ballad makes her bawl, the better. She and Parton seem to have this in common, too.

In the John Sebastian–penned "Lovin' You," Parton explores a positive love song from the perspective of a woman waking up every morning, so deeply in love with her husband that she can't imagine ever leaving him. Banjo and drums are high in the mix by the end of the song, which sports a Melanie "I've Got a Brand New Pair of Roller Skates (You've Got a Brand New Key)" style. Dolly's vocals, while still familiar, are exploring new territory stylistically, and she definitely pulls it off.

"Cowgirl and the Dandy," written by Bobby Goldsboro from the male perspective as "The Cowboy and the Lady," seems tailor-made for Parton. Goldsboro released it himself, and both Brenda Lee (1980) and John Denver (1981) had hits with the song. Seasoned with acoustic guitar leads and fills layered on a bottom crust of synthesizers, this song finds the signer stranded at an airport and meeting a wealthy gentleman in the bar who appears to be the complete opposite of her countrified, rhinestone self. Surprisingly, they hit it off. And forever afterward, "There's a little bit of class in this ole cowgirl," Parton sings with an audible wink, "and a little bit of country in the dandy."

"Two Doors Down" (Parton) was the A side of the single that debuted on the Country Chart March 18, 1978, b/w "It's All Wrong, But It's All Right." Released to pop radio, "Two Doors Down" made it to number 19 on *Billboard*'s Pop Chart. Interestingly, the song sent to pop radio was a different version than the one that originally appeared on the 1977 album. The new version was subbed in for all pressings of the album from early 1978 forward.

The song kicks off with twin fuzz-edged electric guitar lines that seem to be having a party with a saxophone—the kind of groove *Saturday Night Live*'s Blues Brothers would have enjoyed. The narrator is sitting alone in her apartment, feeling sorry for herself over a failed relationship that, honestly, she hadn't held out much hope for anyway. He hadn't made any promises, and now he was gone. After listening to the sounds of her neighbor's party two doors down, she finally decides to move on. "Think I'll dry these useless tears and get myself together," she vows. Instead of more tears, she says, "I think I'd really rather join them two doors down." It goes well, of course, and soon she's inviting her new love back to her place . . . two doors down.

Smack back to the country with the next song, Dolly launches into the sweetly spiritual, acoustic "God's Coloring Book" (Parton). "As Soon as I Touched Him" (Helms-Hirsch) mixes spiritual and sensual images, beginning with a grand piano intro. Lines like "As soon as I touched him I was born again" put the listener in mind of the story of the woman in the Bible who touched the hem of Jesus' garment and was healed because of her faith. She knew that if she just touched him, she would be delivered from the chronic hemorrhaging she'd suffered with for 12 years, and she was. Soon the listener realizes this is quite another story, although described with the same kind of spiritually intense language. The singer is drawn to the man like a magnet; he tells her she was "sent to him," they sleep together once, he leaves forever, and she happily bears his child. Go figure.

The album ends with another cover, Kenny Rogers's "Sweet Music Man," the story of a woman saying goodbye to her traveling musician lover. Parton's voice soars in harmony on lines like, "You touched my soul with your beautiful song." She is almost in awe of the man's musical talents, but she's grown weary of the man himself, who "surrounds himself with people who demand so little of him."

HEARTBREAKER

On the imaginative album cover of *Heartbreaker* (1978), Dolly, wearing a long pink long-sleeved, tight-waisted ruffled dress with extremely high-heeled, strappy metallic pink shoes, is leaping through the canvas of a painting of a rose garden on the left. On the right, closer up, she's leaning on a white shelf with her right leg propped up a step, skirt parted nearly to her underwear line, looking thoughtful. On the back of the album we see the other half of Dolly coming through the picture, with a large, dreamy image of her floating on the left. Not quite Alice falling through the looking glass, the design is curious.

On the inside of the LP cover is a large two-panel vertical photo of Parton in all her pink, filmy splendor. She's wearing a wavy blonde wig parted on the right, a golden butterfly flutters at her lower left side, and flower petals are strewn around her feet. Perhaps this is what Aphrodite would look like if she were a country music star.

Side 1 starts with "Really Got the Feeling" (Billy Vera, Lon Price), in which the singer observes, "You're a gentle man, and a gentleman is getting mighty hard to find these days." The single debuted on the Country Chart November 25, 1978, rising to number 1.

The last two songs are Parton originals, "Sure Thing" and "With You Gone." The former is the feisty narrative of a young woman planning a night out on the town. She could have a date, but she'd rather go stag and dance with a different man for every song. The trumpets and trombones punctuate a funk beat, and Parton's voice squeaks with anticipation: "The guy who strikes my fancy will be the one to dance me home."

The mood shifts dramatically in "With You Gone," as the lonely singer sits alone in her room, in tears. There's an unexpected key change in the chorus, and the trombones, bari sax, steel guitar, congas, acoustic guitars, and electric bass weave a mesmerizing groove, somewhere between a samba and a reggae beat. Just when you think you know Dolly Parton, she throws you a curve. In fact, she probably enjoys throwing you a curve.

The Blues Brothers spirit is back on "Baby I'm Burnin'" (Parton), with an aggressive, in-your-face horn intro propelled with funk guitar. Flaming lyrical images represent the singer's passion, accented with an effect that sounds like a space gun whenever she mentions the word "fireworks." The keys move up and the intensity increases to a big finish. The single debuted on the Country Chart on November 25, 1978, going to number 48. In December it went to number 25 on the Pop and number 11 on the Adult Contemporary Chart.

"Nickels and Dimes" (Parton and Estel) starts off with an acoustic guitar and reflects on the singer's early career as a street musician playing for tips. "If you remember a child on the corner of time," she sings, then she's thanking you for the tips—the "nickels and dimes." Like the narrator in this song, Parton never forgets her humble beginnings or the people who helped her along the way.

In "The Man" (Parton), written in a serious-sounding minor key, the singer describes a man who may have a few rough and rugged edges on the outside, but inside he's the kind of person a girl can trust. At the end of the song we discover the narrator is describing her father. A buzzing sound effect is peppered throughout the song, and Parton tries a new vocal effect in which she hits a note hard, backs off, and then bounces back immediately—something like a human reverb chamber.

The title cut, "Heartbreaker" (Wolfert-Sager), debuted on the Country Chart on August 19, 1978, rising to number 1 for three weeks while also climbing to 37 on the Pop Chart and 12 on Adult Contemporary. The song is reflective. The narrator is sitting alone, thinking about her past with this man who has disappointed her. "Heartbreaker . . . sweet little love maker," she sings quietly, "couldn't you be just a little more kind to me?"

"I Wanna Fall in Love" (Parton) sports a sassy attitude with electric bass and guitar, a horn section, and drums lining out a disco groove. The singer is weary of having a new lover every night and longs to really fall in love with one man—someone she can simply be herself with.

Heartbreaker was certified gold for sales in excess of one million on August 16, 1978. Disco remixes were made of "Baby I'm Burning" and "I Wanna Fall in Love" on a 12-inch single called "Dance with Dolly," which became a big hit at dance clubs.

GOODNESS GRACIOUS, GREAT BALLS OF FIRE!

Certified gold for sales in excess of one million on November 11, 1979, hit songs on the radio from Parton's album *Great Balls of Fire* included "Sweet Summer Lovin'" (#7 on the Country Chart, #77 on the Pop Chart) and "You're the Only One," a number 1 song on the *Billboard* Country Chart for two weeks, which also went to number 59 on the Pop Chart.

In the Parton original "Star of the Show," the metaphor for a relationship is membership in her lover's band. They had a great duet, and he invited her to be the "star of the show." All goes well until the duet becomes a trio and Parton exits. She won't play second fiddle and she insists, "I'm nobody's co-star; I just play leading roles."

In "Down" (Parton) the narrator is someone who has always helped out her friends. Now she's the one who's been left and forgotten, and she's feeling depressed. It doesn't last long, though. By the end of the song she's accepting the current situation as temporary, and she's making plans to get back on her feet and to be as generous as she was before.

"You're the Only One" (Sager-Roberts) is a song of realization. The singer apologizes for breaking her lover's heart. She wants to reconcile and desires with all her heart to go back to their first love. It ends with a recitation that even Porter Wagoner would be impressed with: "Sometimes you've got to go away to realize what you've left behind."

Some absolute superstars of the acoustic/bluegrass music world show up as sidemen on this album, including Ricky Skaggs, David Grisman, and Herb Pedersen. The Beatles song "Help!" (Lennon-McCartney) is presented with a spare, almost bluegrass arrangement, featuring Skaggs and Pedersen, two of the finest harmony singers and arrangers to walk the planet, singing with Parton, high in the mix. The song starts a cappella, with the vocals joined first by an acoustic guitar and then drums. Grisman on mandolin, along with the electric bass, banjo (Pedersen), and lightly tasteful electric guitar and percussion, provide an effective backdrop for the imaginative take on this rock classic. Herb, Ricky, and Dolly bookend the song with an a cappella three-part harmony ending. The Beatles have never been so fun.

Side 1 ends with another Parton original, "Do You Think That Time Stands Still." This one sounds a little more country, with a steel guitar in the band and a backup choir of soul singers who pop out of the loft at the end of the song. The singer's man left her without even saying goodbye. Now he's back again, begging for a second chance, but it's just too late. Things have changed and she's rearranged her life. Time "never has" stood still, and "it never will" stand still. The arrangements and instrumentation are new, but these are some of the same relationship themes Parton explored in her 1960s duets with Porter Wagoner. (Tom T. was right. Ninety-nine percent of songs are all about "this ole boy" and "this ole girl.")

Side 2 kicks off with the uplifting romantic hit "Sweet Summer Lovin'" (Tosti). Parton's lead vocal, light and doubled, bounces euphorically along on top of an acoustic guitar–driven rhythm section anchored by a steadily thumping, rather sexy electric bass. She wakes up in love and feels like "running barefoot through the dandelions." A spritely flute break at the end of the song flutters over Pedersen's steady banjo roll, and then the song ends with two flutes in harmony, soaring like twin bluebirds into the sky.

"Great Balls of Fire" (Blackwell-Hammer) offers a nod to Jerry Lee Lewis's hit version of the song, but—as one might expect—Parton's version squeals a little with girlish flirtation. The song increases in sexual tension and energy, propelled by a frenzied big horn production to the finish.

"Almost in Love" (Parks-Thiele) starts out quietly, with steel guitar, keyboard, and accordion. It's a conversation between a young woman and her mother. "When he holds me, the air is thick and sweet," the daughter confides. She's trying to decide if this is the love she's been waiting for, the one she can leave home for. The melody ends on an unresolved chord. Like the girl in the story, we're not sure what the future will bring . . . but we're hopeful.

In "It's Not My Affair Anymore" (French), the singer has seen her lover out with another woman and she realizes things are over. "Sandy's Song" (Parton) starts out gently with an acoustic guitar, building to a full orchestral arrangement complete with a harp. The narrator is overwhelmed by the power of the love she feels, and she promises to love her man until "green grass turns lavender blue" and "when horses and chariots chase down the wind." The album ends with a sweetly introspective oboe line. The opposite of this song, in concept, shows up several years later as the title track of Parton's Grammy-winning *The Grass Is Blue,* in which the colors of nature turn upside down to reflect the singer's disturbed and heartbroken emotional state.

SHE'S RIDING IN A WHITE LIMOZEEN . . .

Skipping ahead to 1989, *White Limozeen* was produced by country/blue-grass star Ricky Skaggs and recorded in Nashville at Fred Vail's Treasure Isle studio. "Why'd You Come in Here Looking Like That" debuted on May 6, 1989, and went to number 1 on the Country Chart. "Yellow Roses" hit the chart on August 26, 1989, and also went to number 1. The title cut went to number 29, "Time for Me to Fly" went to number 39, and the Don Francisco–penned contemporary Christian standard "He's Alive" also went to number 39.

The title cut, "White Limozeen" (Dolly Parton and Mac Davis) kicks off in tempo with the singer's footsteps as she strides down the California side-walk. Backed by a jazzy Dobro and spirited vocalists who sound like they just stepped out of a black gospel choir loft, Parton sings about the new girl in town, dreaming of seeing her name up in lights someday. Well, she makes it all come true, of course. She may have "met the devil in the city of angels," but she never lost sight of her diamond, star-studded dreams. And when her family comes to town to visit, they're met by a chauffeur with a little red bow tie and a long, white luxury car.

With an estrogen-driven, "girls gone wild" feel, the narrator in "Why'd You Come in Here Lookin' Like That" gets on her good-looking man "with a wanderin' eye and a travelin' mind" for attracting too much attention, with his tight jeans and even tighter derriere. This man who could "stop traffic in a gunny sack" frankly doesn't need to be wearing those high-heeled boots and dancing around with a different woman every night. The emphasis of the first word on the first syncopated note of the first line grabs the listener's attention immediately—probably as much as this guy's outfit. (I imagine him looking like Marty Stuart.)

With "Yellow Roses" Parton proves she can still write and sing a straight-ahead country song as well as or better than anyone. In a sentimental tone, the singer recalls how her husband of many years always brought her yel-low roses—"the color of sunshine"—on every special occasion of their lives together. Now he's gone, loving someone new, and the scumbag chose to say goodbye the same way: "with a single yellow rose."

"It's Time for Me to Fly" (Kevin Cronin) features Mark Casstevens, Steven A. Gibson, and Vince Gill on guitars; Ricky Skaggs on guitar and mandolin; Eddie Bayers on drums; Mike Brignardello on bass; Barry Beckett on piano; Lloyd Green on steel guitar; Stuart Duncan on fiddle; Bela Fleck on banjo; and Curtis Young, Lianna Young, and Lisa Silver on background vocals.

As one might guess by the list of stellar studio musicians, this song is a bluegrass romp with drums, steel, and keyboards sprinkled into the recipe. In fact, this arrangement sounds a lot like Skaggs's own country band in the mid-'80s that spearheaded the new traditionalist movement in country music. The singer has had enough of her false love, with his petty jealousy and intolerant attitude, and "It's time for me to fly," she sings on banjo- and fiddle-propelled wings.

"He's Alive" (Don Francisco) is one of the most dramatic songs Parton has ever recorded. Musicians on the single include Craig Nelson, bass; Eddie Bayers, drums; David Huntsinger, piano and keyboards; Mac McAnnally, acoustic guitar; Reggie Young, electric guitar; Farrell Morris, percussion; Nashville String Machine, strings; and the Christ Church Pentecostal Choir, directed by Landy Gardner, on choir vocals.

The song is the simple and powerful story of the resurrection of Christ, told from the perspective of Peter, the disciple who, when push came to shove, denied three times that he even knew Jesus. If you've never heard this song, put the book down, go buy the single on iTunes, and put on your shouting shoes.

NASHVILLE COFFEE TALK WITH FRED VAIL

Nashville producer/studio owner Fred Vail spoke about his experiences with Dolly Parton in the studio in a January 2010 interview, but first, a little background information. Vail began his 50-plus-year career in the music business working in radio and records as a DJ at 15 and a country music program director at 17. As a high school senior in California in 1962 he started booking artists such as Jan and Dean, Smokey Robinson and The Miracles, and The Righteous Brothers into school assemblies, graduation parties, and teen clubs.

Fred produced the Beach Boys' first major concert on May 24, 1963, and was hired the same night by the band to be their "advance man," emcee, and marketing manager. Vail came up with the idea for *Beach Boys Concert*, the band's landmark 1964 album, which became their first number 1 hit and gold album. Vail was with Brian Wilson when he wrote and recorded "Fun, Fun, Fun," he was present at the *Good Vibrations* sessions, and he was with Wilson when *Pet Sounds* was mastered.

Vail became the Beach Boys' manager and the head of their own Brother Records label in 1969, at the age of 25. He joined Capital Records as a promotion and marketing manager in '72, moving to RCA Records a year later. He resigned in 1974, and on the advice of his friends Waylon Jennings and Johnny Russell, he moved to Nashville that spring to do independent radio promotion and marketing for Jennings, Jimmy Dean, Earl Thomas Conley, Ronnie McDowell, Alabama, Olivia Newton-John and John Travolta, Eric Clapton, George Clinton and Parliament, GRT, and RSO Records.

Fred opened the doors to Treasure Isle Recorders, Inc., in 1980, the studio he still owns and operates in Music City. Celebrating 30 years in 2010, Treasure Isle is the oldest independent recording studio in Nashville still under its original ownership and management. According to Vail, Treasure Isle was the first multitrack digital studio in Nashville and the fist LEDE (an acronym for "live end—dead end") room in the city. In addition to Parton, he's also recorded Emmylou Harris, Linda Ronstadt, Miranda Lambert, Michael W. Smith, Jars of Clay, James Taylor, Alabama, Vince Gill, Keith Urban, B. B. King, Rodney Crowell, the Beach Boys, Johnny Cash, Waylon Jennings, Isaac Hayes, and John Denver, among others. In more recent years, the debut albums from Jason Aldean, Lyle Lovett, Travis Tritt, Pam Tillis, Foster and Lloyd, Highway 101, and Little Texas were all recorded at Treasure Isle.

Vail worked with Dolly Parton twice. The first time was in 1973, he said. "I had left Capital Records and gone to work for RCA," he recalled. "In those days all the promotion staffs were full line, which means there was no specialization. So if a record came out and it was pop or top 40, you worked it. If it was rhythm and blues, you worked it. If it was classical, you worked it. There were probably maybe 30 staffers scattered around the country. I had the Southeast, so I had Georgia, Tennessee, South Carolina, and North Carolina. My job was to promote and market RCA products, to set up new displays [at record stores], and develop airplay from radio stations.

"The thing was," he continued, "out of these 30 or so people who were covering the country, only about five or six of us really had any passion for country music. It was kind of an unofficial rule that your first allegiance was to the pop music department because it made the money. It was 70 percent of the budget. Country was maybe 8 percent of the budget. You weren't told *not* to work country records, per se. You could probably never find anyone who would admit that. But if it came down to it, you were supposed to work the pop product. They were a hot pop label. They had Lou Reed and David Bowie, and they had Elvis who was crossing over, and they had a lot of super acts at the time who were very, very popular. John Denver was hotter than a firecracker. Henry Mancini was on the label. There were a lot of iconic acts, and basically only five or six of us really liked country music."

Vail made a personal commitment to promote country records with equal zeal in his territories. "I had some really good breakout country stations in my market—one in Charlotte, one in Knoxville, there was one in Raleigh, North Carolina, one in Columbia, South Carolina, and there were a couple more that were really major, powerhouse stations in the South, which has always been a country market. I kind of made a name for myself with the country artists, because they weren't used to being treated so well when they came into a town," Vail said. "Sometimes the promotion guy wouldn't even show up to meet them. They'd just go do their gig and get on their bus and head home. With me, I'd go to the gig and I'd hang out with them and I'd turn them on to restaurants, and we'd chat and I knew all about their music. They knew I was a fan, as well as a dedicated employee. I got to know Waylon [Jennings]. Dickie Lee and Johnny Russell were on the label, and they all became real good friends. It was one of the reasons I moved to Nashville, which is an entirely different story."

There were a couple of things that made Dolly Parton stand out in Vail's mind, he says. (No, not those two things. . . .) "Around the summer of '73 Chet Atkins did a benefit in Knoxville, which is where he was from, at the Dean Hills Country Club, and he brought in all these different country artists for a celebrity golf tournament and big dinner," Vail recalls. "It was a fund-raiser for some charity. Among those that came in were Porter and Dolly, and Bill Anderson came in and George Lindsey—'Goober' from *The Andy Griffith Show*, and of course I went over there to cover Porter and Dolly because they were on the label and they were a hot duet. I got the chance to meet them and talk to them, and I was really familiar with their music and the fact that she'd grown up in east Tennessee. I was really impressed with her charm. She was really friendly and still had the big hair. It was really cool," Vail smiled. "Most of her stuff, particularly her duets with Porter, was very country. There was nothing crossover about her. You weren't going to get a record on any of the pop stations because they weren't anywhere close to mainstream.

"When 'Jolene' came out in 1973 and I heard that record, I had a unique situation going on in the Charlotte market. There were two top 40 stations and one what we used to call 'easy listening' or 'middle of the road,' WBT, was a 50,000-watter and it had an all-night truck-driving show. I'd go down there sometimes and hang out with the all-night DJ, Bill Miller. Sometimes he'd even put me on the air and I'd introduce an artist. With 'Jolene,' I heard it and I thought, 'You know, I think that could be a crossover record. I really do.' I told my bosses, and they kind of pooh-poohed it. Like, 'OK, that's interesting. How's the David Bowie doing? How's the John Denver doing?' Then I said 'No, I think this has potential.'"

WAYS was the number 1 station in the market and WIST was the competitor. "These were both AM stations," Vail continued. "There was a big country station there too, that we always got played on, but they had longer playlists. . . . 'Jolene' was going up the country chart pretty well, and I took it over to a DJ named Jay Thomas at 'Big WAY' and he thought it was an interesting record, but he wasn't a believer. He wasn't one who would get on every record that came down the pike. So I took it over to WIST and I started working on him, figuring if he gave it a shot he might force WAY to get on the record. This was Scott Christenson at WIST. I just kind of wore him down. I believed in it so much. I said, 'Just give it a shot. I think it's a great record.' And he did. He gave it a shot, and sure enough, it started to get

really good response and WAY added it, and then they saw that it was starting to get airplay in the Southeast—in Columbia and Knoxville and Charlotte
and some of the secondaries. So then they decided they'd rerelease it to the
pop market, and it became a pretty big record. She was looked at as a country
artist until 'Jolene.' Then all of a sudden she was going mainstream . . . and it
really got her away from the reliance on Porter, which started the whole shift
to her being a single [solo artist]."

In February 1974 Vail left RCA and was planning to go back home to
California. "Waylon Jennings had always told me before I did that, I ought
to come to Nashville because he knew that I had a passion for country," Vail
said, "but he knew I also knew the rock world because I'd been with the
Beach Boys and I'd been with radio and kind of knew about different kinds
of music. He and Tompall Glaser had just started a publishing company together, and they said, 'Well, we can't afford to pay you a whole lot of money
and you're free to take on additional clients, but we'll give you an office and a
phone and we'll give you a hundred and a half a week, and you can start doing
independent promotion out of our office.'"

Fred moved to Nashville in April 1974, where he worked in promotion for
six years with some country artists—but also some pop acts like Eric Clapton,
Parliament, and Funkadelic. "Al Coury had been my boss at Capitol when he
was VP there," Fred recalls. Eric Clapton had recorded "Lay Down, Sally"
and Vail called Coury up and said, "'You've got this Clapton record out. I
think it could be a crossover country record.' He said, 'You're kidding. Eric
Clapton on country radio?' I said, 'Yeah. I think it's a great record.' I said,
'I'll work it for you and let me see what I can do in just a couple of weeks.
You don't owe me anything.' I said, 'If I can get it on a couple of key stations,
will you hire me to work the record?' And he said, 'Sure.' So I picked up a few
stations, and it was kind of neat because Clapton has always been a very hip
artist. A lot of country radio DJs and music directors came out of pop radio,
and they were still into pop. So you'd go to them and say, 'I've got this new
Clapton record. I'd like to play Eric Clapton for you,' and of course to them
it was kind of hip [to be playing Eric Clapton as a country DJ.] It ended up
going top 30; I think it went to 26. But it was gold. It was a big record."

After a while Vail got burnt out on promotions. Some singles were easy
to believe in and get behind. But just as often, there were "records that you
didn't even think deserved a shot that were big hits because of politics or
other factors that entered into it," he said.

Vail and a studio musician friend who was teaching himself to be a recording engineer, David Shipley, got into the studio business—first purchasing
the old Richey House in the Fi-Sci Building at 49 Music Circle West from the
Richey brothers, Paul and George (the latter was Tammy Wynette's husband.)
They called it Island Recorders. A competing tenant ended up buying their
space in order to expand, so Vail and Shipley took the money and built a new
studio in Berry Hill, which he named Treasure Isle Recorders. "We opened
up on my dad's birthday, September 27 of 1982," Vail recalls. "We had a

new console and we still had a lot of the gear from the old Island Recorders. We started work immediately. There'd been kind of a moratorium on studio construction; there hadn't been a studio open in five or six years. There were still some great studios, but there weren't any new studios. So we were able to incorporate all this new technology, including the LEDE design concept in building. We were kind of the new kids on the block, and it was the perfect time—right around the time that I call the changing of the guard.

"Frank Jones and Owen Bradley and Chet Atkins were legendary by then," Vail continued, "but there were also these young Turks who were starting to develop a name for themselves—James Stroud, Tony Brown, Paul Worley, Ed Seay, Doug Johnson. These guys were starting to become prominent players. We had a new studio, and what better chance do these guys have to develop a new sound and to break the ties with the old Nashville than to work in this new Treasure Isle Recorders? For about five years we were a really hot studio. We were getting all these new acts—The Desert Rose Band, Hwy 101, and Pam Tillis. And what happened was, Ricky Skaggs, who in my opinion is one of the real consummate musicians, was an artist on Epic. So he had heard about our studio and really liked it. He did a couple of his albums there, and then he did a Whites album there, and then he came to me and said, 'I'm going to be producing the new Dolly Parton album and I'd like to do it here. *White Limozeen* was kind of a turnaround album for her."

Vail wouldn't say Parton had "gone Hollywood. That's not right," he clarified, "but she kind of needed a fresh start. She needed to relaunch her country image, for want of a better word. And that was the album, with 'Why'd You Come in Here Looking Like That?' Back then we spent around five weeks on [recording] an album. It wasn't every day. She'd be in for three, four days, and then she'd go do a gig and do a TV thing, and then she'd come back. Then while she was gone, Ricky might do some overdubs. She was there quite a bit. I think Mac Davis came in for that album and did a guest spot, which was real cool. Wolfman Jack came to the studio to talk to her. He was in town and he came to visit. It was a big photo op. *The Midnight Special* was on at the time, and Wolfman was a big-time DJ, so that was kind of cool. This would have been '89, and of course it was still a vinyl industry. You actually put out records—and cassettes. Now that did end up coming out on CD, too.

"It was really a magical album," Vail smiled fondly. "I tell this story when I give tours of RCA Studio B [as a volunteer for the Country Music Hall of Fame and Museum.] When I was 14 years old and going to bed in Sacramento 2,200 miles from here, holding a little transistor radio under my pillow so my folks don't know I'm listening to the radio when I should be asleep, getting ready for school, and I'm hearing all these great records coming out of B—Don Gibson and Hank Snow, Floyd Cramer, Elvis, Roy Orbison—all these great records, and then every time I go down there it's like a flashback. I grew up worshipping all those great artists who recorded in that studio. Sometimes I get all teary eyed. . . . Studio B for a true Elvis [Presley] fan is a

Mecca, I'll tell the story about the Elvis record, 'Are You Lonesome Tonight,' and then I'll tell the story about Dolly."

Which is?

"We play bits and pieces of 35 to 40 records," Vail continued. "Roy Orbison will do 'Crying' and 'Only the Lonely,' and Jim Reeves will do 'He'll Have to Go,' and Hank Snow will do 'I've Been Everywhere.' For Elvis, we'll do 'Are you Lonesome Tonight?' and 'Little Sister,' and from The Browns we'll do 'The Three Bells.' With Don Gibson, 'Oh, Lonesome Me,' which was the first hit that came out of B, and when we get to Dolly I always play two songs. I play 'Coat of Many Colors,' which is her favorite song—it's autographical, about her mom and growing up in east Tennessee. And then I'll play 'I Will Always Love You,' which is probably her biggest copyright, and I'll tell them this record predated the Whitney Houston cut and also the duet with Vince Gill. But I'll tell them about Dolly and how cool she is, and about how talented and gifted she is, and how we're so proud of her in this community and what she's done to turn people on to Nashville. Then I'll tell them the story about when she was working at my studio. I remember it distinctly. I was usually the first one there. I'd get there at 8:30 or 9 o'clock and one of the first things I'd do is I'd get the coffee going for the musicians who were going to come in at 10 o'clock. I didn't pay any attention—I was over at the sink. It was before the fire. Back in February of '07 we had a huge fire, and it burned the lounge and the lobby. . . . Anyway, here in the room there was a bar that went out, and here there was a sink, an ice maker, and a coffee machine. So I'm in between the bar and making coffee right there, and I wasn't paying any attention. I think I may have had the news on or something. All of a sudden I feel somebody behind me. There's not much space between the counter where the coffee maker is and the bar to squeeze two people in there. I felt something, and it was Dolly, right behind me, pushing her well-known anatomy into me. I turned around and said, 'Good morning.' I tell people, you don't know what it's like until you've had Dolly wake you up on a Monday morning with her well-known anatomy. So that's the Dolly story. And of course, she didn't have a wig on. At that time it was kind of dishwater blonde and real short, and I don't think she ever wore a wig when she recorded."

Vail remembered Dolly's assistant and longtime friend, Judy Ogle, being with her, "but her husband never came down," he said. "I don't think there is a Carl Dean," he laughs, skeptically. "I want someone to prove it to me."

Vail ticked off on his fingers the number of artists with "God-given talent" that he's had the pleasure to work with over the years. He mentions Brian Wilson, Elton John, Ricky Skaggs, Vince Gill, Waylon Jennings, and then Dolly Parton. "She's a national treasure," he stated simply. "A lot of times now you hear about Pro Tooling and editing and sampling a vocal. Back in the RCA days they didn't have those tools. You either had it or you didn't. In the late '50 to the early '60s when you went in to record, you didn't have any of that technology. You had two choices. If you made a mistake or the guitar player made a mistake, or if the piano player came in too early, you had two choices. You could either take it from the top and do it again, or you could do a razor edit. The engineer could cut the old session out and they'd splice the new take onto it, and it would sound good. . . . When Pro Tools came in you could do punches and all that, but they didn't have it for *White Limozeen*. Dolly is a magical singer, and I would hear scratch vocals, a reference track that she would be singing with the musicians, and I'd say, 'You don't even have to come back and do a vocal overdub. That's as good as it's going to be.' There are very, very few artists who have that kind of ability."

Vail said Skaggs and Parton worked well together in the studio. "I think she respected Ricky because he was a consummate musician, and by that time he'd done several albums and was producing himself, basically. I think she respected him and got a lot of input from him. This was over 20 years ago. . . . She might have known what she wanted, but they worked together and she had enough confidence in him to where she pretty much left it up to him. I don't remember any heated arguments or anything like that."

In addition to her songs—especially the story songs like "Coat of Many Colors" that are based on real things that happened in her life, Vail said, "I really like the fact that she's never really played it safe. She's always been willing to expand the envelope. She's the real deal. From what I can tell, she's always been the real deal." Parton's voice, Vail thought, "has got that old, mountain-y quality to it, but at the same time it's very contemporary. It's so pleasant. She sings in a range that's very listenable. There are some people that if you hear them too much, you kind of tune out on them. Maybe they're too shrill. But with Dolly, you could hear her sing all day. It's really pleasant."[4]

DOLLY DANCES WITH THE MOON

We'll hear from Parton's longtime producer, Steve Buckingham, in a later chapter, but let's skip ahead to 1993 to check out the music on *Slow Dancing with the Moon*, which was certified gold on April 19, 1993, and then platinum on October 5, 1993.

Produced by Buckingham and backed by "The Mighty Fine Band," this recording features Parton on the cover in a classic sepia-toned photo with just a hint of rose-colored tinting on her lips. With her head tilted slightly and looking contemplative, Parton is dressed in a full-length satin gown with a plunging neckline and a tightly fitted bodice with seven buttons down the front. There's a gathered skirt below the dropped princess-style waistline, and she's holding a small bunch of daisies. Dolly is standing under a cloudy night-time sky with a full moon lighting the way, above her left shoulder.

Side 1 starts out with "Full Circle" (Parton, Mac Davis), with Rodney Crowell and Lari White chiming in on vocal harmonies. The story is told from the perspective of a couple who have been together for years. They've been through everything together and came "full circle," and they're still together and still friends. "Romeo," described in a previous chapter, is a collaboration with several younger country artists who were thrilled to work with Parton:

Tanya Tucker, Mary Chapin Carpenter, Kathy Mattea, Pam Tillis, and Billy Ray Cyrus (Miley's dad).

"(You Got Me Over) a Heartache Tonight," written by Parton and Larry Weiss, is a duet with Billy Dean. Like the old duets with Porter, the two switch lead lines back and forth in musical conversation. They're not sure if they're lovers, or friends, or even if they'll ever see each other again, "But against your warm body I felt so alive, and you got me over a heartache to- night," the narrator sings.

"What Will Baby Be" is a haunting Parton original, with Irish singer (now transplanted in Nashville) Maura O'Connell and songwriter/producer Carl Jackson providing the vocal harmonies and Paddy Corcoran on the uilleann pipes. In the song a young couple marries, and they're already fighting when a baby comes along. The child grows up surrounded by "angry words and spiteful actions," and the singer wonders how this will affect the child. Young people reflect what they grow up with, she sings, and that "depends entirely on you and me" as parents. Parton loves children, and they absolutely adore her. This song shows her regard for young ones and the crucial importance of raising them right.

"More Where That Came From" (Parton) features harmony vocals from Alison Krauss, Ricky Skaggs, and Mary Chapin Carpenter; Marty Stuart on the mandolin; and Jo-El Sonnier on the accordion. The singer has been through "hell and half of Louisiana lookin' for a man like you," she says. Now that she's found him, she tells him she wants to have his "clothes in my closet, my name on your mail." She's just getting started on the task of loving the guy, and there's more where that came from.

The peace-themed pop anthem "Put A Little Love in Your Heart" (Jackie DeShannon, Randy Myers, and Jimmy Holliday) is performed with the Christ Church Choir. Parton didn't write this one, but it's a good match for an at- titude that seems to permeate a lot of her spiritually toned original material: can't we just accept each other and all get along?

"Why Can't We" (Allen Shamblin, Austin Cunningham, and Chuck Can- non) features harmonies from Cannon, Michael English, and Emmylou Har- ris. The peace theme continues with this song, which talks about how the wind, the soil, and the seed work together in nature to bring a harvest. The singer watches children of different races playing happily together in a play- ground and wonders, "They were playing together. Why can't we?" The in- strumental arrangement utilizes acoustic guitars against simple percussion in a spare mix, with tasty fills on mandolin and fiddle. Emmylou Harris shines on the tenor line on the chorus.

Chet Atkins contributes guitar on "I'll Make Your Bed," written by Parton, and bluegrass sibling superstars Rhonda and Darrin Vincent provide seamless vocal harmony. The narrator is not particularly domestic, but she promises her love he will never go hungry, and she will make his bed. "I'll clothe you in dreams . . . feed you with love, show you a magic that few have dreamed of," she promises. This song, like a number of Parton compositions, ends in a happy combination of syllables (doo doo dooo, dee dee dee) and humming. It's the kind of thing a happy woman would hum under her breath around the house—a joyful sound. It's the trademark sound of Parton's music spilling out of her soul—sort of a musical heavenly language, like speaking in tongues is for some of her early Church of God buddies back in east Tennessee.

"Whenever Forever Comes" (Parton) is a duet with Collin Raye. It's another positive message song about a love that has lasted for a number of years and is still going strong. In the future, the couple hypothesize, "We'll float on a cloud through eternity" on tandem heavenly clouds—kind of a celestial bicycle built for two, perhaps. "You'll gather the stars; you'll give them to me," they sing to each other.

"Cross My Heart," written by Rachel Dennison; Frank Dycus; and Dolly's brother, Randy Parton, includes harmony vocals from the golden throats of Ricky Skaggs and Vince Gill. Again, this song makes the promise of true love forever. In fact, the content of the entire album seems to be focused on either world peace and understanding, or love songs written from the perspective of a mature woman still in love and in a long, valued relationship worth working for and fighting for. The songs run deep with contentment. There's no fluff here.

"Slow Dancin' with the Moon," the title cut written by Mac Davis, describes a young girl as a "sweet little cherry blossom, blooming before her time." Like her, the narrator remembers growing up absorbed in her teenage dreams, "slow dancing with the moon." As adults, we're encouraged not to give up the childlike wonder, in hopes that our own very wildest dreams still might come true. Parton's spirit personifies this attitude. Hope is one of the woman's four food groups, and she's been that way since she and Judy Ogle were best friends in elementary school.

The last cut, "High and Mighty" (Parton), performed with the Christ Church Choir, is a serious praise anthem with a clearly African American gospel groove. Parton's heartfelt voice begins with just a piano backup, but then the bass-grounded singers come in humming and the tambourine kicks things up a notch. God is "high and mighty. Oh, mighty is his power," Parton proclaims. "He is there with the answers." As the scriptures say, if we lift up the name of the Lord, all men will be drawn to him. Parton launches into a mini sermon recitation, in which she encourages listeners to come to God the way they are, as seekers. "You shall know the truth, and the truth shall set you free," she quotes. Nothing is impossible. We just need to look *up* a little more.

In a photo found in the liner notes, producer Steve Buckingham is standing next to Parton, holding up a tabloid publication with the headline "Dolly Parton Will Never Sing Again." They both appear to be laughing their arses off about that.

"You can read the quotes of all the artists who appear on this album and get some idea of what Dolly's peers think of her," Buckingham noted in the liners. "But it goes beyond the fact that she is one of the great singers . . . or one of our most recognizable superstars of our time. I believe the reason other creative people react to Dolly is the same quality that attracts a little girl in New York, a secretary in Los Angeles, or a coal miner in east Tennessee. There is a spiritual side to Dolly that shines through it all. And remember, when she has everyone laughing with a lyric like 'Romeo,' she is the same person who has us listening with tears in our eyes to 'What Will Baby Be' on this album . . . or 'I Will Always Love You' or 'Coat of Many Colors' in the past. God has blessed me with the opportunity to work with Dolly and have her as a friend."

As Buckingham said, her musical guests on the album were obviously thrilled to be involved with the project. Rodney Crowell called Parton "part Mozart, part Aphrodite, part Mae West . . . a poet in a well-tailored suit." Pam Tillis commented, "There's singers and there's entertainers. There's stars and super stars. No question which category Dolly Parton resides in. I've known her all my life and I still couldn't believe I got to sing with her." Kathy Mattea said Parton is "one of the most consistent human beings I know in this business. . . . She has a wonderful spirit." Billy Dean said simply, "Now I know what it's like to sing with an angel." Mary Chapin Carpenter agreed, adding, "No other voice I know combines such sweetness with such strength, simplicity and emotion." And Alison Krauss said, "Nothing will ever top getting to sing with Dolly Parton. Now I can die." Emmylou Harris said, "Dolly Parton first came over my radio speakers 25 years ago, and still every time I hear that voice I'm astonished all over again." Master guitarist Chet Atkins smiles in his photo with Parton. Holding his guitar, he's seated and she's standing close enough that her well-known twin attributes are hitting him right in the neck. "Dolly Parton is one of God's great examples of talent, beauty, and femininity," he stated. "She has more talent that I've got in my little finger," he jokes good-naturedly.

Porter Wagoner and his Wagonmasters with Dolly Parton take the Grand Ole Opry stage December 8, 1967, with some fellow entertainers and program sponsors. Note Don Warden at the steel guitar, Speck Rhodes looking over Don's shoulder, and Buck Trent (with the banjo), Ramona and Grandpa Jones, and Frosty the Snowman on the right. (© Les Leverett. Used by permission.)

Dolly Parton is pictured here at one of her first performances on the *Porter Wagoner TV Show* in November 1968. (© Les Leverett. Used by permission.)

Dolly Parton takes the stage her first night as a member of the Grand Ole Opry on January 11, 1969. Comedian Speck Rhodes (left) looks on. (© Les Leverett. Used by permission.)

Dolly smiles at the crowd from the back of a convertible at the first Dolly Parton Day parade in Sevierville, Tennessee, on April 25, 1970. Her sister, Stella Parton (left), is riding in the car with her. (© Les Leverett. Used by permission.)

Dolly Parton, perched on the back of a convertible at Sevierville's first Dolly Parton Day parade, is dressed in stylish frills and a fancy hat. The high school marching band is just in front of her. (© Les Leverett. Used by permission.)

A young Dolly Parton takes the stage April 25, 1970, tambourine in hand, for the First Dolly Parton Day in Sevierville, Tennessee, at her old high school. (© Les Leverett. Used by permission.)

Dolly Parton sports a set of glamorous eyelashes in a 1970 photo. (© Les Leverett. Used by permission.)

Dolly Parton, 1971. (© Les Leverett. Used by permission.)

Dolly Parton and Porter Wagoner sing one of their well-known duets on *The Porter Wagoner TV Show*, April 12, 1971. (© Les Leverett. Used by permission.)

Dolly Parton and Porter Wagoner perform in April 1971 at the second Dolly Parton Day in Sevierville, Tennessee, held at the Sevierville High School. Note the gymnasium scoreboard above their heads. (© Les Leverett. Used by permission.)

Porter Wagoner shows off one of his trademark rhine-stone-studded Nudie jackets on the porch of his television show set with Dolly Parton, May 19, 1971. (WSM-TV Studios, Nashville, Tennessee) (© Les Leverett. Used by permission.)

Opry stars Dolly Parton and Porter Wagoner take the stage at RCA Records' show at Nashville's Municipal Auditorium during the first Fan Fair, April 1972. (© Les Leverett. Used by permission.)

Dolly Parton and Porter Wagoner accept the Vocal Duo of the Year from the Country Music Association in October 1971. (© Les Leverett. Used by permission.)

Porter Wagoner and Dolly Parton play the Opry at the Ryman Auditorium for the last time on March 2, 1974, before the show moved to the new Opry House. (© Les Leverett. Used by permission.)

Dolly Parton and Porter Wagoner sing one of their signature duets at the Grand Ole Opry on March 2, 1974. (© Les Leverett. Used by permission.)

Dolly and Porter Wagoner visit backstage with Paul and Linda McCartney, comedian Speck Rhodes, and others at the Grand Master's Fiddling Contest at Opryland, during CMA's 3rd Annual Fan Fair celebration held June 10–16, 1974. (© Les Leverett. Used by permission.)

Dolly Parton accepts the CMA Award for Female Vocalist of the Year October 13, 1975. Mac Davis looks on, from the left. (© Les Leverett. Used by permission.)

Dolly Parton sings at the 50th anniversary of the Grand Ole Opry on October 16, 1975. (© Les Leverett. Used by permission.)

Dolly Parton picks up the five-string banjo to play one of her songs on the Opry, September 17, 1977. (© Les Leverett. Used by permission.)

Dolly Parton and her parents, Lee and Avie Lee Parton, are seated in the audience at the 1978 Country Music Awards. Parton was named Entertainer of the Year that night. When Johnny Cash and Ronnie Milsap announced her name, she had to walk to the stage holding a borrowed coat in front of her to cover the rip in her dress. In her remarks Parton said she was honored to win the award, but about five minutes before she was hoping she wouldn't get it—after the seam let go in her dress. "It's like my Daddy always said," Parton remarked. "This comes of putting 15 pounds of mud in a 5-pound sack." (© Les Leverett. Used by permission.)

Dolly Parton pauses briefly before sharing her heart in a song, December 22, 1979. (© Les Leverett. Used by permission.)

Dolly Parton connects with the audience at the Opry on December 22, 1979. (© Les Leverett. Used by permission.)

Dolly Parton performs at the Grand Ole Opry in 1980. Note Jane Fonda (left) came onstage as an impromptu background vocalist that night. Fonda and Parton co-starred in the movie *9 to 5*. (© Les Leverett. Used by permission.)

As the expression on her face clearly shows, Dolly's bliss is playing her music for the fans who love her. (May 10, 1980.) (© Les Leverett. Used by permission.)

Dolly Parton pauses for a moment backstage at the 2000 International Bluegrass Music Awards in Louisville, Kentucky. (Photo by Becky Johnson.)

An almost speechless Dolly Parton accepts the award for Bluegrass Album of the Year for *The Grass Is Blue*, with producer Steve Buckingham (left), at the 2000 International Bluegrass Awards in Louisville, Kentucky. (Photo by Dan Loftin.)

Dolly Parton performs at the 2000 International Bluegrass Music Awards in Louisville, Kentucky. (Photo by Dan Loftin.)

Left to right: Steve Buckingham (producer) and Dolly Parton pose with the Bluegrass Album of the Year trophy they just received onstage for *The Grass Is Blue* (Sugar Hill Records) at the 2000 IBMA Awards in Louisville. (Photo by Becky Johnson.)

Journalist Nancy Cardwell poses with bluegrass supergroup The Grascals and Dolly Parton at a "meet and greet" backstage in Virginia, the summer of 2004. Left to right: Danny Roberts, Terry Eldredge, Nancy Cardwell, Dolly Parton, Terry Smith, Jamie Johnson, David Talbot, and Jimmy Mattingly. (Photo courtesy of Nancy Cardwell.)

Left to right: John McEuen, Dolly Parton, Vince Gill, and Steve Martin pose for a photo after listening to a take at Nashville's Ocean Way Studio October 6, 2008. Gill and Parton sang a duet on "Pretty Flowers," for Martin's album, *The Crow: New Songs for the Five-String Banjo* (Rounder), produced by his high school friend and picking buddy, John McEuen of The Nitty Gritty Dirt Band. (Photo by Nancy Cardwell.)

Post-Porter Duets and the Trios

Albems and songs in this chapter: *Trio*, *Trio II*, *The Winning Hand*, *Burlap and Satin*, *Once Upon a Christmas*, *Real Love*, "Islands in the Stream," *Eagle When She Flies*, "Rockin' Years," *Honky Tonk Angels*, *Something Special*, "I Will Always Love You," *The Crow: New Songs For The Five-String Banjo*, "After the Gold Rush," "When I Get Where I'm Going," *The Grascals & Friends: Country Classics with a Bluegrass Spin*

DOLLY PARTON: HIGH PRIESTESS OF HARMONY

Dolly Parton has one of those voices that listeners tend to either love or hate. But even her fiercest critics will agree that she has a totally *unique* tone and style—a one-in-a-million voice.

Given her signature timbre, it's even more impressive that Parton has been able to blend her voice so well with so many different artists in classic duets and trios. Most country critics believe Porter Wagoner and Dolly Parton simply defined what a country music duet should sound like. Since then, she's recorded enormously successful singles with such artists as Kenny Rogers, Willie Nelson, Mac Davis, Ricky Van Shelton, and Vince Gill.

The trios with female vocalists have resulted in some of her best recorded work, on platinum-selling albums *Trio I* with Linda Ronstadt and Emmylou Harris (1987), the follow-up *Trio II* in 1999, and 1994's gold-selling *Honky Tonk Angels* with Loretta Lynn and Tammy Wynette.

PARTON/HARRIS/RONSTADT

If there were a Mount Rushmore of goose bump–inducing country music albums, the faces of the Dolly Parton, Emmylou Harris, and Linda Ronstadt trio should be carved in stone for the two heavenly albums they produced in 1987 and 1999 on Warner Brothers and Asylum, respectively.

On the album cover of *Trio,* a stage curtain is pulled to the right to reveal a photo of Parton, Ronstadt, and Harris dressed in rhinestone cowgirl finery, leaning on a fence in front of a Western scene, perhaps from some John Wayne movie. On the flip side we see them in sepia tones, dressed in long, elegant white lacy dresses. On the album sleeve the three singers appear in their skivvies as cartoons, ready to be cut out into paper dolls. They have a couple of outfits apiece, complete with the little tabs to fold over the dolls' shoulders.

One of the joys of LP albums released in the 1970s and '80s, back when liner note reading was a highly enjoyable sport among music fans, is an album sleeve like the one that comes with *Trio.* The complete lyrics to every song are written out on the back, along with songwriter names and IDs for each instrument played and each harmony sung—so you know precisely with whom you are singing along. *Trio* was produced by the renowned George Massenburg, with John Starling as music consultant.

The album debuted on the *Billboard* Country Chart March 28, 1987, hitting number 1 for five weeks and also going to number 6 on the Pop Chart. *Trio* won the Grammy for Best Country Performance by a Duo or Group in 1987. It was certified gold and platinum for album sales in excess of one million. Four singles charted on the Country Chart: "Telling Me Lies" (#3), "Those Memories of You (#5), "To Know Him Is to Love Him" (#1), and "Wildflowers" (#6)

Emmylou Harris sings lead on "The Pain of Loving You" (Dolly Parton, Porter Wagoner), with Dolly on the high tenor part and Ronstadt on the lower, baritone part. Their harmony blend is breathtaking, and it's only the first song! A reprise of this song appeared in 2011 as a Dolly Parton/Terry Eldredge duet on *The Grascals: Country Classics with a Bluegrass Spin* (Blugrascal Records), distributed by Cracker Barrel Old Country Store.

Twin fiddles (or rather, a viola with a fiddle) kick off "Making Plans" (Johnny Russell, Voni Morrison). Parton's singing a high lead, with harmonies from Harris and Ronstadt stacked underneath her. Dolly's voice trembles with sadness as she sings, "I'm making plans to be lo—oh—oh—onesome, while you're making plans to leave," as Lindley's emotional mandolin tremolo hovers in the background. The glorious three-part harmony lasts through almost the entire song, except for a solo bridge and tag at the end from Parton.

The inimitable Emmylou Harris steps to the lead microphone on "To Know Him Is to Love Him" (Phil Spector), with Parton floating above on the high-trapeze tenor line and Ronstadt supporting from below on baritone. The lyrics are resolutely positive up until the bridge, when the narrator confides, "Someday he will see that he was meant for me!" followed by a triple layer 4-5-4-3-2-1 note slide down the scale that's simply a small piece of heaven. The key modulates up for the last chorus, and the mandolin and Hawaiian guitar provide the instrumental altro.

Linda Ronstadt chooses Jimmie Rodgers's "Hobo's Meditation" for her first lead vocal, which asks the musical question, "Will there be any freight trains in heaven, any boxcars on which we might hide?"

Emmy and Dolly's harmonies are stacked above Linda on the choruses, and they end the song in hopes that hobos indeed will have plenty of rides, respect, and money in the hereafter.

An autoharp introduces "Wildflowers," identifying the song immediately as a Parton original with mountain roots. Parton sings the lead, comparing her growing-up years to wildflowers that can pick up their dreams and go, since they "don't care where they grow."

Ronstadt reveals the full power of her voice in all its belting splendor in the climax of "Telling Me Lies" (Linda Thompson, Betsy Cook). Again, Linda sings a low lead and the other two parts are stacked on top for the choruses. The story is from the perspective of a woman who has tried—more than once—to make a relationship work with a man who is simply not honest with her. "You don't know what a man is, until you have to please one," she warns. "Don't put your life in the hands of a man with a face for every season." After Ronstadt kicks it out on the last chorus (making listeners glad to have ears), the dynamics soften for a floating, gentle three-part harmony ending: "telling me lies," accompanied by a piano.

Side 2 begins with Jean Ritchie's "Dear Companion," a song that sounds like it could have come from the British Isles decades ago. Harris starts out the verses, she is joined by Ronstadt on a low harmony, and then Parton chimes in for the last two lines. Feelings of loss and mental distraction brought on by grief pervade the song. The instrumental fills are cleverly provided by mandolin, fiddle, and autoharp.

Parton takes the lead on "Those Memories of You," written by the Nashville Bluegrass Band's Alan O'Bryant. The song has a bluesy, lonesome feel, emphasized by Maura O'Connor's wailing fiddle and Steve Fishell's sobbing Hawaiian guitar. The narrator wakes up, trembling from dreams of a love that is gone. All that's left are the haunting memories. Parton sings a high lead, with the two parts below her on the choruses.

Ronstadt leads out on Kate McGarrigle's "Hard Enough," another tender "love gone bad despite my best efforts" song. Linda sings the first part of the verses, backed by an elegant cello and subdued piano. Emmy comes in on tenor for the next two lines, and then Parton flies to the top with a high baritone part for the saddest line of the song. Unable to find the time for a simple conversation with her love, who is gone too much, the narrator sings, "So I'll just pin this note within your coat, and leave the garden gate unlocked." She's had enough, a pensive clarinet echoes the thought, and then all three singers come in for the last line. She's saying good-bye.

Dolly Parton sings lead on the traditional favorite "Rosewood Casket," which features an arrangement she learned from her mother, Avie Lee Parton. A mountain dulcimer kicks off the song, which tells the sad tale of a young girl who is dying from a broken heart. The "casket" is actually a little wooden box where the narrator keeps a packet of love letters from her untrue beau. The harmonies are so seamless and full, it's difficult to hear who is doing what exactly, but it sounds as if Harris's and Ronstadt's lines are stacked below Parton, and then Dolly adds a high baritone (doubling) part on top, for the last two lines of each stanza for a heavenly harmony sandwich.

"Farther Along" is a traditional standard that all women harmony singers who love gospel and/or country music attempt, and none do it better than this particular trio. Emmylou Harris sings the first verse, the harmonies come in on the chorus, and then Linda Ronstadt takes the lead on the last two verses. The key modulates during the last instrumental break, and the singers end in fervent hope. . . . There are some things in this life that are beyond understanding. Nonetheless, we're urged to "cheer up" and "live in the sunshine," with faith that we'll understand things a bit better "by and by," emphasized by a revival-style piano and organ.

Trio II, featuring the same three women, was produced again by George Massenburg and released on the Asylum label in 1999. It debuted on the Country Chart on February 27, 1999, going to number 4 there and to number 62 on the Pop Chart. John Starling worked as associate producer, and the entire CD was dedicated to the memory of acoustic bass monster (and a former member of Emmylou Harris's Nash Ramblers band), Roy Huskey Jr.

The set list includes a Carter Family favorite, "Lover's Return," with Ronstadt on lead, musing, "Oh no, I cannot take your hand. God never gives us back our youth." A loving heart was slighted, and it's too late to make things right. Linda keeps the lead for a Harley Allen classic, "High Sierra," in which she admits, "I've been right, but mostly wrong—wrong about you, right about me."

Emmylou Harris chooses a Parton original, "Do I Ever Cross Your Mind," and a video was created for the Neil Young–penned song "After the Gold Rush," with Parton on lead vocals. No one really knows what this song is about—perhaps the end of the world. Perhaps it's a dream. It's a beautiful piece of poetry, whatever it means. Parton has said that it's one of her favorites.

"The Blue Train" is a Jennifer Kimball/Tom Kimmel song, with Ronstadt singing lead, Emmylou Harris singing most of the harmony, and Parton coming in at the end of the choruses. Dolly sings lead and tenor harmony on Del McCoury's "I Feel The Blues Moving In," and Emmylou Harris covers the baritone. The blues-edged song from bluegrass patriarch McCoury is anchored by David Grisman's lonesome mandolin and Alison Krauss's moaning fiddle. Both songs have a decided bluegrass groove, a genre all three singers appreciate and enjoy singing from time to time.

"You'll Never Be the Sun" is a Donag Long song chosen by Emmylou Harris about "losing the part inside when love turns round on you, leaving the past behind." The entire album is permeated with a delicious, melancholy sorrow—regret over failed love affairs and lost chances, youth, and lives.

"He Rode All the Way to Texas," a John Starling tune sung by Parton, is a about a "movin' kind" of man who hopped a freight to Texas, not shedding a tear "for the girl he left behind."

"Feels Like Home" is a Randy Newman song that gives Ronstadt room to shake the rafters on the chorus, and the harmonies build to a full three-part tidal wave once again. It's probably the only remotely positive song on the album. The narrator is hopeful about a new relationship that makes him feel like he's coming home again, but he's just been through a rather lonely patch up to this point.

The last cut, appropriately enough, is "When We're Gone, Long Gone," written by Kieran Kane and James Paul O'Hara (country music's "The O'Kanes"). "When we're gone the only thing that will have mattered," Harris sings with Ronstadt on the high tenor part, "is the love that we shared and the way that we cared."

Although this is still a trio album, not all three singers appear to be on every song. Sometimes the lead will dub in a harmony part—two Lindas with an Emmylou, two Emmylous with a Linda, or two Dollys with an Emmylou—likely because of the difficulty of coordinating all three schedules. The overall feel isn't as cohesive as on the first project, but it's still incredibly beautiful, with exquisite harmony and instrumental arrangements.

The graphic design on *Trio II* features childhood photos of Harris, Ronstadt, and Parton. Linda is in a white First Communion dress, and Dolly is in her famous "coat of many colors." Emmylou appears in a tutu, in a marching band uniform with a snare drum, and with her puppy. Dolly is standing in wildflowers, and Linda, originally from Arizona, is dressed up in a cowgirl outfit.

Instrumentation on both *Trio* albums is stellar, and credits are listed in an appendix of this book. On the second album Dennis James plays the glass harmonica on one cut, a curious instrument that Benjamin Franklin invented after watching someone play music by rubbing the tops of water glasses.

REMINISCING WITH JOHN STARLING, MD

During a 2010 interview with John Starling, associate producer of *Trio II* and music consultant on *Trio I*, he recalled how the Trio project first got rolling. "In the late '70s they got together and did some tracks with Brian Ahern," Starling said. "They weren't real happy with the tracks and didn't finish them, but they kept talking about the possibility of doing it again. In '85 or '86 they really started talking again; they were in a hotel room in Nashville talking about this and trying to figure out how to put it together."

Starling, who was practicing medicine in Montgomery, Alabama, at the time, remembers getting "this phone call from Emmy or Linda. They said they wanted to do this and they wanted me to help them. I'll never forget it. I got together with George [Massenburg]. Basically, he wanted to make it sound good, so he said, 'Your job is to help pick out the material and be in the studio to help with arrangements.'

"We had a great time in Nashville," Starling recalls. "I remember this was maybe a couple of months before we started the project. We all got together at Dolly's house for a week and for five or six days would go out there every day and sit and listen to music. At the end, we voted on what we wanted to take a stab at. We figured out we'd do 15 or 16 tracks and dump two or three. That was the idea."

Starling met Emmylou Harris back in the '70s when she was playing a show at The Birchmere, where The Seldom Scene—the group Starling played guitar and sang with—had a standing Thursday night engagement. "Emmy was on the road with Gram Parsons, and at one of their shows in Texas—Houston or Dallas—they shared a bill with Linda Ronstadt," Starling continued. "That's how they got to know each other. Linda came to town [DC], and Emmy talked her into coming over to The Birchmere after one of her shows. After the show we would go to my house or the banjo player's house [Ben Eldridge] and sit and pick until three or four in the morning. She called that night, and we were playing at the Cellar Door. I think maybe we also called Ricky Skaggs, who was working for the Virginia Electric and Power Company then. That's how we got to know each other. We all shared an enthusiasm for music."

Ronstadt had guested on the Scene's classic *Old Train* album, so when she got sick on tour in the neighborhood she called her old friend Dr. Starling. "She had one date in Washington [DC] and one in New York, but she had a temperature of 103," Starling recalled. "She canceled the last two shows on the tour and called me and stayed at my house. We were in the studio at that point and were practicing at my house. She was feeling better and was having fun, so she just hung out there for two weeks. Lowell George [founder of Little Feat] was on the road with Linda. Little Feat had broken up for a brief period of time. He came over to the studio, and George Massenburg was the engineer. He [Lowell George] said, 'This guy should be cutting hits in L.A.' Linda recorded one track off of our best records: 'Keep Me from Blowing Away' on her *Heart Like a Wheel* album, and she sang on a song of ours. George and Linda and I went over to the radio station in Washington; it was the number 1 station for 18- to 32-year-olds. They played a lot of Little Feat and when they found out he was in town, they invited us, too. Lowell did 'Willin'' live on the air, and Linda and I sang harmonies. I've heard the tapes—they needed a little Auto-Tune, I think," he laughed. "They begged him and Billy Payne to put Little Feat back together."

Ronstadt was having such a good time on sick leave in DC, she lost track of time. "Her manager, Peter Asher, had to call her and say, 'When are you coming back?'" Starling laughed. "He flew out to get her."

Massenburg was a generous producer, giving Starling the freedom to provide a lot of influence. "The first time I met Dolly was when I went to her house," Starling recalled. "Oh listen, she's delightful. As humans, we all kind of tend to be rather full of ourselves, but some of us delightfully so. That would be a good title for a book about Dolly: *Delightfully So.*"

Starling was present at all the *Trio* sessions except for the end of the second album. They were recorded at The Complex in West L.A., and also at Woodland Studios in Nashville and Ocean Way Recordings in Hollywood. "They [Parton, Ronstadt, and Harris] started having problems with how to promote it, with their separate careers and trying to meld something together [to tour and perform]," Starling said. "All three of them were being pulled in 50 different directions at once. The second record was done in 1994, and it didn't come out until 1998. The record label couldn't get them to agree to how they were going to promote it. Linda took a lot of tracks and put them on an album of hers. Then a new woman at Warner Brothers took over and said, 'The world doesn't realize this album is out there!'"

Starling, of course, was still trying to be a doctor down in Alabama. "I just told them I had to be away for a while," he smiled. "I had a pressing need to get back, so my partner wouldn't shoot me. George and I mixed the first album together.

"We all agreed that we wanted to get whoever was singing the lead vocal on a particular track—we wanted to get that live if we could," he said. "None of the harmonies were done at the same time, but a lot of the vocals were live (recorded with the musicians). At least one of the harmony parts was over-dubbed; most of the time it was both."

Starling, who is a retired ear, nose, and throat (ENT) specialist, explains his unique perspective on biology and music. "The corpus callosum is a portion of the brain between the right and left lobes," he explained. "The right side is the emotional, artsy lobe and the left is the logical, obsessive-compulsive side. The corpus callosum is how the two sides of the brain communicate. If you play music for someone and did a CT scan while the person was listening to music, one portion of the brain that really lights up is the corpus callosum. Music helps the right and left sides of the brain talk to each other. This is one of the reasons music has been such a great boon to us. Most musicians have different life views, and I can tell you from being in a band if it weren't for music, we never would have known each other. The only time we ever talked about politics backstage was when an election was coming up. We laughed at each other, would go on and play, and then go home."

Specifically, Starling was in charge of material and arrangements on the *Trio* projects—a job that required both parts of his brain to work together. "As a producer, you can only really help people who have a good idea of where they're going," he noted. "They particularly wanted to try and make a

fairly down-home record. It sort of fit all three of them—Linda the least, but it was her idea to do it. She basically did all the communication and handled all the payouts and management and that sort of thing. They had a traditional foot firmly on the pedal. A couple of times I was wanting to get a little more away from that, and they would come right back and say, 'No.' As a matter of fact, they wanted to use an acoustic bass on every track. I finally talked them into an electric on one or two tracks that were real slow. They wanted to do a traditional-feeling record. Linda was pop, Emmy was a folk artist who had made her way into country with a different approach, and Dolly has always been that way. Ever since the *Trio* records, Dolly has stayed in that mode. One of the reasons is that bluegrass has such cartage—it's easy to transport. You throw your guitar in the car and go. Going place to place with all the gear—some rock bands give up because they can't afford to be on the road. Some of the country players performing around here are playing some of the clubs as solos. They can do it. Dan Tyminski was here in a duet. Vince Gill has been here as a solo act."

Used to the limited budgets most bluegrass bands deal with when it's time to record, Starling was pleased to be given a green light on pretty much anything he suggested. "At that point money wasn't an issue," he recalls. "I thought I'd died and gone to heaven, being able to get Mark O'Connor and David Lindley in the studio together. I was such a Jackson Browne freak— I heard him [Lindley] playing lap steel and fiddle with Jackson Browne. I had never met Mark O'Connor before. I remember Mark was just warming up [in the studio]. David looked at me and said, 'I shall never touch the instrument again.'

"It was done in L.A., and we brought out some Nashville people. I found out L.A. musicians did charts differently from Nashville. I can remember Alison Krauss asking me, 'Whose idea was it to have me play on this?' And I said, 'All of us.' On the second album Sam Bush was supposed to play mandolin, but the day before they had a snow and ice storm in Nashville and he slipped and fell on the ice and broke his arm. He called and said, 'I can't make it.' 'Oh my God,' I thought. 'What are we going to do now?' Sam said, 'Of course, Grisman is out there.' I called him up and said, 'We're going to need you in two days.' He said, 'I've got something to do, but I'll cancel it to get to play with Dolly.' Everybody who participated in it had fun," Starling said. "The fun part was making the music. The hard part was the business end of it. I know Dolly had to turn down offers, to do this."

Looking through the liner note for *Trio 1*, Starling remembered that the fiddle was added to the steel on "Making Plans" on the spot, just because Mark O'Connor happened to be there—an off-the-cuff, good decision, as it turns out. "Hobo's Meditation" was a song Linda Ronstadt brought to the project, Starling said. "We were both enamored with Jimmie Rodgers."

Dolly wrote "Wildflowers," and "Linda Thompson wrote 'Telling Me Lies.' She [Thompson] had been married to a famous musician and he cheated on her. Linda [Ronstadt] sings with attitude on that one. Boy!

"'Those Memories of You' is a song that a gentleman I met while I was in Montgomery named Alan O'Bryant wrote. Alan plays with the Nashville Bluegrass Band, but at the time he was playing with Claire Lynch, and we would get together from time to time. The song was written about this girl that Alan dated one time from Birmingham, who was an heiress to some big fortune. Then he ended up getting married to someone else later. NBB never did that song. I recorded it on my second solo album, *Waitin' on a Southern Train*, and Alan and Claire sang on it. When we were going over the songs they asked me for some stuff, and I just sang it for them. Dolly said her husband was upstairs listening, and he really liked that song. She decided she wanted to do this. Bill Monroe had the publishing. 'Memories of You' became a big hit for Kathy Mattea, as well. I remember the week [we were making decisions about material at Parton's house]. Somehow people found out where I was staying and I would go down in the morning to leave, and the front desk would say, 'We've got some packages for you.'"

About "Farther Along," Starling remembered, "Specifically, Emmy and I sort of arranged that in the studio. We wanted to try and make it as simple as possible, without making it boring. We started out with Billy Payne, Little Feat's keyboard player, playing piano on it. At end of the day Dolly said, 'You and Emmy arranged this thing. You should claim the arrangement.' Then we ended up getting sued for allegedly stealing the arrangement from a gospel band in the 1930s. It was written in 1902. I think after it was all said and done, Emmy's lawyer just said to give them the money. I got a courtroom lawyer up there. Music lawyers don't like to go to court. I would hang out in the balcony. The music lawyer in Nashville gave the claim to the musicologist. The version that I liked was one The Byrds did. They used a six minor chord, and I wanted to use a six minor chord every time. The girls said, 'No.' I said, 'Let me do it one time.' If you change one chord, they lose [cases like this]. So they ended up dropping their part of the suit.

"We went out to Dolly's house to work on arrangements for the first *Trio* album," Starling recalled. "Dolly had just had some kind of surgical procedure done. I remember she was in her pj's and nightgown the whole time. The second time we met at Linda's in San Francisco for five or six days and worked on material. Once again, we had so much fun doing the record," he smiled. "Doing a record is so much different than going out on the road."

Looking down the *Trio II* set list, Starling stopped at "I Feel the Blues Movin' In." He said, "I'll never forget playing the Del McCoury version in the studio. Jim Keltner was Ry Cooder's drummer. They just had that big California earthquake in L.A. We got up there and he was still shaking. When we did that song, he went out there and started playing a double-time drum thing. We said, 'Jim. Half time.' And he said, 'Oh, half time.' He played the bluegrass version," Starling laughed. "And I'll never forget when Alison did her fiddle overdubs. It was all set up to do one afternoon. It was like a party, and we all just enjoyed the heck of her doing the fiddle tracks—all three of us and George and the three girls."

All three of the singers liked the song "You'll Never Be the Sun," Starling said. "You know, we didn't succeed at everything," he confided. "One of the things we wanted to do was do some real Irish music. We even flew an Irish piper from Belfast to L.A. for the first album. He reunited with this Irish girl who played keyboard, and we tried tracking at a practice session the night before at Linda's house. I had my doubts, but I thought, 'Oh my God, this is going to be great.' [Later, after our little party he] went to Venice, California, and got totally smashed and got thrown into the drunk tank. George had to go bail him out. He thought he'd get a little hair of the dog that bit him. The girls put their heads together and said, 'Well, this is our fault.' So we sent him home and he didn't [record anything on the album at all]."

Harris brought in a copy of the Starling original, "He Rode All the Way to Texas"—Claire Lynch's version. "I said, 'I'm staying out of this,'" Starling said. "I didn't vote, but the three girls did."

Ronstadt brought "Feels Like Home" to the table, Starling said, and they all intentionally agreed to make "When We're Gone, Long Gone" the last song on the album.

Starling defined a producer's job as "being paid for being enthusiastic about music," he smiled. "Nobody is any good at anything unless they have an ego. You have to have the confidence to do it. I wondered if I would have problems dealing with egos, but they intentionally tried to see that no one's ego got in the way and it worked. That was the most fun. Nobody [had the attitude that] it was 'my way or the highway.'"

The business part of the project was the most challenging, Starling said. "That's what ends up breaking up a lot of good music," he noted. "At the time I remembered that in a communist country the state decided what kind of music you listen to, or in a deeply religious country, they decided. The free enterprise entertainment system is a two-edged sword. It allows you the freedom to do what you do, but it's easy to get cynical."

When asked specifically about Parton, Starling said, "Her contributions go way beyond just making the music. I think Dolly always said it the best. She said you can make a lot of money looking like a prostitute. She laughs about it. She'd take that attitude, and sell [music] that I love. That's what I loved about Dolly Parton and still do. She sang on Emmy's last album, so I got to talk to her again. I had so much fun working with her. She has it figured out. Take modern music . . . for example, Lady GaGa. If you want to just have an attitude, you can make a lot of money with just an attitude—a visual attitude. Amy Winehouse is another one. After a while, it's a part of the act. But then, somebody like Susan Boyle comes along and just wows people."

When Parton found out Harris and Starling were sued over their "Farther Along" arrangement, Dolly told them, "I just quit accepting demos from people. As soon as you do that, somebody's going to sue you." Starling ruefully noted, "If anything is a success, there's going to be a lawyer on a [ladder] rung above you.

"Working on this thing has been one of the high points in my life," Starling continued. "One of the things Linda said, was . . . she's from the Southwest, and a lot of her musical roots are Mexican American. She quit college to go to L.A. and join the Stone Ponies. . . . The first time she heard the song '(I Think I'm Gonna Love You for a) Long, Long Time,' she pulled the car off on the side of the road. It was the first time she'd ever done that. She wanted to do this kind of material, and the only two people she knew in the Nashville field were me and Emmy. It was their idea to call me."

Starling said Parton was "pretty easygoing" in the studio. "In some way, everybody learned something from what we did," he commented. "I learned about dealing with them as people, and how the music sounded—and a lot of the credit for that goes to the players. One particular strikeout we had was a Staples Singers song. I can't remember the song it was, but Ry Cooder was playing on it and he sounded just like Pop Staples. But to try to have three white girls sound like three black girls, it just wasn't making it. Ry Cooder told me, 'You know, I love the song too, but it's just not working out. What they should do is 'Rank Stranger,'" Starling laughed. "But that [Staples Singers song] was one song they had made their minds up on. . . . For a while, it looked like 'Farther Along' wasn't going to work. For the most part, I think the albums were mostly a success. We switched leads and mixed it up as much as we could get away with artistically."

George Massenburg "has talked about Linda getting a new outlook on music and how it's done," after working on the *Trio* projects, Starling said. "I enjoyed getting to know Linda Ronstadt with the Seldom Scene, and of course in the meantime I was trying to practice medicine, doing an ENT residency at Walter Reed [Army Medical Center]. I remember one day when my boss's son came up to him and said, 'Dad, do you think you could get The Seldom Scene to come where I can hear them?' He called me into the office and started giving me crap about [playing music and being gone]," Starling smiled. "The Seldom Scene played The Red Fox, and then The Birchmere. We played one night a week, and never did get too involved with traveling. [Band leader/mandolinist/vocalist and an absolute character in outrageous pants] John Duffey wouldn't fly at the time. John said, 'I have two rules for this band. No big deals. Let's just have fun. Second, we're not going to do 'Roll in My Sweet Baby's Arms' over and over again,'" Starling smiled.[1]

FRED FOSTER'S WINNING HAND

Parton was included in a 1982 collaboration on Monument Records with Kris Kristofferson, Willie Nelson, and Brenda Lee produced by her old friend Fred Foster. In the liner notes for *The Winning Hand,* Foster thanks "Almighty God, who put me on intersecting paths with Brenda, Dolly, Kris, and Willie. Four of the true originals artistically, and four of the best friends any one man ever had. It is their friendship I treasure most of all."

On the album cover the four artists are pictured in double images on playing cards: Kristofferson as the king of diamonds, Nelson as the king of hearts, Parton as the queen of diamonds, and Lee as the queen of hearts.

On this double album, the tracks consist mostly of unreleased material recorded for Monument in the mid-1960s. Kristofferson and Lee contributed new vocals, and some of the older recordings were edited to create duets. The Dolly Parton original "Everything's Beautiful (in Its Own Way)," with Willie Nelson's vocals added, made it to the top 10 on the *Billboard* Country Chart. In early 1983 a television special aired in celebration of the album, and all four stars sang together—for the first and only time. Johnny Cash hosted the program.

In "Ping Pong" (Boudleaux Bryant), Parton and Kristofferson sing together on a light-spirited novelty song that compares the narrators' love affair to a game of table tennis as they sing, "My heart is falling in a ding dong, ping pong game with you."

Dolly's vocals blend with Willie Nelson's on "Happy, Happy Birthday, Baby" (Margo Sylvia, Gilbert Lopez), and Parton sounds almost more like Brenda Lee than Lee does herself on this album. The lyrics are from a young girl who is writing a birthday letter to her ex-boyfriend, feeling a little blue because she's not the one who is celebrating with him.

"Everything Is Beautiful (in Its Own Way)," not to be confused with the Ray Stevens song of the same name, is the Parton original she performed when she auditioned for Porter Wagoner's television show. Her vocals are combined again with Willie Nelson's here. In classic east Tennessee Parton form, the lyrics describe the beauties of nature and the joy in witnessing the simple changing of the seasons.

Parton's first radio hit as a songwriter, "Put It Off Until Tomorrow" (Parton, Bill Owens), is performed on this album with Kristofferson. On side 4 Parton sings one by herself: "The Little Things" (Parton, Bill Owens), mentioned in a previous chapter. Her last cut is "What Do You Think About Lovin'," sung with Brenda Lee in an up-tempo rockabilly groove. Their voices blend like those of sisters from the '50s.

In liner notes for *The Winning Hand*, Johnny Cash recounted that his "one claim to her fame is that I introduced [Dolly Parton] first on the Grand Ole Opry, even before she had her record contract. As the years went by, I watched her grow as an artist and a writer," he added. "I've always loved everything I've ever heard or seen her do."

In an almost stream of consciousness style that morphs into a humorous long poem, Cash talks about how his son, John Carter Cash, enjoyed having his picture made with Parton backstage once. And Johnny recalls one random incident when he ran into her again backstage somewhere and she quipped, "We never did get together, did we, Cash?" Cash says he was too puzzled to answer, and Dolly just smiled and walked off. He notes how Parton "turned me to the Bible a long time ago when I first heard 'Coat of Many Colors,' the story of Joseph. She brought June and I a little closer together with 'What Do You Think About Loving.'"

Cash goes off on a tangent about the prophet Elijah, who ran 80 miles to get away from Jezebel, an evil woman in the Bible whose "morals were lower than frogs. She fell out of a window and was eaten up by dogs." But then he gets back to Dolly—whose heart is "as warm as sunshine, and her soul fights for all things pure." She has "a voice as true as tomorrow, a delivery that heals, songs that make you wonder how she knows just how you feel."

BURLAP AND SATIN: WILLIE AND DOLLY

On the album *Burlap and Satin* (1982), Parton sings again with Willie Nelson on the song "I Really Don't Want to Know," written by Dan Robertson and Howard Barnes. In the lyrics a couple wonder about how many lovers the other one has been with in the past. They wonder, but they don't really want to know. "Even if I ask you, darlin', don't confess," Nelson sings.

On the album cover a close-up of Dolly's face appears, with her first name in white cursive in the top left corner. Big-eyed and dewy, she wears perfectly done makeup and a large light blonde wig. Silver hoop earrings and feathers clipped in her hair complete her accessories, and she's wearing a peasant blouse–style top. On the back of the album she is portrayed in a full body shot, mature and beautiful at 40. With a nod to her album title, her blouse is satin and her skirt is gauzy burlap with a slit up the left side. The elbow-length sleeves are trimmed with the same lace and ribbon that outline her low-cut neckline, and she is lying on dark red satin bedsheets with black satin pillows.

Continuing with the pillow theme, Parton turns in a sweet version of Hank Locklin's "Send Me the Pillow That You Dream On" on this album, and she also includes several original songs worth checking out. In "Jealous Heart" the narrator, who imagines the worst from her lover, criticizes herself: "Don't you hate yourself for the fool you are, when you're cursed with a jealous heart?"

In "A Gamble Either Way" (Parton), the main character could be from the same neighborhood as "Fancy," in the Reba McEntire song. Except this girl was a "Cinderella slave" and unloved at home, until she matured at 13 and suddenly everyone wanted her, as she was "passed back and forth by strangers." She runs away at 15 and resorts to a life of prostitution. Playing card imagery is used, as Parton sings, "Win or lose, you have to play the hand that life has dealt you, and it's a gamble either way."

Dolly moans, "Life's a mill and I've been through it," in her original "Appalachian Memories," the story of a poor family that leaves the mountains for work, "hitching their station wagon to a star" in hope of work and better times up North.

In "A Cowboy's Ways" Parton notes that "even love can't change a cowboy's ways," and "One of Those Days" notes a sense of déjà vu. Everything about the day reminds the singer of the time when she was still in love. "Calm on the Water" is a John the Revelator–style dream sequence song, reminiscent of the last book in the Bible. The narrator sees Jesus standing on a mountain, little children lay flowers at his feet, and wild animals walk tamely at his side. Full of compassion, joy, and love, Jesus tells the singer, "Your questions are many, but the answer is love. I'll draw all men unto me if I be lifted up."

DOLLY PARTON AND KENNY ROGERS: ANOTHER RIGHT COMBINATION

Kenny Rogers is one of Parton's favorite duet partners. She's commented in interviews that his cool vocal tone is a great match for the warm, passionate style of singing she favors. Whatever it is, it works. The two have released a number of successful recordings.

Once Upon a Christmas, recorded with Kenny Rogers for RCA in 1984, was certified gold and platinum on December 3, 1984, and later sales went double platinum by October 25, 1989. Their duets include "A Christmas to Remember," "Christmas Without You," "The Greatest Gift of All" (which went to #53 on the *Billboard* Country Chart and #81 on the Pop Chart. "I Believe in Santa Claus," "Once Upon a Christmas," and "With Bells On." In 1997 the album was reissued, removing a couple of Rogers's solo cuts and adding Dolly's song from *The Best Little Whorehouse in Texas* movie score, "Hard Candy Christmas." The album debuted on the Country Chart on December 15, 1984, and went to number 12, as well as to number 31 on the Pop Albums Chart in *Billboard.* Parton and Rogers also appeared together on a critically acclaimed CBS television special called *Kenny and Dolly: A Christmas to Remember,* on December 2, 1984.

Parton's solo album in 1985 for RCA, *Real Love,* included another duet with Rogers (the title cut), which went to number 1 on *Billboard*'s Country Chart and number 91 on pop radio. The entire album was nominated for a Grammy and went to number 9 on the Country Chart, after debuting at radio on March 9, 1984. The project also included a number 1 hit for Parton that she sang solo, "Think About Love," and "Tie Our Love in a Double Knot" went to number 17.

Probably the first song most fans think of when they recall that unmistakable Parton/Rogers vocal blend is "Islands in the Stream," written by Barry Robin and Maurice Gibb of the Bee Gees (the Brothers Gibb). It appears on Kenny Rogers's album *Eyes That See in the Dark* (RCA AFL1-4697), which hit the triple jackpot: number 1 on the Country, Pop, and Adult Contemporary Charts in August–September 1983. Interestingly, it hit number 1 on the Pop and AC Charts first, on August 27, climbing to number 1 on Country on September 3. Actually, it isn't surprising at all. It's a pop song. It's just that country music had been influenced by pop music enough by the '80s that it fit both places.

"Islands in the Stream" was recorded in 1983 and produced by Barry Gibb, Karl Richardson, and Albhy Galuten. Musicians on the cut included Barry Gibb, Maurice Gibb, Tim Renwick, and George Terry on guitars; Ron

Zeigler, drums; Albhy Galuten and George Bitzer on piano; George Bitzer, Albhy Galuten, and Maurice Gibb on synthesizers; Joe Lala, percussion; Larry McNeely, banjo; and Pete Graves, Whit Sidener, Ken Faulk, and Neal Bonsanti on horns.

Set to an irresistibly catchy melody, the song is a conversation between two lovers who are metaphoric islands in a stream of romantic love and emotion, incredibly attracted to each other and hoping this will be "the year for the real thing." Rogers starts out on lead in verse one, Dolly jumps in on a harmony line halfway through the verse, and they sing the chorus together. Parton sings lead on the second verse and chorus. There's not a lot to the song lyrically, but it's easy to sing along with and the melody is impossible to get out of your head—the trademark of many popular pop songs.

DOLLY WITH RICKY VAN SHELTON

"Rockin' Years," a duet with Parton and Ricky Van Shelton on *Eagle When She Flies*, was produced by Steve Buckingham and released in 1991. Written by Floyd Parton, the single debuted on the *Billboard* Country Chart on March 2, 1991, and went to the number 1 spot. The album, produced by Buckingham with Gary Smith, went to number 33 on the Country Chart after an October 19, 1991, debut.

In a slow-paced, straight-ahead country love song—a conversation between a man and a woman who are committed to each other for the long haul— the singers promise to stand by each other through their "rockin' years," in rocking chairs on the porch. It's the perfect love song for artists who aren't teenagers any more, and one their middle-aged fans can relate to.

COUNTRY MUSIC'S PIONEERING HONKY-TONK ANGELS: DOLLY, LORETTA, AND TAMMY

Honky Tonk Angels, by Dolly Parton, Loretta Lynn, and Tammy Wynette, was produced by Steve Buckingham and Parton for Sony Music Entertainment/Columbia Records. In an interview released to country radio as a promotional piece in 1993, "The Honky Tony Angels Story," Parton says, "Kitty Wells kind of opened all the doors for us. I love Tammy and Loretta. They're so real. There's three of us still living who were pretty big in country music around the same time, and we were very similar as writers," she noted. "There was that kinship, that sisterhood. [I thought] you know, it would be a shame, a disgrace for us not to record something together. I think they're great. I thought we'd be great together. The reason we called it 'Honky Tonk Angels' is because Kitty Wells kind of started things for all us girls in country music. We wanted it to be simple."

Loretta Lynn added, "I used to sing 'Honky Tonk Angels' eight times a night"—that is, until a drunk came up to her onstage and informed her there was already one Kitty Wells and she needed to stop trying to sing like Wells and sing like herself if she was going to make it. "I thought about it later and said, 'You know, that old boy is right,'" Lynn laughed.

The set list includes two Parton originals, the perennial "Put It Off Until Tomorrow" and "Let Her Fly"; Lynn's "Wouldn't It Be Great"; and Wynette's "That's the Way It Should Have Been." They borrowed a track from their old friend, the late Patsy Cline, on "Lovesick Blues" and added harmony parts.

The three country music icons chose several old favorites—"Silver Threads and Golden Needles," which climbed to number 68 on the *Billboard* Country Chart and was made into a video; "Please Help Me I'm Falling (in Love with You)"; "Wings of a Dove"; "I Forgot More Than You'll Ever Know (About Him)"; and Parton "Dolly-ized" the lyrics to "I Dreamed of a Hillbilly Heaven" (Hal Sothern and Eddie Dean), adding a few names to the song—including Loretta's, Tammy's, and her own—before the singer wakes up to realize she was only dreaming.

The album was a hit, debuting on the Country Chart November 20, 1993, and moving to number 6, as well as to number 42 on the Pop Chart.

In the achingly sad "That's the Way It Could Be," Wynette imagines the way things could have been—the way they should have been, if the couple in the song had met "way back then" and things had been different.

Lynn's "Wouldn't It Be Great" deals matter-of-factly with a husband's alcoholism. The singer vehemently urges her man to "throw the old glass crutch away and watch it break."

Parton's "Let Her Fly" is a song set at the funeral of the singer's mother. "She's an angel; let her fly," she sings. "She's gone on to Glory in her home in the sky." In the promo interview Parton said the song was inspired by her grandmother, Renie Owens. "She loved flowers and always lived by the river and always had these beautiful roses and flowers," Parton recalled. "When I bought my old home place, there was a creek running through it so I built a replica of Grandma's house. I sit there on that little porch and everything's like Grandma's house, with a swinging bridge over the creek. One day two or three years ago I was sitting up on the porch and it was just like Grandma was there with me. I started crying, and my friend Judy started crying. It was like she was there. She was like an angel, so I called it 'Let Her Fly.' It was a message to God, asking him to make a place for her."

In Buddy Sheffield's poignant "Sittin' on the Front Porch Swing" the narrator feels that life has somehow passed her by because she never found the right man to marry and never had children. "Why do I sit at night and long to hold their babies," she wonders, as she's "sittin' on the front porch swing." Parton said she came across the song when she was hosting her syndicated television show and thought about doing it with the Linda Ronstadt and Emmylou Harris trio, but she ended up thinking it would be better for the trio with Loretta Lynn and Tammy Wynette.

In the promotional interview Wynette recalled the first time she heard Loretta Lynn on the radio. "I was in the cotton field picking cotton, and I thought, 'My gosh, that is so different from anything I've ever heard.' Dolly and I first came to town just about the same time; I think it was the same year I first heard from Dolly. She was doing some demos for Monument Records and doing some songwriting, and she brought one over called 'If I Could Again Be a Little Girl, Still Clinging to Mom's Apron Strings,' and it was a song I recorded on one of my first albums. I always felt very good for either or any of the three of us, or any of the female artists, when we had a hit record because there were so few of us. I never felt any kind of competition. I felt more like they were getting something good and I was getting something good, and it was good for all the women combined. At the time, it was very hard for a woman to work in the business. I know I was told they didn't like to book females because they didn't like to patronize the bar and didn't like to talk to the people in the clubs. And I thought we was going there to sing! But I kept thinking that Dolly and Loretta were doing the same thing I was doing, and we could prove a point, somehow, and we could make a difference. I feel very close to them because it was a struggle when we first came to town to do anything."

Parton said when she first heard Wynette she was immediately struck with the richness and quality of her voice—something "we hadn't had since Patsy Cline," she notes, and she liked the subjects she sang about. "They (Lynn and Wynette) were both ahead of their time," Parton said, "doing those feminist songs. Loretta was doing songs about 'the pill' and women's rights, even though she didn't have any rights. Tammy's songs were more about standing by your man and 'I Don't Want to Play House'—about the problems that real families had."

In the interview Steve Buckingham asked the women why they thought so many of the songs on this album have endured over the years. "They're songs that touch people's hearts and souls," Parton said. "The subject matter is always going to be there. When you write a love song, love's always going to be love. Take a song like 'Please Help Me, I'm Fallin'.' How many times a day do you see someone who turns your head? You don't have to run away with them, but that don't mean you don't follow them down the road a piece," she giggled. "Problems don't change. People don't change. It's the same old thing year in and year out, over and over from the beginning of time 'til the end of it we'll deal with the same stuff. That's what's so great about these songs. They touch those particular emotions."

DOLLY AND VINNIE

One of Parton's most famous duets, "I Will Always Love You" with Vince Gill, appeared on the *Something Special* album (Columbia, Blue Eye Records, 1995). Gill starts out verse one, his soaring tenor voice choking with emotion: "If I should stay, I would only be in your way. . . ." Parton comes in on the lead for "Bittersweet memories . . ." Gill takes the lead again on the third verse, with Parton echoing and speaking.

The album debuted on the *Billboard* Country Chart on September 9, 1995, climbing to number 40. The single with Gill went to number 15 and was nominated for a Grammy. When Parton came to the stage to meet Gill (who was hosting the CMA Awards in 1995) to accept the trophy for Vocal Event of the Year, she wisecracked to the audience, "Aren't you all about sick of this song by now?"

In 2009 Parton teamed up with Gill again for the Steve Martin–penned song "Pretty Flowers" on the well-known actor and comedian's album *The Crow: New Songs for the Five-String Banjo* (Rounder).

NEW TRIOS AND DUOS

A couple more notable duets appear on the *Something Special* album, including "Crippled Bird," a Parton original that she sings with Alison Krauss and Suzanne Cox. With some of the most celestial harmonies this side of heaven, the narrator compares her broken heart to a bird with a broken wing, unable to ever fly again. The spare, piano-based accompaniment with the focus on the three women's achingly beautiful harmonies captures the quiet devastation of heartbreak.

In "No Good Way of Saying Good-Bye" (Parton) Nashville Renaissance man Carl Jackson—a gifted producer, songwriter, instrumentalist, and singer—joins Dolly. Jackson sings like a tenor songbird, matching Parton's vocal line perfectly at every turn and flourish. "It's the hardest thing I'll ever do in my life," they sing, "saying good-bye, but loving you still." It's too late to start over, and the narrator in the song just doesn't have it in her to try any more.

Parton sings again with Krauss and Cox with another cut of "After the Gold Rush" on her 1996 album *Treasures* (Rising Tide/Blue Eye). The song won the Best Country Vocal Collaboration Grammy for Parton with Ronstadt and Harris, and a music video was released to television with the Parton/Krauss/Cox version.

One of her most memorable recent duets was with current country music superstar Brad Paisley. "When I Get Where I'm Going" debuted on October 8, 2005, on the *Billboard* Country Chart, reaching number 1 on March 4, 2006. From Paisley's album *Time Well Wasted* (Artista), the song also went to number 39 on *Billboard*'s Pop Chart, number 1 on the *Radio and Records* Country Chart, and number 2 on the Canadian Country Chart. It won two Academy of Country Music Awards and was certified both gold and platinum for digital single sales, with more than 200,000 copies legally downloaded, in June 2006.

Written by Rivers Rutherford, George Terren, and Brad Paisley, the song catches a glimpse of heaven. Written from the perspective of someone who has lost his grandfather, the narrator is contemplating his own death. He doesn't want his friends to cry for him when he's gone, because he's going to be walking the hills of home with his grandpa, matching him "step for step" in a place where there are only tears of joy. Pause for a moment and think about that image. Then the narrator thinks about the joy of arriving in heaven and seeing God's face as he sings, "I'll stand forever in the light of his amazing grace."

Dollywood and Hollywood

Albums and songs in this chapter: *9 to Five and Odd Jobs*, *The Best Little Whorehouse in Texas*, "Hard Candy Christmas," "I Will Always Love You"

DOLLY PARTON, ENTERTAINMENT BUSINESS ENTREPRENEUR

Parton's entertainment business interests include the Pigeon Forge, Tennessee–based theme park Dollywood; the Splash Country water park; and the combination rodeo/fried chicken dinner theater Dixie Stampede—the latter with additional locations in Branson, Missouri; Myrtle Beach, South Carolina; and Orlando, Florida.

Parton and her longtime manager, Sandy Gallin, operate Sandollar Productions, which has produced films such as *Father of the Bride* and its sequel, *IQ*, *Shining Through*, *Straight Talk*, and *Buffy the Vampire Slayer*, as well as television programs including the *Buffy* series and its spin-off, *Angel*. Parton's production company is called Southern Light Films.

Dollywood is the 24th-most-popular amusement or theme park in the United States and in the top 50 worldwide, with nearly three million annual visitors. Although she has not made her net worth public, 2003 press reports estimated Parton's net worth to be in excess of $300 million, and in 1988

Nashville Business magazine ranked her as the wealthiest entertainer in country music, with a personal fortune estimated at that time of $500 million.[1]

On July 3, 2010, a one-hour special titled *Dolly Celebrates 25 Years of Dollywood* aired on the Hallmark Channel. Parton's guests included Miley and Billy Ray Cyrus, Kenny Rogers, Reba McEntire, Brad Paisley, and Kenny Chesney, among others.

"I've often joked that I want to be a female Walt Disney," Parton said in a May 2010 article. "In my early days, I thought if I do get successful, I want to come back here and build something special to honor my parents and my people. I've always been a big dreamer, but this has gone far beyond my hopes and dreams."[2]

DOLLY CONQUERS HOLLYWOOD
AND RETURNS TO TELEVISION

Along with creating a vastly successful family vacation destination with a mountain theme (and a few hundred rhinestones and butterflies thrown in for pizzazz) at Dollywood, Parton also has a proven track record in Hollywood as a bona fide movie star, with starring roles and original music in movies like *9 to 5* (1980), *The Best Little Whorehouse in Texas* (1982), *Rhinestone* (1984), *Steel Magnolias* (1989), and *Straight Talk* (1992). Parton's song "Travelin' Thru" from the 2005 film *Transamerica* was nominated for both a Golden Globe and an Oscar in 2006.

Back in 1987–88 Parton hosted a television variety show on ABC called simply *Dolly!*, which fans remember as sort of a cross between the *Carol Burnett Show* and the *Barbara Mandrell Show*—with Parton's own personal stamp on it. Although it was canceled, she did pick up a People's Choice Award for Favorite Female Performer in a New Television Series and Favorite All-Around Female Performer in 1988. In recent years Parton has set her sights on Broadway, writing all the music for a 2009 production of *9 to 5*, which began touring nationally in 2010.

The overall sound on Parton's album *9 to 5 and Odd Jobs* (1980) is jazzed up significantly from her earlier RCA country albums, with heavy electric bass and drums, rocking electric guitars, horns, rock/pop electronic keyboards, and pop background vocals. Dolly's supple, emotional voice speaks more than one language, and from the '80s on she would never be confined to only country music parameters. Parton claims it was never her intention to leave country music. Rather, she took her country-roots-based talent and amazing voice with her into the world of mainstream music.

Debuting on the *Billboard* Country Chart on December 30, 1980, the album went to number 1 and stayed there for an amazing 10 weeks, also going to number 11 on the Pop Chart. The album was certified gold on March 6, 1981. The single "9 to 5" went to number 1 on the Country, Pop, and Adult Contemporary Charts, staying at each for 2 weeks. It was also certified gold for single sales over 500,000. Another single, "But You Know

I Love You," also went to number 1 on the Country Chart, as well as number 41 Pop and number 14 AC. Parton's version of the old chestnut about a house of ill repute, "House of the Rising Sun," went to number 14 for country radio and number 77 for pop.

On the *9 to 5 and Odd Jobs* album cover "working girl" Dolly Parton is wearing a ball cap trimmed with a red bandana and a yellow daisy and is dressed in a work shirt and blue jeans, with high-heeled silver shoes, of course. There's a red hose coiled around her right shoulder and a paint roller in her left hand, and she's also carrying a hoe, a rolled-up scroll of paper that may have come from an architect's drafting board, a watering pail, a coffee mug, a lunch bucket, a pair of work boots, a carpenter's T square, and some other tools . . . and she's pulling an old-fashioned lawn mower. There's a red briefcase with paper, pens, needle and thread, and red nail polish spilling onto the floor. And there's a manual typewriter at her feet. One wonders how she managed to carry all these things for the photo shoot. In the back cover photo Parton is reading a magazine, sitting on a chair at home. The clock says it's about seven minutes before 7 p.m. Coffee cup in hand, she has her fuzzy slippers on and a dog yawns at her feet. She's probably finally getting home after a long day at the office.

On the insert inside the album packaging Parton appears in office attire and a modest (for her) wig. Her mouth is open, and she's jubilantly tossing a handful of time cards into the air. On the wooden office desk behind her is a typewriter and a black telephone. There's a water cooler in front, and of course she's still wearing high-heeled shoes.

Parton wrote the theme song for *9 to 5* while on the set for the movie of the same name, creating the typewriter-like rhythm section by tapping her long fingernails. On the single, the pulsing rhythm reflects a rushed morning before work, as the singer "tumbles out of bed and stumbles to the kitchen" to pour herself "a cup of ambition." She's in a situation with a boss who doesn't appreciate her work, but that's not likely to diminish her dreams one bit.

The intro to "Hush a Bye Hard Times" (Parton) is lifted from the Stephen Foster song "Hard Times (Come Again No More)," with bluegrass legends Bobby and Sonny Osborne (of "Rocky Top" fame) absolutely nailing the vocal harmonies. The song is an up-tempo, modern version of the Foster tune, and times are hard at home. The wolf's howling at the door and the cupboard is bare.

"The House of the Rising Sun," arranged by Parton and Mike Post, is a rocked-out, R&B-flavored cover of the classic song. Parton changes the lyrics slightly, belting out that her father was a gambler and her mother died when she was just a girl, "and I've worked since then to pleasure the men at the House of the Rising Sun."

"Deportee (Plane Wreck at Los Gatos)," by Woody Guthrie and Martin Hoffman, is a sad, piano-accompanied, tender treatment of an issue that remains in the news today. The Mexican worker singing is either illegally in the country or his work contract has run out. He's 600 miles from the border, and he and his immigrant friends are being chased like "outlaws, like rustlers, like thieves." Perhaps they're in Arizona?

"Sing for the Common Man," written by Freida Parton and Mark Andersen, is a modern tribute to the common working man (or woman), which is the theme of the entire album. Parton's protagonist in "Working Girl" is a stylish, aggressive young woman who will not give up as she bravely climbs a career ladder, refusing to "look down until it's from the top."

"Detroit City," the Danny Dill/Mel Tillis standard, is the first outright country song on the album, dripping with steel guitar and trademark country electric guitar riffs. Parton embellishes a bit on the melody in the chorus, and then the strings come in. The last verse is a recitation.

"But You Know I Love You" (Mike Settle) is a strong cover that Parton definitely makes her own. The "traveling life" and the "dollar signs" are keeping the two main characters apart, but they seem to be willing to work to make their long-distance love work.

"Dark as a Dungeon," the Merle Travis–penned coal miner's lament, starts with a fingerpicked guitar and gets an intensely introspective vocal treatment. Parton absolutely pulls all the feeling of this old chestnut. Strings and synthesizers come in on the second verse, but for the most part it's just Parton's lead vocal and a guitar.

"Poor Folks Town," by Parton, explores the "we don't have a lot of money, but we're rich in love" theme that she's been writing about since the 1960s—one of her universal songwriting themes.

A separate *9 to 5 and Odd Jobs* movie soundtrack CD was released, which pictures Parton on the cover with her costars, Lilly Tomlin, Jane Fonda, and Dabney Coleman. Songs taken directly from the movie score are featured, including Parton singing the theme song, "9 to 5."

The Best Little Whorehouse in Texas (1982) album features music from the original motion picture soundtrack, with Burt Reynolds and Dolly Parton. "This much fun just couldn't be legal," the subtitle reads . . . which turns out to be true!

In this movie Parton plays the part of Mona, a madam in charge of a house of ill repute, and Burt Reynolds is the local officer of the law. They're also romantically involved. Parton and Reynolds are pictured on the album cover, smiling in a friendly way at each other. The drawing in the lower right corner is a Victorian "chicken house" with silhouettes of young women in the doorway and windows, with a big moon shining off in the distance and cacti growing on the right and left. It is Texas, after all.

The inside photo shows Parton at her most voluptuous. Standing in front of a window with long red curtains, she's holding a large, feathery black fan and wearing a black sequined dress with silver rhinestones.

The music opens with "20 Fans," written by Carol Hall and narrated by Jim Nabors, a description of the ceiling fans that get a good workout in the house, cooling down the girls and their guests.

Following "A Lil' Ole Bitty Pissant Country Place" is "Sneakin' Around," written by Parton and sung as a duet with her costar, Burt Reynolds. Mona likes a number of things, including "fancy, frilly things, high-heeled shoes and diamond rings, ragtime bands, and Western swing," and of course, sneaking around with Burt Reynolds's character.

Three orchestra numbers follow, which attempt to sound rural: "Court Yard Shag" (Carol Hall), "The Aggie Song" (Carol Hall), and "The Side-step" (Carol Hall), performed by Charles Durning.

"Hard Candy Christmas," which went to number 8 on the *Billboard* Country Chart, was written by Carol Hall and performed by Parton and the "Whorehouse Girls" in the movie, who have the blues at Christmastime—but are still determined not to let "sorrow bring [them] down." The lyrics play on the traditional old-fashioned hard candy the girls remember getting in their stockings at Christmas, and the hard time they're currently having with the holiday blues.

Parton's popular "I Will Always Love You," sung this time while looking Burt Reynolds in the eye, went to number 1 on the Country Chart and number 58 on the Pop Chart. The entire album debuted August 28, 1982, on the Country Albums Chart in *Billboard* and went to number 5, as well as to number 63 on the Pop Chart.

THE LIGHTS OF BROADWAY!

The Broadway production of *9 to 5* opened April 30, 2009 with a string of sold-out shows but closed after 24 previews and 148 performances. Allison Janney played the role originated by Lily Tomlin; Stephanie J. Block played Fonda's part; and Megan Hilty played Parton's character, Doralee. Parton was awarded the L.A. Drama Critic's Musical Score Award on March 16, 2009, for her songwriting on the project. Parton did not act in the show, but she wrote all the music for it.

The world premier of the *9 to 5: The Musical* tour began at Nashville's Tennessee Performing Arts Center on September 21, 2010, running through September 26. Diana DeGarmo, a former *American Idol* finalist, played the part of Doralee Rhodes.

In a September 2010 interview Parton said writing for the stage is "less binding" and "much freer. I could write the stories longer, in more verses," she explained. "In radio you have to keep it to a couple verses, a bridge and chorus, and keep it under three minutes. But with the stage, you can just write until finished! I found that liberating."[3]

In another interview Parton talked about the challenge of writing songs in the musical for the Franklin Hart character, the office boss villain. Dolly said she "holed herself up in her lake house" and pretended to be Hart. "I got up on the stairs in my manly voice, and tried to feel like a man would feel," Parton laughed. "Now, I have six brothers, and all my uncles, and my dad, so I know men inside and out. I love men, so I know all of their different personalities. And I've known lots of male chauvinists. But I got such a kick out of it. It was the biggest thrill. I kept thinking, 'Oh, women are going to kill me for saying such awful things.'"[4]

The issues presented in the movie and musical are still current, Parton said. "I've always used my femininity as a tool, and I don't mind saying so. I looked like a cheap dumb blonde and I often said when I first came to town that it served me well, because people thought they were going to be going to bed with me. But before we got to bed, I had the money and I was gone," she laughed. "I really feel like I'm suited to this," she said about writing for musicals. In fact, she said she enjoyed writing musical scores "so much so that when I finished *9 to 5,* I went to work on writing my life story as a musical, too. I think I get this. . . . I think it could not have worked out more perfect."[5]

Hungry Again:
The Acoustic/
Bluegrass Albums

> Albums and songs in this chapter: *Hungry Again, The Grass Is Blue,*
> *Little Sparrow, Halos and Horns, Eagle When She Flies,* "Rockin' Years,"
> *Slow Dancin' with the Moon,* "Romeo," *Treasures, Honky Tonk Angels,*
> "Silver Threads and Golden Needles," "I Will Always Love You" (with
> Vince Gill), *Something Special,* "After the Gold Rush" (with Alison
> Krauss and Suzanne Cox), *Just Because I'm a Woman*

PARTON RETURNS TO HER MUSICAL ROOTS

In a 1997 interview Parton, who described herself as "middle-aged, no longer viable at radio and not knowing what I should be doing in my musical
career," returned to the Tennessee mountain cabin of her youth to fast and
pray for a week and "write like I was hungry again," she said. "The result,"
biographer Alanna Nash observed, "is an album that revives her reputation as
a *country* singer/songwriter and allows her to sing, to *testify* even, with the
kind of authentic, fiery passion absent from her recordings for nearly three
decades. . . . *Hungry Again* isn't just Dolly's return to her rural roots. It's the
sound of an artist who's found herself again."[1]

After coming home musically with *Hungry Again*, Dolly recorded a trilogy of acoustic, bluegrass-based music with some of the finest sidemen in
the genre for the flagship bluegrass/Americana label, Sugar Hill Records.
According to former label owner Barry Poss, Sugar Hill conducted a survey

of fans and label employees, asking them what artist they would most like to hear record a bluegrass album, and Parton won, hands down. Intrigued, Dolly and producer Steve Buckingham recruited contemporary bluegrass giants such as Jerry Douglas on the Dobro, Sam Bush on the mandolin, Stuart Duncan on fiddle, Byron Sutton on guitar, Smilin' Jimmy Mills on banjo, and bassman Barry Bales to play on the album. Award-winning vocalists Claire Lynch, Alison Krauss, "Man of Constant Sorrow" Dan Tyminski (the singing voice of George Clooney in the movie *O, Brother Where Art Thou?*), Rhonda and Darrin Vincent, the Nashville Bluegrass Band's Alan O'Bryant, and Keith Little sang harmony on songs from the repertoires of Flatt and Scruggs, the Louvin Brothers, and Johnny Cash, along with Parton originals.

In liner notes Buckingham said, "The excitement and energy were so obvious, both from Dolly and the musicians. The band was absolutely amazed at her vocals. I really believe that a lot of people have forgotten she can sing like this. If Dolly can turn the heads of these singers and musicians, I can only imagine what the public will think. This was completely natural to her and, I believe, reaffirming." Top studio and award-winning fiddler Stuart Duncan said, "Dolly Parton has the power. She continues to inspire the world with her singing and her personality. Regardless of genre, she delivers every song with precision, emotion, and strength. To hear her sing bluegrass is like coming home again for the first time. She always sounded jazzy and grassy to me, and I always try to play as passionately as she sings. This recording may be the most important fun I've ever had. Thank you, Dolly. You're so in tune!"

HUNGRY AGAIN

In one of the most informally dressed photo shoots of her life, the all-original *Hungry Again* (1998) album cover presents Parton in a pair of faded blue overalls with the gallouses twisted and tied in front. (According to an Arkansas legend, if you twist an overall gallous, you won't be struck by lightning. Perhaps the same is true in Tennessee.) Dolly is sitting cross-legged on a wooden porch swing, and a bit of green grass in the yard is visible in the background. Heart-shaped holes have been carved out of a weathered oak post to the left and the middle board in the porch swing. Parton is gazing pensively off to her right, quietly smiling to herself. She's wearing a blonde wig with a long braid draped over her left shoulder, hanging down almost to her waist. On the back of the CD booklet she's smiling a little more, and her long-sleeved black cotton shirt is unbuttoned down past her bibs. On the back of the CD jewel case she's pictured in a brown minidress with spangly designs around the low U-shaped neckline and down her shoulders. Leaning against a blue car with her right high-heeled foot propped up on a little brown suitcase, Parton is surrounded by six men, all dressed in textured brown suits—something between corduroy and velour. There's a bass fiddle tied to the top of the car and the band's ready to go. This must be the "Blue Mountain Songbird" PR photo! (See song description below.)

The couple in "Hungry Again" has been together long enough to have settled into a comfortable routine. They've lost the romantic spark in their relationship, so they decide to "love like we're hungry again." The arrangement is simple, acoustic, and direct. Dolly's cousin and co-producer Richie Owens plays Dobro, Gary "Biscuit" Davis plays the five-string banjo, Gary Mackey's on mandolin, and Rhonda and Darrin Vincent provide seamless bluegrass sibling vocal harmonies.

In "The Salt in My Tears" the protagonist has committed the sin of not being true to herself and has allowed herself to be overshadowed for years by a lover who lied and cheated, and "ain't worth the salt in my tears." The melody is catchy and memorable, and Parton's vocal soars when she sings about how the narrator's man never cared about her.

In "Honky Tonk Songs" the narrator is singing into her beer, taking every sad song the jukebox plays to heart personally. The man she loved left her for a woman half her age, and she idly wonders why there aren't more women singing songs "about the heartaches and the tough breaks and the men that's done 'em wrong?" The "Honky Tonk women chorus" includes Jennifer O'Brien, Joy Gardner, Rhonda Vincent, Rachel Dennison, Judy Ogle, Teresa Hughes, Ira Parker, and Lois Baker.

"Blue Valley Songbird" is a musical short story about a young girl mentally and physically abused by her father. Her mother, who seems to be powerless in the situation, urges the singer to "run while you can," and the girl hits the road at age 15 to become a bluegrass singer. She writes letters home in care of the minister at the town church—given secretly to her mother so her dad won't find out where she is. Understandably, she's a little crazy . . . but she "sings like a bird and she writes like a poet." She wears a blue dress with blue shoes, rides around in a blue Cadillac, and takes the stage with a band dressed in blue at her side. With instruments tied to the top and the sides of her Caddy, the Blue Valley Songbird is ready to sing tonight. Richie Owens provides a Kona guitar in the mix, and Mark Brooks plays the upright bass (after dragging it off the roof of the car and tipping out the blue rainwater, one assumes.)

"I Wanna Go Back There" is told from the perspective of a man and woman who want to go back to when things were simpler—back "to the time when love was tender and fair." The tempo is swingy and positive, and the listener wants to go there, too.

"When Jesus Comes Calling for Me" starts with a recitation—a child remembering an old man everyone in town knew, who lived alone. When he's not out plowing with "Muley," he spends a good part of his latter days sitting on his creaky old rocking chair on the front porch, optimistically waiting for Jesus to come calling for him. The melody is catchy in an old-timey sort of way and the mood is sincere. This song should be listened to more often.

"Time and Tears" is an up-tempo bluegrass song with the banjo high in the mix. The singer emphasizes that she definitely did *not* change her whole life around, just to have some man "come back with your same ole act, thinking I'll understand."

In "I'll Never Say Goodbye" the narrator can't accept the fact that her man has cleaned out his closet and shelves, loaded up his car, and gone. She never actually said goodbye, and the door to her heart is still open. This song is another of the "girl is a little crazy after having her heart absolutely broken" variety that Parton writes so well.

"The Camel's Heart" features double-time bluegrass harmony and rhythm behind moderately paced lyrics. The woman singer has put up with more than the amount of hurt her heart can take, and this last incident is "the straw that broke the camel's heart," in a play on the expression "the straw that broke the camel's back."

"Paradise Road" is a commentary on the power of imagination and songwriting, which sounds autobiographical for Parton. With the power of imagination, the singer explains, "I could change my situation any time I chose." Dreams have taken the place of warm clothes and a meal, at times—a sentiment that recalls Parton's childhood days. Rhonda Vincent shines on the harmony vocals.

Sung to the tune of "Amazing Grace," "Shine On" is an anthem of encouragement. The message is that we should all help each other when help is needed, and more than anything, we should reflect God's love in our hearts and actions. "God gave us all a special gift," Parton and the choir of family and friends at her grandpa's old church sing, and we should let it shine. Cousin Richie pulls out an autoharp and a bouzouki this time, and the choir includes Richard Dennison, Jennifer O'Brien, Joy Gardner, Rhonda and Darrin Vincent, and Louis Nunley, with Jimmy Boling and the House of Prayer Congregation—featuring the Partons: David, Bobby, Rachel, Randy, Cassie, Willodeene, Lee, and Dolly.

In liner notes from Parton herself, she says, "Sometimes to know just how far you've traveled, you've gottta go back to where you began. Sometimes to know how good you've been eatin', you need to go hungry again. These two statements pretty much sum up the frame of mind I was in when I wrote and recorded this new CD. Not knowing exactly what I should be doing in my musical career or in my life at this point, I asked for guidance. I knew in my heart that my music had always been my Number One priority. It was the songs that I wrote and sang that took me out of the Smoky Mountains and took me all over the world. My songs are the door to every dream I've ever had and every success I've ever achieved. No matter what else I've had the good fortune to do, my first love is still my music. I'm still hungry for hit records, still hungry to sing, and still hungry to write songs for myself, as well as for others."

At the end of her sabbatical at the cabin in Tennessee, Parton had written 37 songs for this album. She asked her first cousin, Richie Owens, to coproduce the record with her. "I felt I should keep it in the family," Parton writes. "We did it all in his basement studio, using his band 'Shinola,' with his kids and theirs running in and out. I just loved it. It was so real, as everything about this album is to me. If you hear a baby crying now and then on some of these tracks, Richie had a new baby girl during the recording of this album."

THE BLUEGRASS TRILOGY

Produced by Steve Buckingham, *The Grass Is Blue* (1999) features an A+ Team band of award-winning musicians with bluegrass pedigrees: Jerry Douglas, Dobro; Stuart Duncan, fiddle; Barry Bales, bass; Sam Bush, mandolin; Bryan Sutton, guitar; and Jim Mills, banjo.

Parton's first full-out bluegrass album ended up being one of the most critically acclaimed projects she has ever released. *The Grass Is Blue* won a Grammy for Best Bluegrass Album of the Year and also the IBMA (International Bluegrass Music Association) Album of the Year in 2000. The album debuted on the *Billboard* Country Chart November 13, 1999, rising to number 24 and number 19 on the Pop Chart. She's pictured on the album cover in a black and white close-up, hugging her guitar to her chest.

"Travelin' Prayer" (Billy Joel) is a quick-tempo bluegrass prayer for the singer's lover, in hopes that he'll return safely. Alison Krauss and Dan Tyminski are at the top of their game singing harmony, and the instrumentalists are on fire.

"I got in a little trouble at the county seat," Parton confides in "Cash on the Barrelhead," making this old Louvin Brothers standard her own story. There are no free rides and everyone's got to pull their own weight. Claire Lynch and Keith Little sing harmonies.

Patty Loveless and Rhonda Vincent provide the vocal harmonies on the chorus of one of the most lonesome, well-written songs in the history of bluegrass to date, Hazel Dickens's "A Few Old Memories."

On "I'm Gonna Sleep with One Eye Open" (Lester Flatt), mandolin maestro Sam Bush, Alison Krauss, and Union Station bassist Barry Bales chime in on the harmonies on this Flatt and Scruggs standard. The singer's husband won't have the chance to step out "between midnight and day" because she's going to keep one eye open while she sleeps.

In "Steady as the Rain," Lynch and Little return for harmonies on this Parton original that perfectly fits the bluegrass genre. Utilizing a storm analogy, the singer's memory is clouded and her tears are "steady as the rain."

In "I Still Miss Someone," written by Johnny Cash and Roy Cash Jr., the narrator admits, "I never got over those blue eyes." She still sees eyes in a crowd, on a day-to-day basis, that remind her of her lover's. She misses his embrace, and the feeling "when all the love was there." Stuart Duncan's fiddle sobs, "Flux's" (Jerry Douglas's) Dobro cries, and Parton and Krauss must be equally pleased to harmonize on such a sad song.

"Endless Stream of Tears" (Parton) is another lonesome, up-tempo original. You won't necessarily die from a broken heart, the singer proclaims, but you might want to. She drowns in "an endless stream of tears," floating along on top of Rhonda and Darrin Vincent's vocal harmonies.

The public domain song "Silver Dagger" begins with just Jim Mills's banjo and Parton's voice on a traditional song about a young woman who is trying to discourage a suitor because her mother's a little overprotective and jaded. Mom also happens to be waiting just inside the door with a silver dagger, in case the young suitor doesn't take the hint to leave.

"Train, Train" is a barn burner sung from the perspective of a woman left behind and a bit ticked off about it. Her man, "the no good so and so" is on a train to Memphis. Alan O'Bryant and Keith Little nail the train whistle harmonies at the end with Parton. Big Mon (Bill Monroe, the father of bluegrass) would be proud.

"I Wonder Where You Are Tonight," a standard written by Johnny Bond, is another trinity classic from Flatt and Scruggs. (The other two "trinity" groups in bluegrass are Bill Monroe and his Blue Grass Boys, and The Stanley Brothers.) Parton proves she's "one of the guys" with the choice of this song, one of the most popular jam session standards in bluegrass music around the world.

"Will He Be Waiting for Me" (Parton) is a song of disoriented uncertainty. Will he be waiting for her, or "will [she] find that this time [she'll] be the one to cry?" In the title cut, "The Grass Is Blue" (Parton), the narrator is so distraught over the sad fact that her love has said good-bye that she has to pretend the opposite of everything is true, just to survive. "Rivers flow backwards, valleys are high," and mountains have become flat after what she thought was truth turns out to be a lie.

"I Am Ready," written by Rachel Parton Dennison, is a celebratory a cappella song from the perspective of a woman who is near death, but she's joyfully, anxiously ready to go to heaven. Her Bible is on the table, and she asks her visitors to read a few verses to her. She can hear "God's heavenly angels singing me on to heaven's shore." Rhonda Vincent, Darrin Vincent, and Louis Nunley provide the spirited vocal harmonies.

Steve Buckingham produced Parton's follow-up acoustic album for Sugar Hill, *Little Sparrow* (2001). This time the material reaches a bit past bluegrass into the Celtic/mountain sound Parton grew up with, and she also throws in a few covers from other genres, "bluegrassed" up. The album won Dolly Parton a Grammy in 2001 for Best Female Country Vocal Performance.

Parton has a thoughtful look on her face in the black and white photo on the album cover. She's sitting backward on an old straight-back wooden chair in a black sweater, and her hair falls down around her shoulders in soft ringlets.

In the title cut, *"Little Sparrow"* (Parton) flies high and feels no pain, in a song with a message similar to the one in the traditional song "Fair and Tender Ladies." Women are warned to beware of men who will crush their spirits like a little bird and break their hearts. Dan Tyminski and Alison Krauss return for vocal harmonies

"Shine" (Ed Roland) is a Collective Soul cover that really shows off Chris Thile on mandolin, Stuart Duncan on fiddle, and Jerry Douglas on Dobro. Actually, there are no weak links in this band. Lynch and Little provide harmony support.

"I Don't Believe You've Met My Baby" (Autry Inman) is the old Louvin Brothers love song of mistaken identity. A woman's arm is resting on the shoulder of the narrator's beau, and he says (we're not sure to whom), "I don't believe you've met my baby." We don't discover until the last verse that the girl is his sister. Alison Krauss also did a memorable version of this song as a guest on the Jerry Douglas album *Slide Rule*.

"Go spread your blue wings and I'll cry my blue tears," the singer shouts to the bird outside her window in "My Blue Tears," written by Parton. The narrator is plainly in no mood for birdsong because the only man she's ever loved has gone. Alison Krauss sings the duet with Parton—another lovely, horribly sad song. Ciaran Curran adds bouzouki and Dermot Byrne the accordion to the mix.

In "Seven Bridges Road" (Steve Young), Sonya Isaacs and Becky Isaacs Bowman from the popular bluegrass gospel group The Isaacs join Parton for a song The Eagles had a hit with. Carl Jackson sings a bass vocal, Jim Mills plays banjo, Bryan Sutton is on guitar, Thile is playing mandolin, Jerry Douglas plays the resophonic guitar (Dobro), and Barry Bales is on acoustic bass.

In "Bluer Pastures" (Parton) the singer left Kentucky for greener pastures, but she ends up going home to the bluegrass state of Kentucky where her love "waits with open arms for [her, she] hopes." A gentle, three-quarter-time bluegrass song reflects on "the grass is always greener" concept.

Trembling with emotion, the singer in "A Tender Lie" (Randy Sharp) begs her man to just tell her once more than he'll love her forever. "How much more damage now, honestly, can one tender lie do?" she asks sadly.

"I Get a Kick Out of You" (Cole Porter) literally kicks off with the amazing Chris Thile on mandolin, followed by Jerry Douglas on resophonic guitar, and then Stuart Duncan on fiddle and Bryan Sutton on guitar swing for a long instrumental introduction before Parton comes in with, "I get no kick from champagne."

Following three Parton originals described in a previous chapter, "Mountain Angel," "Marry Me" and "Down from Dover," comes "The Beautiful Lie"—in which Parton is accompanied solely by Duncan's fiddle. "In the Sweet By and By" is a traditional hymn about meeting our loved ones again in heaven. The song starts out quietly, and then builds to a Celtic choir with Mairead NiMhaonaighi singing a verse in Gaelic and accompaniment on the bouzouki, accordion, whistle, and harmonium. The album ends with a haunting reprise of the title cut, "*Little Sparrow*."

Parton produced *Halos and Horns* (2002), the third in her bluegrass trilogy of albums, herself, assisted by Gary Davis and her touring band at the time, the Blueniques. All the songs in this collection are Parton originals except for the two rock covers, "If" and "Stairway to Heaven."

"Halos and Horns" explores the constant struggle between good in evil in our hearts. April Stevens and Darrell Webb sing harmony. "Sugar Hill" is a quick-paced love song about skinny-dipping and falling in love. "Not for Me" is about depression. The singer feels that "birds sing for everyone but me," but like the Joe Btfsplk character in the Little Abner cartoon who was constantly followed by a black cloud, all the narrator gets is rain. "Hello God" is an earnest series of questions for the Creator, with a request for help.

"If" (David Gates) is Parton's acoustic cover of the pop song popularized by the group Bread. One of the sweetest love songs in history, probably sung at a thousand weddings, the song has probably never been done with a Scruggs-style banjo before.

On "Shattered Image" Randy Kohrs's Weisenborn guitar powers the almost Cajun groove on this song that talks about how people can hurt each other deeply with criticism. Beth and April Stevens, who performed for many years on the bluegrass circuit with The Stevens Family and later as The Stevens Sisters (including several years at Dollywood), provide vocal harmony with a timbre almost identical to Parton's.

"These Old Bones," described previously, is followed by "What a Heartache," which notes that love isn't always what it appears to be. "I'm Gone" is a "happy to leave home" song with the banjo high in the bluegrass mix. The singer grabs some chewing gum, a magazine, a change of clothes, buys a one-way ticket on the train, and tosses her wedding ring happily out the window.

"Raven Dove" is a song about heaven, with images drawn from the book of Revelation. When the lion lies down with the lamb and when "a child tames the beast, nations shall gather and bow at his feet," then we shall know peace, the singer believes.

"Dagger Through the Heart" is a "cheated on" song, and "If Only" presents two of the saddest words in the English language—regarding profound regret in a relationship that has gone wrong.

"John Daniel" is the story of a modern-day prophet, and "Stairway" (Jimmy Page and Robert Plant), of course, is the Led Zeppelin classic. No one on the planet but Dolly Parton would have thought of doing this song bluegrass style, and probably no one else could have pulled it off.

REFLECTIONS FROM STEVE BUCKINGHAM, PRODUCER

The *All Music Guide* credits Steve Buckingham with producing more than 200 albums. He's been awarded 11 platinum and 19 gold albums, as well as 27 number 1 singles. Buckingham has produced singles that charted in the top ten on 11 different charts: pop, country, rhythm and blues, jazz, adult contemporary, Americana, bluegrass, Christian, Hispanic, Triple A, and dance.

He teaches a course called "How Rhythm and Blues and Rock 'n' Roll Tore Down the Walls of Desegregation" at the University of Richmond in Virginia, and also at Vanderbilt University in Nashville, and he's worked with a who's who of musicians from multiple genres—in addition to Dolly Parton, folks like Linda Ronstadt, the Chieftains, Ricky Skaggs, Shania Twain, Loretta Lynn, Tammy Wynette, Sinead O'Connor, Mary Chapin Carpenter, Ysuf Islam (Cat Stevens), Dionne Warwick, Brenda Lee, Joan Osborne, Norah Jones, Nanci Griffith, Ladysmith Black Mambazo, Bela Fleck, Allison Moorer, Vince Gill, Isaac Hayes, Kim Carnes, Sam Bush, Buddy and Julie Miller, Chet Atkins, Del McCoury, Vern Gosdin, and many more.

Buckingham got into music while playing beach music in Virginia and the Carolinas, and he worked as a session musician out of Atlanta, L.A., and Muscle Shoals, Alabama. In 1978 he produced "I Love the Nightlife," a hit for Alicia Bridges, and he moved to Nashville, where he served as vice president of A&R for Columbia Records for 10 years, and he later worked as senior vice president at Vanguard and Sugar Hill Records.

In a 2010 interview Buckingham talked about his 18-year professional relationship with Dolly Parton. "We met in '89," he recalled. "Ricky Skaggs was producing Dolly's album *White Limozeen*, and I was producing *Kentucky Thunder* [an album for Skaggs and also the name of his band], so we were both working at the same studio, just across the hall from each other. Ricky would be over there working on Dolly's album, while I'd be in the control room working on his album. The following year I was VP of A&R at Columbia, and Dolly asked me if I'd help her work on her new album. She wanted to cut it with her road band, and she said some of the 'bigwigs' in New York told her she couldn't do it by herself with her band, so she asked me if I'd help her. I did. That was *Eagle When She Flies*. We ended up coproducing that together."

Buckingham's first impression of Parton in the studio was that she was "always up, always her effervescent self in the studio, a total pro." From the beginning of their work together, Buckingham said Dolly was "very pleasant, but very businesslike. She was very serious—and still is—about her work, her art, her writing, her performing, her production. . . . Focused."

Parton brought songs she was considering for the album and either played them live for Buckingham or played a cassette. "One was her brother Floyd's song, 'Rockin' Years.' She wanted to do a duet on it, and at the time I was producing Ricky Van Shelton. I couldn't think of two people who were more different than Ricky Van Shelton and Dolly, because she is so outgoing and he is quiet and reserved. But the first day we got in the studio together, it felt like a hit. And it was. The album went to number 1 and the single went to number 1, so that's how we started."

When Buckingham came onboard with the project, Parton had already given all her artist (royalty) points away to her band. "I said, 'I'll do it,'" Buckingham said, "'but you don't have to pay me production points or anything. I'll just do it to help you.' But I remember once the album went platinum, I got a check from Dolly out of her own personal account, and she paid me like I'd been the sole producer. Nothing came from Sony, because I wasn't down on the contract for any points. She paid me out of her own pocket, which is the only time in my career that anybody did that."

The two trusted each other, which is probably why their working relationship lasted 18 years—a length of time that's "kind of unheard of," Steve said.

In the studio he said Parton is "always dressed. She says that if somebody sees her one time and they say, 'I saw Dolly Parton,' then she wants to look like Dolly Parton. She's always camera ready, always on time, always prepared, and she knows what we're cutting that day. We would always go over songs together, with me playing guitar or one of the other guitar players or a piano player. We would always go over stuff and have the keys. I'd do the charts, and especially when we did the bluegrass albums, it was nothing for us to get six, seven, or eight tracks the first day."

On both *The Grass Is Blue* and *Little Sparrow*, Buckingham cut seven or eight tracks the first day, "which is really flyin'," he smiled. "She was always ready. I was always prepared with preproduction. That's one of the reasons we worked so well together. She's fast and I'm fast. There was never a lot of that 'sitting around waiting.'"

Buckingham booked the musicians, and he used Gary Paczosa as an engineer. On the *Eagle as She Flies* album, Buckingham said Parton "just wanted to do a good country album. She wrote most of the material. With Dolly, she'll write new songs for an album, and then she'll go back and take old songs she's got a lot of times. She did this on most of the albums we did, where she'll rework one of her old songs—like 'Endless Stream of Tears' on *The Grass Is Blue*. She keeps a file in her head of songs. She never puts them away. She can always go back and bring them back out."

No one is really sure how many songs Parton has written—mainly because she writes constantly. "I've read somewhere around 3,000," Buckingham said, "but I think that's just an arbitrary number. She writes all the time—pieces of things, complete things; it's rare that you bring up a song of hers that she doesn't remember. . . . I mean, she'll remember everything. If not, she'll get the words from her office. Then she'll sit there and maybe rework the lyrics. It's fascinating to watch her work."

The label heads in New York were anxious for Buckingham to be spending time with some of their younger artists rather than focusing too much time on Parton, Buckingham said, even after the platinum album *Eagle as She Flies*. When they were getting ready to do *Slow Dancing with the Moon*, the topic came up again. Buckingham told them, flatly: "Dolly is going to be around much longer than most of the new artists we're signing now."

Regarding her songwriting habits, Buckingham said, "She keeps notepads everywhere. Any of her houses that I've ever been in—here, L.A., anywhere, there are notepads in every room. In her car there's always a notepad and a pen. They're kind of like a reporter's notepad, with a pen. She's constantly writing things down—whether it be a title, a lyric, an idea for a song, or anything. It could be the name for a restaurant, or for a clothing line."

It's difficult to imagine anyone being able to remember new melodies for that many song ideas at once. "She would always keep boom boxes wherever she was, so she could put a cassette in. I even went out and bought her a mini disk recorder with a microphone on it, because sometimes it might be something so great that we could take and put it on tape, or play the digital and use it as a basis. But she never really tried to use it. As far as I know, she's still using cassettes today. And it's worked."

The concept for *Slow Dancing with the Moon* was duets, Buckingham said. "These records were all on Columbia, and this record went platinum, too. She had the idea of doing the song with Billy Ray Cyrus, 'Romeo.' She came in and played it while we were in the studio, working on the album. It was just a collaboration of her with the other girls we got on there—Mary Chapin Carpenter, Kathy Mattea, Tanya Tucker, and Pam Tillis . . . and Billy Ray. I remember none of us really knew him, but the night he came in to sing, he was really soulful, really good. He was really a nice fellow, and I know all the girls were on the video."

The concept for the *Treasures* album, Buckingham said, was that it was a collection of songs Parton liked that were written by other people. "She loves Cat Stevens, and I know Yusuf Islam. She'd heard 'Peace Train' on a Lifesaver (candy) commercial and asked me who that was, on there. I told her it was Ladysmith Black Mambazo. We ended up getting them and cut the song in New York with them. I think this was the only album that there were none of her songs on there. They were all songs that she liked the original artists who did them. I got the guests for that album—if there were certain people she liked their voices, or didn't know how to get in touch with them. It was an unusual concept."

The collaboration with Tammy Wynette and Loretta Lynn, *Honky Tonk Angels,* was "totally Dolly's idea," Buckingham said. "She said, 'I want to do an album with Tammy and Loretta before one of us goes.' I had worked with Tammy in the mid-'80s. She was the first country artist I produced, and we did two albums. I'd never worked with Loretta before, but I remember the first day the three of them got together with me over at [engineer/producer] Allen [Reynolds's] office and each one of them brought in songs. We sat in a circle and the three of them pretty much picked out the material.

"That was like a summit, having the three of them together," Buckingham smiled. "There's a lot of footage I've got of that. I ran a DAT and recorded the whole time in the control room, to catch the stories. Columbia did a lot of filming in the studio. It was incredible. One night we had cut the old song "I Dreamed of a Hillbilly Heaven.' Dolly was rewriting the lyrics, and she was faxing them back and forth with Buddy Killen, who was the head of Tree Music, about trying to find the original lyrics. And Buddy would fax back over a verse, and Dolly would rewrite it to kind of fit them. And the one night we did 'It Wasn't God Who Made Honky Tonk Angels,' Kitty Wells came in. So we had the four of them together. It was pretty amazing. The only one missing was Patsy Cline, and we even took an old track of Patsy Cline and put the three of them on there with Patsy. It was a track, oddly enough, that Columbia owned, even though she was not on Columbia Records. So we had every one of the country queens on that album. That was something."

The main memory Buckingham has about the *Honky Tony Angels* sessions is that "we laughed all the time," he said. "Dolly's got the greatest sense of humor. She was always cracking jokes. It was just great. . . . It was fun. It was historic. They did 'Silver Threads and Golden Needles' on the CMA Awards that year, and the video. It was a shock, just a few years after that, when Tammy died. That was the last gold album Tammy had, and to this day, it's still the last gold record Loretta has had. I remember Dolly brought in some songs that she had written and maybe had recorded before, and redid them and reworked them for the three of them."

With a professional history like Buckingham's, you have to wonder if he ever wakes up in the morning and asks, "How did I get here? How did this happen in my life?"

"[Dolly] asked me if I thought we could do a duet on 'I Will Always Love You' with Vince [Gill]," Buckingham continued. "I've known Vince since he first moved to Nashville. He was the hottest thing at that time, and it was very difficult to work it out. I called Vince and of course he wanted to do it, but I had to work it out with his managers and MCA. I remember that night when we did 'Honky Tony Angels' and 'Rockin' Years' and 'Eagle When She Flies'—those albums were done over at a studio on 17th Street that Ray Stevens owns, but back then it was called Nightingale, and after that it was called 17 Grand. We cut a lot there. . . . We did *Slow Dancing with the Moon* here at Sound Stage—a lot of it. We cut the tracks over there and came over here and did vocals. Most of it was done over at the old Nightingale Studio, except for the night we did 'I Will Always Love You' with Vince, which we did over at Sound Shop. And I mean, as soon as Vince opened his mouth, she just looked at me like, 'This is going to be unbelievable.' And it was. It was magic from the start. I had got Vince's key ahead of time, so we cut the tracks. But we cut the vocals that night together, and it was stunning. We did that on the Opry."

On the *Treasures* album, one of Parton's favorite songs was "After the Gold Rush," Buckingham said. "She changed a lyric, and it was recorded with Suzanne Cox and Alison (Krauss). Alison has been on every Dolly album I've produced. I don't think Dolly was aware of Alison when we did *Eagle When She Flies*, but I remember the first night she came in. She was 18, as I recall, and was not very well known outside bluegrass circles. Gary Paczosa had worked with her. . . . I know the night Alison came in Dolly did not come into the studio because we thought it might be too overwhelming. When people first meet Dolly, sometimes they get a little overwhelmed."

Krauss has said in numerous interviews that she immediately started crying the first several times she met Dolly Parton in person. "She did," Buckingham smiled. "Alison and I are great friends, to this day. I remember her parents were still living in Illinois, and she was holding the phone up to the speaker saying, 'That's me, with the queen!' She's been on every album I've done [with Dolly], and some other people."

In the studio, Buckingham said, "usually we cut the track with Dolly, and then add the guest vocalists and certainly the background vocals. We cut Vince and Dolly together; after we'd done the track we cut the vocals together."

Parton's Blue Eye Record Label came about after Parton was having hits with Buckingham on Columbia. "Sony approached her finally, about having her own imprint—her own label," he said. "She had the idea to call it 'Blue Indigo' because of a dream she had. But there was some copyright reason she couldn't use the name 'Blue Indigo.' So she called it 'Blue I Records'—with the letter 'I.' She told the people at Sony, 'I'll do it if Steve can be my partner.' So we opened Blue I Records basically for Dolly."

The name evolved into Blue Eye Records. "That's what it became," Buckingham said. "That's her eye. She doesn't have blue eyes; she has hazel eyes. There was some reason the letter 'I' was confusing people, so she changed it to 'Blue Eye'—the logo being her eye, colored blue. I think the first album we did on Blue Eye/Sony was *Something Special*—the one that had the duet with Vince. I was in Dolly's offices and did that for two years. Then Doug Morris at Universal approached us about doing the same joint venture with Universal. That was in '97. The first album we did on that . . . was the *Treasures* album. I think the next album was when she did *Hungry Again,* herself.

"That was about the time that I was approached by Welk Music out in Los Angeles to come with them. They had Vanguard Records. I went to Dolly and I said, 'You know, this is nothing to do with me being unhappy with you,' because we'd worked, at that point, for nine years together. I said, 'I've got the chance to do this,' and she said, 'Do it. It's an opportunity for you to do other kinds of music you like,' and so it was announced on a Friday that I was leaving Blue Eye/Rising Tide/Universal to go with Welk Music/Vanguard, and the following week Universal came in and closed Rising Tide. Not because I left, obviously, but they been planning on it—which none of us knew. It caught everybody off guard. Dolly was moved over to Decca, and that's why some of those albums there—like *Hungry Again*— show up as Decca.

"Then the early part of '99 or spring of '99 it was announced in the papers: 'Dolly Parton Dropped from Decca Records.' In June of '99," Buckingham continued. "By that point I was flying to L.A. every month to have a meeting at the Welk offices in Santa Monica, and Dolly gets on the plane with me, and she's sitting two rows in front of me. I walked up to say hello, and she screamed and it was like old home week. Whoever she was sitting with, she made them switch with me so we could sit together, flying out to L.A. On the way out I asked her, I said, 'Do you have plans for this evening, when we get to L.A.?'

She said, 'No,' and I said, 'Why don't we go to dinner?' This was June of '99 and we went to dinner that night at a great Italian restaurant in Santa Monica that's been there forever, and I was telling her about my new gig with Welk and Vanguard. I was telling her, 'We bought this bluegrass label called Sugar Hill that's been around forever.' I said, 'Have you ever thought about doing a bluegrass album, because a lot of people within Sugar Hill said they would love to see you do a bluegrass album.'"

Just kind of on a whim, Buckingham said, Parton replied, "Yeah, let's do it. I own myself. I can do whatever I want." So in less than a month the label got together with her attorney, and she let me pick all the musicians. She was sending me songs. She said, 'Why don't we do it in August, because I'll be tied up in July. . . . We put the deal together, got the band, the studio, Gary (Paczosa), the studio was the Sound Kitchen down in Franklin, and 35 days later we were cutting the album. She was sending me songs, and she called me one day from the set of the movie and said, 'I just wrote the cut for the title of the album, *The Grass Is Blue*,' and she played it for me over the phone. She wrote it on the set of this *Blue Valley Songbird* (movie), and she was sitting on the bus, playing it for me over the phone, on her guitar. I got a rough cassette of it a few days later, and she and I and Bryan Sutton got together a few times and worked out the charts and keys and everything."

It was Parton's idea to do "Traveling Prayer," the Billy Joel song; "Cash on the Barrel Head"; and "I Still Miss Someone."

"It seems like 'Steady as the Rain' was a song that she reworked," Buckingham said. "I know 'Endless Stream of Tears' was one of her older songs that she reworked for this. 'Silver Dagger' was an old folk song by another title, and she wrote these beautiful lyrics to it. 'I Wonder Where You Are Tonight' was her idea. 'Train, Train' was by some Southern rock group. We didn't even know who the publisher was. We talked about doing this album in June, we're in the studio in August recording, and it was out by October. It was unbelievably fast. We cut at least seven or eight tracks the first day with these musicians. All the solos—everything was live except the background vocals."

Buckingham said he didn't know if "Dolly thought anything was going to come of it, but it came out and got the best reviews she ever got, that I was ever aware of"—along with a Grammy, a CMA, and an IBMA award.

"I guess it was the following October, when she performed at the IBMA Awards show in Louisville, Kentucky," Buckingham continued. "It was a magic night. The band from the album played that night—Jerry [Douglas], Stuart [Duncan], Bryan [House], Jim [Mills]—everybody was there. I think we did two songs, maybe 'Traveling Prayer' and "The Grass Is Blue' put together as a medley. Rhonda and Darrin Vincent sang harmony at the IBMAs. We performed at the Grammys just two months later, and it was nominated and won. She was dumbfounded at the IBMA Awards," Buckingham said. "It's the only time I've ever seen her speechless. I've been around her when she's won Grammys, I've been around her when she was inducted into the Songwriters Hall of Fame in New York, the Kennedy Center Honors in

Washington, the Hall of Fame here (Nashville), and I've never seen her that surprised and overwhelmed as that night she won the IBMA award for Album of the Year. She was truly knocked out. Marty [Stuart] was the host. We had a ball. It was a magic night. I guess it was after we did *Little Sparrow*, we played at MerleFest. That was another magic night, with Doc Watson."

By July of 2000 they were back in the studio, working on *Little Sparrow*. "It was her idea to do 'Shine,'" Buckingham said. "It was her idea to do all the outside tunes—'Tender Lie.' 'I Get a Kick Out of You' was certainly her idea. I remember bringing in the Sinatra version and the Ella Fitzgerald version, and we did charts. 'I Don't Believe You Met My Baby' was from the Louvin Brothers. She wrote, obviously, '*Little Sparrow*' for the album, and some of these others. We went down to Ocean Way. It was the same band, except Sam Bush was on the road with Lyle Lovett. I knew Chris Thile, because they were a young band on Sugar Hill and Nickel Creek had just started to take off. He was, I think, just 19 when he did that album, and he blew everybody away. I remember the opening of 'I Get a Kick Out of You.' It was Thile that came up with that. He did such an unbelievable solo, it raised the level for everybody else. And again, everything was live except for the background vocals.

"This reminds me of another one we did," Buckingham added. "It was called *Live, from Home*. It was a live album with Rhonda and Darrin Vincent as one pair of background singers, Alison (Krauss) and Suzanne (Cox) as one pair of background singers, and we had everybody—a gigantic acoustic band. We had some of the McCourys, some of Alison's Union Station, Ron Block and Dan Tyminski. We were switching mandolin players and guitar players. We had Randy Scruggs; we had David Lindley and Roy Huskey Jr. It was like an acoustic orchestra. Alison was crying at that concert. We taped four concerts. We brought this group from Ireland called Altan for the live album, and they sang on the [*Little Sparrow* album also]."

In particular, they worked the Irish musicians and influences into "In the Sweet By and By," "My Blue Tears," "Mountain Angel," and "Down from Dover."

"Whereas *The Grass Is Blue* was the pure bluegrass album," Buckingham explained, "I thought of *Little Sparrow* as the mountain album. My idea was if we had done a trilogy, was to do an almost pure mountain, Irish thing. I've still got all the CDs I put together of all the old traditional songs that were known by one title in Ireland and another title in the bluegrass world. When we got ready to do *Little Sparrow*, the bar had been raised by *The Grass Is Blue* because it won all those awards. The reviews were phenomenal. It was almost like there was no place to go but down, but it was even better."

"Shine" won a Country Female Vocal Performance award from the Grammys, and the video got a lot of airplay.

"The funny thing about the video," Buckingham said, "is that Stuart [Duncan] was on the road. Jerry Douglas was out of town. I think the day we shot the video for 'Shine,' Sarah Watkins was playing the fiddle in the video, and it was Stuart's fiddle being played. I think Sean (Watkins) was miming the Dobro. The only reason we did that was because Jerry and Stuart were out of town and the video had to be shot on a particular day. I was kidding Sarah, saying, 'People are going to be saying you play just like Stuart Duncan'"—which, of course, is a compliment in anyone's book, and Watkins would agree.

Parton has a specific way she likes to work in the studio, Buckingham said. "She likes to come in, cut the tracks quick, sing live, put it away for a week or two when her voice is really strong, and then she'll come in and sing all of her vocals in one day. It's a second set of vocals. She does the live vocal, and then goes into the studio and literally she'd sing each song. She'd stand in the studio and have her glasses on, and has her water and her tissues and takes her earrings off so they don't rattle, and we had all the little things we needed to do. She sits there with her glasses down on her nose and looks at the lyrics and makes notes, and she sings each song two or three times. If she felt like she still hadn't captured it, she would say, 'Let me do it one more time.' She'd give me another set of vocals, but she does it all in a day—less than a day. We'd start at 10 and we'd then take a break for lunch and she'd fix food for us. Then we'd be done by two or three o'clock in the afternoon with her singing all the vocals."

Buckingham didn't make a lot of suggestions to Parton, as a rule. "She knows her voice," he said. "She knows when she's got it. And then it was a case of me, after she was gone, spending the next week comparing live vocals to the vocals she'd redone and picking. I could go back in my notes to see which vocal we used on each one, but half the time it was the live vocal. Her voice gets tired like anybody's," he continues, "but most people would not come in and do all their vocals in one day. . . . Yeah, she sings great. She's still got great pipes."

Parton is famous for bringing her home cooking into the studio for lunch, for everyone. "It's Southern cooking," Buckingham said. "You never know what she's going to bring. One of her favorite things, and the musicians go crazy over it, is her chicken and dumplings. When we cut tracks I would always cater lunch, but Dolly would also bring in food for everyone, too. She would always bring food in for Gary [Paczosa] and me when we were working on just her vocals. When she's out there doing her vocals, it's the serious, focused, intense Dolly. She's pleasant, but totally professional."

In 2001 when it was time to do the third Sugar Hill bluegrass album, Buckingham was spending a lot of time going back and forth to Richmond, Virginia, because his mother's health was deteriorating. The end of 2001 and the beginning of 2002, Parton had already started working on demos for the next album with some musicians from Dollywood, and they were recording in Knoxville.

Buckingham was needed at home and Dolly decided to use the demos on the album because they were turning out so well, so she produced *Halos and Horns* on her own, with Gary Davis assisting.

"In 2002 I went to her with the idea of putting together an album of people doing her songs," Buckingham said. "It was a tribute album, but we didn't want to call it a tribute to Dolly Parton," he explained. "It just evolved as I started putting it together. The *Halos and Horns* album came out. She did a tour and did songs from all three albums. The Blueniques were her touring band before she worked with the Grascals. It took a different path than these two. These two were black and white albums, almost like a film noir thing, the way the music is, and the *Halos and Horns* went a different direction. But you know, Dolly was the artist and the producer. . . . I threw my efforts into this one, *Just Because I'm a Woman*. It didn't start out that way but eventually I thought, 'Man, it would be cool if it were all women doing her songs.' I remember putting together two or three CDs of people doing Dolly songs. It was a list of the song titles, and I remember talking to the staff at the label, at the Nashville office. I said, 'If you had to pick out a title for this album, what would it be?' And it was Molly Nagel Driessen who picked it out. 'Just Because I'm a Woman,' she said. 'That would be a great title, with all these women on it,' and I said, 'Yeah, it would.'

The big surprise on the *Just Because I'm a Woman* album, Buckingham said, was that Alison Krauss chose to do "9 to 5." "I love what they did with it," he says. "I knew Shania (Twain) was a Dolly freak, and I knew she loved 'Coat of Many Colors.' The other one that really surprised me was when Norah Jones said, 'I want to do 'The Grass Is Blue.' And of course, she kills it. Mindy Smith was the only unknown artist on there. I was producing Mindy and I put her on the album for two reasons—one, because I thought she was great, and two—I thought it would help her career, which it did. It was just really fun. It was a headache, like it always is when you've got multiple artists and multiple record labels and multiple managers, but we got it together. I went to Ireland and put on Sinead O'Connor, and Dolly even did a video of 'Dagger through the Heart' that was influenced by Sinead O'Connor's 'Nothing Compares to You' video."

Parton recut "Just Because I'm a Woman" for the new album, but decided to do something different than the original country version. "She said, 'Let's do an old soul version, an R&B version,' and that's what we did, with Reggie Young and Barry Beckett from Muscle Shoals and Memphis, and I played on that one with Reggie. She said, 'Well, this is kind of weird to put a song I sing myself on a tribute album,' and I said, 'Well, we'll make it a bonus track. It's not like you're paying tribute to yourself.' Anyway, that thing did great. It sold great."

Parton was touched by the varied group of women who wanted to record her songs, Buckingham said. "And that year we did 'The Grass Is Blue' at the CMA Awards, it *tore* the place down. I played in the band that night, and we started out with the bluegrass version of the song, with Sam Bush, Bryan Sutton, Jerry Douglas, and Rhonda and Darrin Vincent—and it was either Bryon House or Barry Bales on bass. Then the lights came over [to the other side of the stage] and it was me and Reggie Young playing guitars, Shannon Forrest played brushes, Glen Worf was playing upright bass, and Norah Jones was playing piano and singing it in her style, with Dolly singing harmony. It tore the place down. It was a standing ovation before we even got to the end of the song. It was one of the most magical things I've ever experienced. It was like that night at MerleFest, and that night at the IBMA Awards."

Buckingham and Parton are still friends, but they're not doing records together now. "I think the last album she did was that *Backwoods Barbie*," he said. "I would have gone more down the course of *The Grass Is Blue* and *Little Sparrow*—deeper into the mountain, so to speak. I remember Emmylou [Harris] and Linda [Ronstadt] both said they loved Dolly doing this stuff, the acoustic stuff. But Dolly's persona is so *big*, it's hard to limit her.

"There was a girl in New York who did the best article I've ever seen on Dolly," Buckingham continued, "and she said it would be convenient if there was just one Dolly Parton, like it would be convenient if there was just one Elvis—the 1950s Elvis, but there's not. There's all the other Elvises—the movie Elvis and the Las Vegas Elvis, and the fat Elvis. With Dolly you get that, too. It's not just the acoustic, mountain girl. There's the—as she calls herself—'the showgirl,' 'the show dog Dolly.' There's the bigger-than-life 'cartoon Dolly.' And again, these are her words. It's difficult for her to limit herself. One thing she does not do is edit herself, in a good sense of the word. Songs pour out of her. Ideas pour out of her. Gary Paczosa used to say one of the great jobs I did was help edit her, because she pours it out. You have to figure out which of the dozens and dozens and dozens of ideas coming at you are the 10 or 12 that you can catch, like in baseball. She's the pitcher and you're the catcher. Which of the 12 balls coming at you are the ones you're going to catch and keep, and work on? I mean, the ideas come like nobody has ever seen. It's like a fountain of ideas. I don't mean that as an insult," Buckingham clarified. "It's a compliment. I've never seen anybody where the wheels are turning creatively. Ideas—not just song ideas, but ideas about a show, a restaurant name, or a clothing name. It just comes all the time. So she had to do those other albums like *Backwoods Barbie* and *For God and Country*, the one for the military. She had these ideas, and she has to explore them. And that's why she is so successful at what she does."[2]

Fiddle virtuoso Stuart Duncan, who played on the first two Sugar Hill bluegrass albums with Parton, had this to say about her: "She absolutely is the most energetic and enthusiastic and generous person you'd want to work for. None of that stuff that you see on camera is fake with her. That's exactly the way she is all the time."

Duncan said she comes to the studio prepared with arrangements for her songs. "If she doesn't like the way the groove is going, she'll tap it out with her fingernails till you get it," he said. "Matt Glaser said about Vassar Clements what I like to say about Dolly Parton: 'She's like an appliance. You just plug her in.'"[3]

Backwoods Barbie and Beyond

Albems, songs, books, and Broadway shows in this chapter: *Backwoods Barbie*, *Joyful Noise*, "Better Get to Livin'," "Jesus and Gravity," *I Am a Rainbow*, *9 to 5*, "I Am Strong," "Viva Las Vegas," "I Had a Dream about Elvis"

A NEW LABEL, A TOURING BROADWAY MUSICAL, AND A NEW RETAIL VENTURE

In *American Songwriter* magazine Edd Hurt describes the music on Parton's 2008 *Backwoods Barbie* album as "her signature blend of ancient modal melodies and optimistic pop confections."[1] Along with the strong material—9 of 12 cuts are originals—one of the most unusual things about this CD is that Parton released it on her own new "Dolly" label at a time when other record companies were reacting to decreased retail sales by downsizing, consolidating, or simply closing up shop. "The majors are going down the tubes," she stated. "They're 'has-beens' like they thought I was. So why not release my own album? Nothing ventured, nothing gained."[2]

Parton spent around $1 million to launch Dolly Records, and she recouped her start-up costs in three months with the release of *Backwoods Barbie*. She made a music video of the title cut, and she sold *Backwoods Barbie Collectors Edition* CDs and pink rocking chairs at Cracker Barrel Old Country Store restaurants. Parton's worldwide "Backwoods Barbie Tour" in 2008 included performances across the United States and Europe, where she sold out major arenas and grossed in the tens of millions of dollars.

In April 2009 the musical theater version of *9 to 5* opened on Broadway, and a national tour of the show launched in Nashville, Tennessee, in October 2010. During that time Parton also wrote a children's book, received an honorary doctorate from the University of Tennessee, opened a gift shop in downtown Nashville called "Trinkets and Treasures," and continued to write the script for a Broadway production of her own life.

Parton was a guest on the popular *American Idol* television show around the time *Backwoods Barbie* came out. "One thing we found out from *American Idol*," said Danny Nozell, Parton's manager and the general manager of Dolly Records, "is that most people don't know that Dolly Parton wrote 'I Will Always Love You,' most people don't know she has sold 110 million units, that she has 25 number 1 singles, that she has 80 albums out, published 3,000 songs. We're not reinventing Dolly. We're just reintroducing her to a younger generation."[3]

New Albums, Movies, Tours, Philanthropic Projects . . .

According to press reports, Parton is working on two new albums—one for dance clubs and a second recording that leans toward gospel and country music. She spent the early part of 2011 in Atlanta shooting a feature film with Queen Latifah called *Joyful Noise,* a movie about two women who join forces to keep a small-town gospel choir from shutting down. Later in the year Parton planned to tour Australia and Europe, and she's also said in recent interviews that she'd like to get involved with more children's projects as she gets older—perhaps more books, music for kids, or even a weekly television show for children.

At age 65 in 2011 and still going strong, Parton finds that dreams are not in short supply. She keeps pulling ideas out of her hat like rabbits. Like the brightly colored butterflies she's chosen as the symbol of her creative spirit and independence, surprisingly diverse and breathtakingly beautiful new projects will continue to emerge from their cocoons and fly—as long as Dolly Parton has anything to say about it. "I want my own cosmetic line, and I want to still produce myself and a few other artists I believe in," she said in 2008. "I'm still interested in TV things, specials, possibly a few more movies if the right things come along. I'm up for grabs, but I've got plenty to do and I never intend to retire."[4]

In a 2008 interview Parton focused again on how important her identity as a songwriter continues to be to her. "I want to be remembered for songs like 'I Will Always Love You' and 'Jolene' and 'Coat of Many Colors.' I'm still livin', so I just want to be thought of as an active person who loved to write, sing, and perform," she said. "But the songwriting was really what I loved the most."[5]

Parton appeared proudly on the cover of *AARP* magazine in May 2009. In this article Parton mentioned plans for a line of clothing and accessories, and the writer estimated her current net worth at between $200 and $400 million. "I wake up with new dreams every day," Parton said. "And the more you do, when you're a dreamer, the more everything creates other arenas you can go into. It's like a tree with many branches, and branches with many leaves."[6]

The more ideas Parton comes up with, the more she seems to reveal the same person she is inside. "The irony of Dolly Parton is that "despite all the reinventions—the plastic surgery, the late '70s foray into pop music, the entrepreneurial projects—she has never really changed," commented Meg Grant in *AARP* magazine. "She still maintains a look and sound connected to her early Nashville days. And her personality is pure backwoods girl."[7]

Parton's Dollywood Foundation, formed in 1988, offers scholarships to students in east Tennessee and supports the Imagination Library, which in 2009 mailed six million books to children in the United States, Canada, and the United Kingdom every month through their fifth birthdays. "My daddy was more proud of the kids calling me 'the book lady' than them calling me a star," Parton said.[8]

In the beginning Parton simply offered $500 to every Sevier County student who graduated from high school, which had the immediate effect of drastically reducing her alma mater's dropout rate. In 1996 she founded The Imagination Library, which now serves more than 1,000 communities.

DOLLY PARTON: BACKWOODS BARBIE

Produced by Kent Wells and Dolly Parton, *Backwoods Barbie* debuted March 8, 2008, on the *Billboard* Country Chart, rising to number 2. It went to number 17 on the Pop Chart, number 2 on the Indie Chart, and number 16 on the magazine's Internet Sales Chart. The album's 27,000 sales its first week out made for Parton's best retail week since *Honky Tonk Angels* (with Loretta Lynn and Tammy Wynette) sold 40,000 units the week of Christmas 1993. "Better Get to Livin'" went to number 48 and "Jesus and Gravity" went to number 56 on *Billboard*'s Country Chart.

On the *Backwoods Barbie* album cover Parton is sitting, shapely legs crossed, on a pile of hay in the back of a vanilla white pickup truck trimmed in pink. She's wearing a short leopard-print dress belted tightly at the waist and cut low in front, with an ankle-length sheer pink jacket. On the inside design behind the CD, four Dolly Barbie dolls pose, one with a guitar. In photos inside the liner notes booklet Parton is dressed like a rhinestone Daisy Mae—fishing from a flat-bottom boat in a stream in the woods, leaning up against her cabin door next to an improvised clothesline, and mowing the grass out back with an old-fashioned elbow-grease-powered mower.

In "Better Get to Livin'" (Parton, Kent Wells) Parton sings the question that people ask her all the time: "What's your secret" for having such a positive attitude? The answer is of a spiritual, self-help nature. To really live, you have to give back to others. Make love your motto. Take a look at where you're going and if you don't like it, "design, refine, and shine" your dreams until they come true. The narrator highly recommends falling on your knees every day to pray, and later in the song she advises, "Be willin' and forgivin' because all healin' starts with you." As well as any other song she's written, "Better Get to Livin'" defines Parton's philosophy of life. She definitely has a strong faith in God and regularly goes to him for guidance and inspiration, but she's also not afraid to pull herself up by her own high-heeled boot straps and get to work making her dreams come true. She has no time or energy for negativity, and she chooses the path of love and forgiveness over grudge holding and pompous attitudes.

"Made of Stone" (Parton) is told from the perspective of a woman who knows her husband is having an affair—in fact, the entire town knows it. She's emotionally frozen, unable to leave him. What hurts her more at this point than the infidelity is his lack of consideration for her feelings. "Do you think I'm made of stone?" she asks him. Does a single thought cross his mind about how his actions might be hurting her?

"Drives Me Crazy" (Roland Gift, David Steele) comes across with a bluegrass disco vibe. A hit previously for Tom Jones and the Fine Young Cannibals, Parton redefines the composition with her unique version. The narrator is a young woman in love to the point of obsession. She can't sleep. Her friends think she's gone off the deep end. She knows she's a little crazy about this guy, but she's enjoying the mind-altering rush of the relationship. Love can be a roller coaster sometimes, when it's just best to hang on for the ride and scream.

"Backwoods Barbie" (Parton) appears to be autobiographical. Parton sings, "Don't let these false eyelashes lead you to believe that I'm as shallow as I look, 'cause I run true and deep." Everything about her appearance at this point may look artificial and glamorous, but inside she's a real person.

The Craig Wiseman/Betsy Ulmer song "Jesus and Gravity" points out the only two things the narrator needs: gravity to keep her feet on the ground, and the Lord to keep her from getting too prideful. "Every time I get too high up on my horse, I fall," Parton sings. Her belief in Jesus is what lifts her spirit up, and the law of gravity is what keeps her feet on the ground.

"Only Dreamin'" (Parton) starts off with a mellow acoustic guitar and a penny whistle. The narrator is also in a dreamlike state. She's in denial about the relationship she's in—or the one she thinks she's in. She doesn't want to know the truth. Parton says she wrote this song on her 60th birthday, when she was in New York City, working on the *9 to 5* Broadway show. All she had to write on in the car was the musical script—which she didn't really want to write on—so when she got to the theater, she said, "I told the girl there, 'I'm writing a song,' and she asked me if I needed a piano. I said, 'Nope, but you don't have a dulcimer on you, do you?'"[9]

Parton wails and romps through the "The Tracks of My Tears" (William Robinson, Marv Tarplin, Warren Moore), an old Motown favorite that was a hit for Smokey Robinson's band, The Miracles, as well as Aretha Franklin, Linda Ronstadt, and the Jackson 5.

"The Lonesomes" is a Parton original that sounds like a jazz standard. She's downright lonesome tonight and her "tears all puddle up in her eyes."

In "Cologne" (Parton) another heartbroken woman—this time "the other woman"—is hurt because her lover asked her not to wear cologne when she's with him. He's afraid his wife will smell another woman's perfume and know he's been unfaithful. "You can't take our secret home, so you ask me not to wear cologne," the singer sadly whispers. She wonders if things will ever be different, if she'll ever be free to do something as simple as wear the scent she wants to when she's with the man she loves. It's not likely.

"Shinola" (Parton) is another lighthearted song about a serious subject. The singer tells her man, in so many words, that his attitude stinks and she's sick of how "everything's about you. I'm getting' out of Dodge," she announces, because this guy doesn't know "love from Shinola."

"I Will Forever Hate Roses" (Parton) is a three-quarters-time country weeper, told from the perspective of a woman whose husband just left her. Parton has recorded the song previously, but it still works today.

The last cut, "Somebody's Everything" (Parton), states a universally held hope. The narrator is a woman who simply wants to be someone's first choice. She wants it all—"romance, love and passion, and magic that will last." Her friends tell her it's a fantasy, but she's set on it being reality. She refuses to settle for anything less than her dream relationship, even if it takes years to find the man.

DOLLY, THE BOXED SET

A four-CD boxed set of Dolly Parton's music was released October 27, 2009, on the RCA Nashville/Legacy label. Titled simply *Dolly*, the 99-song collection was compiled by Rob Santos, and it's a veritable treasure trove for Parton fans.

Parton's black silhouette, holding a guitar and facing away, is pictured on the cover. She appears to be looking at the sun just coming up over the hills. Extensive liner notes from Holly George-Warren and an introduction from Laura Cantrell are included, along with exquisite photography of Parton and her album covers over the years.

In a 2009 review of *Dolly*, the boxed set, Michael McCall writes, "That Parton's career hasn't previously received the honor of an in-depth collection illustrates how the full scope of her creative strengths sometimes gets downplayed in the klieg-light glare of her status as an iconic superstar." Fans mostly recall her songs about growing up in the mountains; her crossover pop hits; and, of course, the classic duets with Porter Wagoner, McCall said, "but her darker material rarely receives the same celebration, although it should. . . . Through all of her phases, Parton's never stopped—she just changed where she looked for inspiration."[10] As the singer and DJ Laura Cantrell writes in the liner notes, whenever she's asked to recommend Parton albums, she asked, "Which Dolly do you want?" Finally, all of them can be found in one place."

"DR. DOLLY"

Five months before the boxed set was released, Parton was on the campus of the University of Tennessee in Knoxville on May 8, 2009, to receive an honorary doctorate of humane and musical letters. "Just think, I am Dr. Dolly!" she proclaimed to the crowd of 1,000 at graduation ceremonies. She started off with a spirited rendition of "Rocky Top," The Osborne Brothers hit that serves as the university's fight song at sporting events and also one of the state songs of Tennessee.

In her commencement speech Parton encouraged the graduating seniors to "work hard and follow their dreams. . . . I was just an average student. And if I had one regret, it is that I didn't further my education. Either that, or that I didn't really kiss Elvis," she laughed. "I did further my education just like you, except you earned your degree in a few short years and it has taken me 45 years after high school to get mine. But nonetheless I am very, very proud."[11]

CHILDREN'S BOOKS

Along with obtaining a college degree, Parton is also now a children's book author. In the introduction of *I Am a Rainbow*, published in 2009 by G. P. Putnam's Sons/Penguin Young Readers Group, she writes, "I dedicate this book to all children everywhere and to the dedicated parents and teachers who help, guide, and show them how to utilize their true colors."[12]

In a simple and direct narrative Parton compares emotions to colors—everything from feeling tickled pick and green with envy, to seeing red or feeling blue. We all feel these colors and moods at various times. "It's not up to you, the way that you feel," she writes, "but how you act is a different deal."

Parton encourages readers to be a rainbow and celebrate all the colors inside themselves, while filtering their emotions through love and kindness for each other.

SOMETIMES SIDEMEN AND MUSICAL COLLABORATORS: THE GRASCALS

In addition to her side projects, Parton is still very focused on performing live. One of her most recent touring bands—and a group she's also recorded with—is the Nashville-based bluegrass band The Grascals. Voted Entertainer of the Year by the members of the International Bluegrass Music Association for two years (2006–2007), the band issued its first four albums on the Rounder Records label. Their latest release, a collection of duets with well-known friends from the country music genre called *The Grascals and Friends: Country Classics with a Bluegrass Twist*, hit the shelves at Cracker Barrel Old Country Store restaurants in January 2011. The Grascals also spent a good part of 2010 opening up for Hank Williams Jr. on his "Rowdy Friends" tour, in addition to playing bluegrass festivals and concert venues across the country, in Canada, and in Europe.

Parton guests on two songs: "The Pain of Loving You," which she cowrote with Porter Wagoner, and "I Am Strong," which was inspired by the band's 2009 visit to the St. Jude Children's Research Hospital in Memphis, Tennessee. Guitarist/vocalist Jamie Johnson said they walked into a cafeteria at the hospital and saw an entire wall decorated with the children's artwork. Each had an emotion illustrated—something like the colors in Parton's children's book. They said, "I am sick," "I am afraid," "I am lonesome," "I am tired"—many different feelings young cancer patients might experience. But at the center of the pictures was a drawing that declared in big letters, "I am strong!" Jamie was inspired to go home and cowrite the song with his wife, Susanne Mumpower-Johnson, and Janee Fleenor.

During a 2010 interview Johnson recalled how the band first met Parton. "We were recording at the same studio, when we were doing our first tracks for the first Grascals album," he said. "The engineer was doing Dolly's new album, and she was cutting some of her old songs with new arrangements." Parton told the engineer "she wanted to go on the road again with her band, but also with a bluegrass band so she could do an acoustic set. [Our fiddler], Jimmy Mattingly, had been in her band for a long time, and Terry Eldredge sang with her for a short while [with the Blueniques, playing acoustic bass]."

Parton listened to the first three songs the new group had recorded: "Me and John and Paul," written by Harley Allen; the traditional "Saro Jane"; and one more.

"She loved the sound and she gave us a chance," Johnson said. "The next thing we knew, we went from playing The Station Inn [a small bluegrass club in Nashville]—which we still love—to walking into her studio/house on 12th Avenue. She came out to meet us, wearing a Grascals cap and shirt, and she hired us. She told us she was the first Grascals girl. We recorded on her next album, and we asked her to be on our album."

Parton split the lead vocals on "Viva Las Vegas" on The Grascals' second Rounder release, with Terry Eldredge. "Dolly was a big Elvis fan, and she'd actually wanted to record 'Viva Las Vegas' for years. We were just lucky to be the ones that she recorded it with," Johnson said.

For their first recording session, Johnson said Parton "gave us the assignment of learning 12 or 13 songs. She said, 'You can work these up at your discretion. You come up with the music, chart them out, and let's record this album.' Basically, it was a lot of old songs from the 1960s—some she wished she had recorded first. We worked them up, and then we went into the studio in same house on 12th Avenue and she rehearsed with us. We went into the studio and recorded those songs, and then the tour started. Everything happened real fast—from the Station Inn to the 'Hello, I'm Dolly' tour, playing in front of 15,000 people a night. Those were our first crowds as a band, which was amazing. It was a huge honor for the Grascals, and for bluegrass music, period. A lot of folks who never heard our type of music before got to hear it when we were out on the road with Dolly Parton.

"We were with her—as her band—for one year, in 2004," Johnson continued. "In 2005 she let us go, and there was no disrespect intended. We didn't expect her to hire us for the rest of our lives. She helped us launch our career. She said, 'I can see it now. You guys are really good at what you do, and if you don't go out now and live your dream and become the Grascals, you'll always just be known as 'Dolly's band.'"

In so many words, she gave the band an "I will always love you" pink slip and said, "Now, go out and do it."

"She gave us the launching pad and fuel for the rockets. . . . And the next tour in the fall, we opened up for her, but we were not her band," Johnson said. For fans who were at one of those "Hello, I'm Dolly" shows in 2004, Jamie Johnson was the guitar player who played the part of "the king" in the "I Had a Dream About Elvis" segment, a song Parton wrote.

"In the 1970s Elvis almost recorded 'I Will Always Love You,'" Johnson said. "The day he recorded it, Colonel Tom Parker called her up and said, 'We're going to record this on one condition—if we get half of the publishing.' Dolly [ever the savvy businesswoman] said no. It crushed her heart because she was such an Elvis fan."

In the stage production Johnson was singing along to a track of Roddie McDowell, who sounds quite a bit like Elvis on this particular song. "Once we were rehearsing and Dolly looked at me and said, 'Do you like to fly?'" Johnson recalls. "I wasn't sure what she meant by that—I was afraid she was going to fly me across the stage on a trapeze wire or something," he laughed. "Well, she meant fly in a plane. She flew me and my wife, Susanne, out to one of her homes in Malibu Beach and we stayed for three days. She had us picked up at the airport, and they took us around to all her favorite restaurants. Then the designer who does all her outfits, and also Kevin Costner's, measured me for the Elvis suit. It was a 1970s model of one of Elvis's stage outfits. I was measured from head to toe, in every place imaginable, even my feet. I had to wear lifts. I'm five feet seven and a half inches, and in those boots I was right at six foot. The whole thing probably cost 15 to 20 thousand dollars.

"For two weeks straight I went to her office on 12th Avenue for dance rehearsals," Johnson said. "I sat there and studied from 8 a.m. to 10 or 11 o'clock. She'd come out around one, and we'd do our dance things from noon to 3 p.m. We became very close friends. She's so down to earth. She grew up a poor girl, and she's no different now than she ever was. She is a very smart person, and so funny. That was a huge honor, and a huge learning experience. She's just one of those good people who have worked hard for what they get."

Johnson's impression of Parton after working with her in rehearsals, on-stage, and in the studio, is that "she cares," he said. "She's the boss, but she also takes your input and processes it. She can play any instrument, so she'll give you the idea of what to play—and then she'll entertain and do her thing. She gives you the road map, and then you take off from there. And you'd better not be late for anything, or you're in trouble," Johnson emphasized. "She's usually there ten minutes early. She'll cut up with you and have fun, but the reason she's there is because she's a great entertainer and artist. She'd bring out food that she cooked for us—biscuits and gravy, that kind of thing. Then we'd work for two or three hours. She would eat a couple of Lays potato chips to coat her voice. She would walk into her kitchen and she'd be cooking chicken and dumplings for lunch, or chicken and noodles. That was the amazing thing. She cooked the food almost every day. If there was something cooked, it was her doing it. She'd cook it slow, which is the best way to do it. At lunch we'd take a break and she'd sit right with us. It was so fun, hearing her laughing and cutting up. She wanted to learn our stories and get to know us.

"In the studio," Johnson said, "we'd all get in there and set up, and she'd bring her bag of chips and drink and go in and sing. She'd usually just need one or two takes. She's still definitely got it. She's good at production, too. She would take our input, but at that point she wasn't the boss anymore. At a recording session she would work with us and encourage us to share our ideas. She'd say, 'If anybody's got anything to say, say it now. Don't you wait until after it's recorded and it's too late!'"

Johnson said he tried the potato chip technique the next time he was in the studio. "But I ended up eating the whole bag," he joked. "I do drink five or six bottled waters when I record one song. I went to the Vanderbilt voice clinic and that's what they told me to do—drink a lot of water. I'll also drink a lot of water if I'm starting to get a cold. Water is the key. I've heard Amy Grant also does the potato chip thing."

Johnson's impressions of Parton as a producer and an entertainer are that "she's second to none. As for the singing—she has got a beautiful voice. She cares, and she's got the gift of an incredible talent," he said. "She uses it well. She's one of those singers that I like to call a songwriter's dream because she tells a story with emotion. When she's hitting the fancy notes, she's singing it from the bottom of her heart. She can sing an up-tempo, happy song, and it's happy. When she sings a slow, sad song like 'I Will Always Love You,' it makes you want to cry. And 'Coat of Many Colors'—I love that! We had rehearsal every day on tour at the same time, and you'd better not be late. She would come out and rewrite the whole set. If she didn't feel the energy from the crowd, she'd change the order or how she did something. It definitely keeps you on your toes. She would do something different every night. We'd rehearse the changes, and she'd ask us for our input. She was there all day, doing television interviews or radio, or waiting on the bus in between appointments. We'd do a 30- to 50-minute sound check, and she'd stay until we got it right. She would walk the stage in her high heels, because she didn't want to trip [later that evening during the show].

"She's just an entertainer," Johnson said. "She would sing 'Coat of Many Colors' in rehearsal as heartfelt as she would on the show, or the first time she ever wrote the song and sang it. Before we walked out on the stage every night she'd say, 'Guys, this is the funnest job on earth. So leave everything you've got out there except your clothes. Leave your heart and soul. You give them your heart and soul, and they'll give it back. Give it to them and mean it, and they'll feel you're accessible to them. They'll know if you're pure or not. If you want them to love you, you love them first.'"

Johnson is a fine songwriter himself. He says he didn't see Parton writing when the Grascals were working for her. "I wish I could have learned more about how she writes," he said. "You know, my Boston terrier passed away on June 15, on my birthday. Dolly used to have a Boston terrier named Peanut Butter. She said she never got another one because she couldn't handle the heartbreak. I called her when Cole Train [his son] was first born. We took him down there to meet her and took a picture. She sends him books every month from her Imagination Library. . . . I don't consider myself as a songwriter in her league, at all," Johnson smiled. "I hope someday I can write a song a tenth as good as 'I Will Always Love You' or 'Coat of Many Colors' or 'Apple Jack.' She is so clever, and very witty with her words. She sits there by herself and does it. I can't. I always try to write with someone better than I am," he confided. "She's like a John Prine, a Kris Kristofferson, James Taylor, Merle Haggard, Willie Nelson, or a Bobby Osborne. She's definitely got a God-given talent.

"When I was at her house, I rolled on every chair and bed in the place, trying to get some of Dolly's talent to rub off on me," Johnson laughed. "She had a guitar setting out, so I tried to write a song on it. But doggone it, nothing came out. I tried real hard!

"There are very few who have that kind of talent," Johnson added, "and who are also smart enough to figure out how to use it. There are very few who can do it all. But even with all that combined together, most artists haven't been able to do the one thing that she does so well, and that's the business part of it. She's very, very smart. She's in this for the love of the music and the people, but she's also in this to make a living for herself and for her family. You've got to have a business mind to find a way to make money for yourself, whether it's in the oil fields, the ballpark, the automobile business, or whatever. She did it in the entertainment business. It doesn't mean you're selling out. She branded her name. When you work with a sponsor or collaborate with another business, it means you're trying to help someone else out with what they're doing, and they can also help you. We shouldn't be suffering and starving in this business. We've got a sponsorship from Mobil Delvac now, and that's because we watched Dolly do what she does—find something you believe in, and give somebody the chance to help you. You can help each other."

Parton's also smart about music publishing, Johnson said. "She told us, 'A young girl named Whitney Houston came along and wiped all my tears away!'"

Grascals' acoustic bass player, singer, and a songwriter himself, Terry Smith said Parton "has got as much charisma as anybody I've ever seen—her and Johnny Cash," he added. "When she walked into a room, it was like she'd been shot out of a cannon. It was like a comet. When she bursts into a room, every eye is on her. Even if your back's to her, you could just feel it. It's amazing, because she's [just] an east Tennessee country girl. She's sweet, and everything you see is what she is."[13]

Smith, or "Smitty," as his bandmates call him, remembered Parton's home cooking fondly. "The most amazing thing she ever brought to me was the chicken and dumplings," he said. "It was a different sauce than most of the chicken and dumplings you eat. It was like a brown gravy—that was the base—a country-style brown gravy with a meaty taste. That was so good. It was delicious. She would bring that to the studio, and she brought it to rehearsal one time. I would love to get the recipe."

Smith's mother, Hazel Smith, is the renowned cooking diva on CMT's television show *Southern Fried Flicks,* where she interviews a country or bluegrass artist and then cooks something for them—while tuning in and out of a movie that's showing on the cable network. Parton's brown gravy chicken and dumplings would likely be a hit on his mom's show.

"I don't think she has been on the show," Smith said. "She should. That would be a great meeting of two country girls, there," he smiled.

Onstage and in the studio, Smith said Parton "was a professional. She expected you to come to the plate and do your job, but there was no real stress. She believed firmly in having fun. She told us that before we went onstage. She said, 'Just leave it all out there and have fun. Just go out there and have a ball.' It was hard not to watch her," he admitted. "I found myself sometimes being a spectator onstage. She's mesmerizing, and I'd find myself watching her. She doesn't like that. She wants you to perform and do your part. She wants you to look at the crowd and look at her, but not to stop moving and just stare. . . . It's easy to watch her, and when you do that you're prone to make mistakes. You've got to watch what you're doing. She's something else."

Smith has been playing bass professionally since he was a teenager, performing with Jimmy Martin, Wilma Lee Cooper, in groups with his brother Billy Boone Smith, The Osborne Brothers (for 13 years), and Mike Snider before he cofounded The Grascals—so he's no stranger to the stage. But he says he learned something from Parton about entertaining.

"We learned to love our audience. They can feel that, and see through phoniness. People can," Smith stated simply. "Dolly is real. She genuinely loves her fans and loves her audiences. The Grascals try to include the audience in on the fun, and I think the audience can feel we are sincere in that. That's the recipe for our success."

Some bands, particularly those who are extremely gifted instrumentalists, end up playing for each other's entertainment in the band, or to impress other musicians watching. That leaves the fan out of the circle. "That's exactly right," Smith said. "It is possible to do that, but include the audience in it. Bill Monroe was good at that," he said. "He was all about competition. He would compete with you onstage. You were not going to outdo him. He was very competitive, but he kind of brought the audience in with it. But that's the key. You've got to bring the audience in and include them. You can't exclude them. Why would you want to go see that?"

In the recording studio, Smith said Parton "was very professional. She had charts worked out. She would leave room for creativity. You could try some things—a lick or something. It was mapped out, but it wasn't so mapped out that it was rigid. But really, I didn't feel a bit of stress. It was just like going to Dolly's living room, and laughing and singing and eating chicken and dumplings."

Terry said the thing that impresses him most about Parton's writing is that "she makes it deceptively simple. It sounds simple. To me, the best stuff is like that. If you can take a profound thought and express it in a simple manner, when you hear it, you say, 'Oh, I could do that.' And then when you try, you can't," he smiled. "In fact, that's the most difficult thing to do. It's easy to write a bunch of profound thoughts. But to express it in a simple manner, the way she does, in a way that people can relate to, it's a lot harder than you'd think. And she does it. It's just like water flowing down a creek. She's a master songwriter; she really is."

As a singer and an entertainer, Smith believes Parton is "from a line of artists that, to me, are not being replaced. They are totally unique. There's nobody like Dolly. Nobody like Johnny Cash, Waylon Jennings, Hank Sr., Hank Jr., George Jones, Loretta Lynn, Patsy Cline, Lefty Frizzell, Carl Smith. They're just totally unique. To me, there's just not that many out there now who are unique. Those artists are not being replaced. Not only great artists, but total characters—absolutely hilarious, and in a lot of cases hard headed people who are just not going to take no for an answer. It's like Johnny Cash said, 'If it don't fit, force it,'" he laughed.

The music industry has changed since Fred Foster's days of refusing to sign anyone who didn't have a totally unique singing voice and talent. Now it's more common to recognize someone who is doing well, and then try to find a new artist who sounds like that person. It's a risk to take a chance on someone who is a little different, or who management might not be able to control creatively.

"Yes, all of those things," Smith agreed. "I mean, why take a chance on anyone different? I understand. It's a safe way to make money. I'm not putting anybody down," he clarified. "It's the way the business kind of became. But Dolly is one of those totally unique people who has done things her own way. She does exactly what she wants to do, too. She's willing to take a chance. She's willing to fail. She's just one of those people—one of those artists."[14]

THE HALL OF FAME

In May 2010 the Country Music Hall of Fame and Museum's core exhibit, "Sing Me Back Home: A Journey through Country Music," was updated and brought forward in time, with a conclusion that takes a glimpse into the future. Oversized portraits on the second floor of the museum depict country music's duet kings and queens: Loretta Lynn and Conway Twitty, Tammy Wynette and George Jones, and Dolly Parton and Porter Wagoner. New video clips and artifacts are also on display—including television clips from the old *Porter Wagoner Television Show* when Dolly had just joined the cast, and in a glass case Parton's handwritten lyrics of her song "Jolene" appear.

A pick satin dress Parton wore early in her career is also on display. A bell-sleeved confection embellished with rhinestones and lace, the gown was made by Parton's longtime designer, Lucy Adams, and worn by Dolly in 1970 to the "Dolly Parton Day" festivities in Sevierville, Tennessee—pictured in this book in photos by Les Leverett.

Parton's sparkly clothes, her impossibly high-heeled shoes, her massive hairstyles, her long polished nails, and her perfectly applied makeup still decorate the heart of a simple country girl from Locust Ridge, Tennessee. Her "getup," as she calls it, is a part of the dream she has worked hard to create and step into, in order to share her music with the world. She looks exactly how she wants to look to present her most precious gift to the public—her songs—and she continues to do pretty much exactly what she wants to do. Her life is literally a daily "dream come true," powered by the faith, hard work, and vision to make all the imagined dreams reality.

In liner notes for *Dolly*, the RCA boxed set released in 2009, Marty Stuart comments on Parton's "evolution from mountain girl to country star to superstar to national treasure to global icon . . . with plenty of altitude left for her future visions and plans. At the core of Dolly's empire you'll find her heart and therein lies the treasure," Stuart said. "Deep within that heart, in a language known only to her and God, secrets were passed. Those secrets became her songs. At the end of the day, it's about the songs. Those songs are her story, and those stories will forever stand as psalms for the ages: heavenly empowered offerings to all of us from the mountain girl who dared to dream."[15]

Awards and Honors

GRAMMY AWARDS

1978—Best Country Vocal Performance by a Female (album), "Here You Come Again"

1981—Best Country Vocal Performance by a Female (single), "9 to 5"

1981—Best Country Song, "9 to 5"

1987—Best Country Performance by a Duo or Group (album), *Trio* (with Linda Ronstadt and Emmylou Harris)

1999—Best Country Collaboration with Vocals (single), "After the Gold Rush" (with Linda Ronstadt and Emmylou Harris)

2000—Best Bluegrass Album, *The Grass Is Blue*

2001—Best Country Female Vocal Performance, "Shine"

2001—Vocal Performance, "Dagger through the Heart"

2003—Best Country Album, *Livin', Lovin', Losin': Songs of the Louvin Brothers* (Parton was one of the artists featured on the album)

2011—Grammy Lifetime Achievement Award

COUNTRY MUSIC ASSOCIATION AWARDS AND NOMINATIONS

1968—Vocal Group of the Year, with Porter Wagoner

1970—Vocal Duo of the Year, with Porter Wagoner (first time given)

1971—Vocal Duo of the Year, with Porter Wagoner

1975—Female Vocalist of the Year

1976—Female Vocalist of the Year

1978—Entertainer of the Year

1988—Vocal Event of the Year (with Emmylou Harris and Linda Ronstadt)

1993—Country Music Honors (first time award given)

1996—Vocal Event of the Year ("I Will Always Love You" with Vince Gill)

2004—International Artist Achievement Award (presented by the BBC)

2006—Musical Event of the Year ("When I Get Where I'm Going" with Brad Paisley)

ACADEMY OF COUNTRY MUSIC AWARDS AND NOMINATIONS

1977—Entertainer of the Year

1980—Female Vocalist of the Year

1982—*The Best Little Whorehouse in Texas* (Tex Ritter Award—to soundtrack, not artists)

1983—Single of the Year ("Islands in the Stream" with Kenny Rogers)

1983—Vocal Duet of the Year (with Kenny Rogers)

1987—Album of the Year (*Trio*, with Linda Ronstadt and Emmylou Harris)

2006—Vocal Event of the Year ("When I Get Where I'm Going," with Brad Paisley)

2006—Video of the Year ("When I Get Where I'm Going," with Brad Paisley)

2007—Pioneer Award

2009—Jim Reeves International Award

INTERNATIONAL BLUEGRASS MUSIC ASSOCIATION AWARDS

2000—Album of The Year, *The Grass Is Blue*

2002—Recorded Event of the Year, *Clinch Mountain Sweethearts* (award presented to album performers Ralph Stanley, Dolly, Iris DeMent, Pam Tillis, Patty Mitchell, Gillian Welch, Maria Muldaur, Sara Evans, Joan Baez, Kristi Stanley, Gail Davies, Chely Wright, Melba Montgomery, Jeannie Seely, Lucinda Williams, and Valerie Smith)

2004—Recorded Event of the Year, *Livin', Lovin', Losin': Songs of the Louvin Brothers* (award presented to album performers Dolly, Joe Nichols, Rhonda Vincent, Emmylou Harris, Rodney Crowell, James Taylor, Alison Krauss, Vince Gill, Terri Clark, Merle Haggard, Carl Jackson, Ronnie Dunn, Rebecca Lynn Howard, Glen Campbell, Leslie Satcher, Kathy Louvin, Pamela Brown Hayes, Linda Ronstadt, Patty Loveless, Jon Randall, Harley Allen, Dierks Bentley, Larry Cordle, Jerry Salley, Sonya Isaacs, Marty Stuart, Del McCoury, Pam Tillis, Johnny Cash, and the Jordanaires)

PEOPLE'S CHOICE AWARDS

1981—Favorite Movie Song, "9 to 5"

1988—Favorite Female Performer in a New Television Series

Favorite All Around Female Performer

1990—Favorite Dramatic Motion Picture, *Steel Magnolias* (award given to the film)

GOLD AND PLATINUM ALBUM AWARDS

USA
Double Platinum Album (more than 2,000,000 copies sold)
Once Upon a Christmas with Kenny Rogers, 1984 (simultaneously certified gold/platinum 12/3/84, double 10/25/89)

Platinum Albums (more than 1,000,000 copies sold)
Slow Dancing with the Moon, 1993 (certified gold 4/19/93, platinum 10/5/93)

Eagle When She Flies, 1991 (certified gold 7/2/91, platinum 8/4/92)

Trio with Linda Ronstadt and Emmylou Harris, 1987 (simultaneously certified gold/platinum 7/14/87)

Greatest Hits, 1982 (certified gold 10/31/83, platinum 10/7/86)

Here You Come Again, 1977 (certified gold 12/27/77, platinum 4/28/78)

Gold Albums (more than 500,000 copies sold)
Trio II with Linda Ronstadt and Emmylou Harris, 1999 (certified gold 11/15/01)

Home For Christmas, 1990 (certified gold 12/27/94)

Honky Tonk Angels, with Loretta Lynn and Tammy Wynette, 1993

White Limozeen, 1989 (certified gold 12/6/91)

9 to 5 and Odd Jobs, 1980 (certified gold 3/6/81)

Great Balls of Fire, 1979 (certified gold 11/13/79)

Heartbreaker, 1978 (certified gold 8/16/78)

Best of Dolly Parton, 1975 (certified gold 6/12/78)

Platinum Single (more than 2,000,000 copies sold)
"Islands in the Stream" with Kenny Rogers (certified gold 10/18/83, platinum 12/7/83)

Gold Singles (more than 1,000,000 copies sold
"9 to 5" (certified gold 2/19/81)

"Here You Come Again" (certified gold 2/1/78)

Digital Gold Single (more than 500,000 copies legally purchased and downloaded)

"When I Get Where I'm Going" with Brad Paisley (certified gold 6/15/06)

Canada
Gold Albums (50,000)

Eagle When She Flies, 11/21/97

Honky Tonk Angels, 04/01/94

Slow Dancing with the Moon, 9/24/93

Greatest Hits, 1/01/85

9 to 5 and Odd Jobs, 04/01/81

Heartbreaker, 12/01/78

Here You Come Again, 03/01/78

Gold DVD (5,000)

Live and Well (11/04/04)

Quintuple Platinum Single (50,000)

"9 to 5," 4/01/81

Quintuple Platinum Album (500,000)

Once Upon a Christmas, 4/13/88 (gold and platinum 12/01/84, double and triple platinum 11/14/85, quadruple platinum 1/21/87)

Diamond Single (10 times platinum) (100,000)

"Islands in the Stream," 01/01/84 (quintuple platinum 11/01/83)

Great Britain (silver album 60,000, gold album 100,000, platinum album 300,000; silver single 200,000)

Both Sides of Dolly Parton, silver and gold, 11/10/78

Single—"Islands in the Stream," silver, 01/01/84

Little Sparrow, silver, April 2001

Very Best of Dolly Parton Vol. 1, silver and gold, April 2007; platinum, June 2009

New Zealand

Both Sides of Dolly Parton, 1987, gold

Once Upon a Christmas, 1987, gold

Trio, 1987, Gold

Single—"Islands in the Stream," 1987, gold

Australia

18 Greatest Hits, 1980, gold

The Netherlands

The Love Album, 1984, gold

South Africa

Single—"Just Because I'm a Woman," 1971, gold

*Partial list of international sales awards

MUSIC CITY NEWS AWARDS

1968—Most Promising Female Artist

1968—Duet of the Year (with Porter Wagoner)

1969—Duet of the Year (with Porter Wagoner)

1970—Duet of the Year (with Porter Wagoner)

1984—Duet of the Year (with Kenny Rogers)

1988—Vocal Collaboration of the Year (with Linda Ronstadt and Emmylou Harris)

TNN/MUSIC CITY NEWS AWARDS

1992—Vocal Collaboration of the Year (with Ricky Van Shelton), "Rockin' Years"

1992—Video of the Year (with Ricky Van Shelton), "Rockin' Years"

1994—Living Legend Award

1994—Minnie Pearl Humanitarian Award

CMT VIDEO AWARDS

1994—Video Event of the Year, "Romeo" with Billy Ray Cyrus, Tanya Tucker, Mary Chapin Carpenter, and Kathy Mattea

2000—Video Event of the Year, "After the Gold Rush" with Emmylou Harris and Linda Ronstadt

CMT MUSIC AWARDS

2006—Most Inspiring Video of the Year, "When I Get Where I'm Going" with Brad Paisley

AMERICAN MUSIC ASSOCIATION AWARDS

1977—Favorite Country Album, *New Harvest . . . First Gathering*

1983—Favorite Country Single (with Kenny Rogers), "Islands in the Stream"

1984—Favorite Country Single (with Kenny Rogers), "Islands in the Stream"

Cash Box Awards

1968—Most Promising Up and Coming Female Artist

1975—Top Female Vocalist, singles

1977—Female Entertainer of the Year, album

1977—Female Vocalist of the Year, album

1978—Female Entertainer of the Year, album

1978—Female Vocalist of the Year, album

1978—Female Vocalist, Highest Debut Single of the Year, "Heartbreaker"

1978—Crossover Artist of the Year

1979—Composer/Performer of the Year

Record World Awards

1975—Top Female Vocalist, singles

1977—Top Female Vocalist, album

Billboard Honors

1978—Country Artist of the Year

1978—Country Singles Artist of the Year

1978—Bill Williams Memorial Artist of the Year

1979—Ranked No. 3 in Top 20 Country Artists of the 1970s

1981—Distinguished Achievement Award

American Guild of Variety Artists Awards

1978—Country Star of the Year

1979—Country Star of the Year

1980—Entertainer of the Year

1980—Country Star of the Year

Nashville Songwriter's Association International, Songwriter Achievement Awards

1968—"Put It Off until Tomorrow" (as recorded by Bill Phillips)

1971—"Daddy Was an Old Time Preacher Man"

1972—"Coat of Many Colors"

1974—"Jolene"

1975—"Jolene"

1975—"Kentucky Gambler" (as recorded by Merle Haggard)

1975—"Love Is Like a Butterfly"

1976—"The Seeker"

1979—"Two Doors Down"

1982—"9 to 5"

1986—Inducted into the Hall of Fame

1991—"Eagle When She Flies"

1992—"I Will Always Love You" (adult contemporary category, as recorded by Whitney Houston)

1995—"I Will Always Love You" (duet with Vince Gill)

Broadcast Music Inc. (BMI) Awards

Million-Air Award (song has been broadcasted 1 million times), "Two Doors Down"

Million-Air Award, "Jolene"

Million-Air Award, "Yellow Roses"

Three-Million-Air Award (broadcasted 3 million times), "9 to 5"

Six-Million-Air Award (broadcasted 6 million times), "I Will Always Love You" (One of only six songs in BMI's catalogue to reach the 6 million or more mark, including works by artists such as John Lennon and Paul McCartney)

1966—Country, "Put It Off until Tomorrow" (as recorded by Bill Phillips)

1971—Country, "Daddy Was an Old Time Preacher Man"

1971—Country, "Joshua"

1972—Country, "The Last One to Touch Me"

1974—Country, "Jolene"

1974—Pop, "Jolene"

1974—Country, "Traveling Man"

1975—Country, "Kentucky Gambler" (as recorded by Merle Haggard)

Country, "I Will Always Love You"

Country, "Love Is Like a Butterfly"

Country, "Please Don't Stop Loving Me"

1976—Country, "Say Forever You'll Be Mine"

1976—Country, "The Bargain Store"

1976—Country, "The Seeker"

1977—Country, "All I Can Do"

1978—Country, "Two Doors Down"

Pop, "Two Doors Down"

Country, "Light of a Clear Blue Morning"

1979—Country, "Baby I'm Burning"

1979—Pop, "Baby I'm Burning"

1979—Country, "It's All Wrong, But It's All Right"

1979—Country, "Two Doors Down"

1981—Robert J. Burton Award for Country Song of the Year (the most played country song of the year), "9 to 5"

1981—Pop Song of the Year, "9 to 5"

1981—Country, "9 to 5"

1981—Pop, "9 to 5"

1982—Country, "9 to 5"

1982—Pop, "Heartbreak Express"

1982—Pop, "I Will Always Love You"

1983—Country, "I Will Always Love You"

1983—Country, "Heartbreak Express"

1983—Pop, "Everything's Beautiful (in Its Own Way)"

1983—Country, "Everything's Beautiful (in Its Own Way)"

1985—Country, "Tennessee Homesick Blues"

1993—Pop, "I Will Always Love You" (as recorded by Whitney Houston)

1993—Pop Song of the Year, "I Will Always Love You" (as recorded by Whitney Houston)

1994—Pop, "I Will Always Love You" (as recorded by Whitney Houston)

1995—Pop, "I Will Always Love You" (as recorded by Whitney Houston)

2003—BMI Icon Award

Note: Dolly has also recorded a couple of songs that she didn't write but brought their writers Million-Air Awards: Three Million-Air Award, "Islands in the Stream," written by Barry, Maurice, and Robin Gibb

Three-Million-Air Award, "Here You Come Again," written by the Barry Mann and Cynthia Weil

ADDITIONAL AWARDS AND HONORS

Grand Old Opry, inducted February 4, 1969

Hollywood Walk of Fame, inducted 1984

Ms. Magazine, Woman of the Year 1986

Guinness Book of World Records, named most successful entertainer (for grossing $400,000 for one performance)

Canadian Country Music Association Awards, Top Selling Album of the Year, *Once Upon a Christmas* (with Kenny Rogers), 1985

Nashville's Starwalk, inducted 1988

East Tennessee Hall of Fame for the Performing Arts, inducted 1988

Small Town of America Hall of Fame, inducted 1988

Sevierville Chamber of Commerce, Citizen of the Year, 1989

Carson-Newman College, Honorary Doctorate of Letters Degree, 1990

Soul Train Awards, Best R&B Song (given to songwriter), "I Will Always Love You," 1994

Inducted into the Country Music Hall of Fame, 1999

British Country Music Association, Top International Independent Label Artist (Sugar Hill/Blue Eye, *The Grass Is Blue*), 2000; Top Female Vocalist—1976, 1977, 1978, 1979, and 1980

Association for Independent Music Awards, Best Bluegrass Album, *The Grass Is Blue*, 2000

National Academy of Popular Music/Songwriters Hall of Fame, inducted 2001

Good Housekeeping Seal of Approval, 2001

European CMA, Female Vocalist of the Year, 2001

American Association of School Administrators, Galaxy Award, 2002

Association for Independent Music Awards, Best Bluegrass Album, *Little Sparrow*, 2002

National State Teachers of the Year, Chasing Rainbows Award, 2002

Junior Achievement of East Tennessee Business Hall of Fame, inducted 2003

Governor's Awards for the Arts, Tennessee Arts Commission, 2003, Lifetime Achievement Award

TV Land Awards: Most Memorable Female Guest Star in a Comedy as Herself, for appearance on 1989 episode of *Designing Women*

Parents as Teachers National Center, Child and Family Advocacy Award, 2003

U.S. Fish and Wildlife Service, Partnership Award, 2003

International Country Gospel Music Association, Gold Cross Awards, Single of the Year, "Hello God," 2003

Country Weekly Fan Favorite Awards, Career Achievement Award, 2003

U.S. Library of Congress Living Legend Award, 2004

Reading Works Award, NashvilleREAD, 2004

Christian Fan Awards, Duo of the Year with Dottie Rambo and Song of the Year with Dottie Rambo for "Stand by the River," 2004

American Legion, James V. Day Good Guy Award, 2004

Country Radio Broadcasters' Artist Career Achievement Award, 2005

National Medal of Arts, 2005 (selected by the president of the United States, the highest honor bestowed by the U.S. government for excellence in the arts)

Phoenix Film Critics Society Awards, 2005, Best Song: "Travelin' Thru"

Sierra Awards, Las Vegas Film Critics Society, 2005, Best Song: "Travelin' Thru"

Lindy Boggs Award for "patriotism, courage, integrity, and leadership through public service," Stennis Center for Public Service, 2006

European CMA, Vocal Collaboration of the Year, with Roy Rivers, "Thank God I'm a Country Boy"

Kennedy Center Honors, 2006

Tennessean of the Year, 2006

Grammy Hall of Fame, song, "I Will Always Love You" (1974 recording), 2007

Songwriter's Hall of Fame Johnny Mercer Award, 2007

Woodrow Wilson Award for Public Service, Woodrow Wilson International Center for Scholars of the Smithsonian Institution, 2007

Gospel Music Association Hall of Fame, inducted 2009

Los Angeles Drama Critics Circle Awards, Best Musical Score, *9 to 5: The Musical*, 2009

Broadway.com's Audience Awards: Favorite New Broadway Song, "Get Out and Stay Out" from *9 to 5: The Musical*, 2009

Broadway World.com's Theatre Fans' Choice Awards: Best Original Score, *9 to 5: The Musical*, 2009

Founders Medal for Education, Daughters of the American Revolution, 2009

Dr. Perry F. Harris Award from the Grand Master Fiddler Championship, 2009

Country Gospel Music Hall of Fame, inducted 2010

Sources: Duane Gordon. www.dollymania.net; www.dollyon-line.com

Discography

Dolly Parton and Friends. *Dolly Parton and Friends at Goldband*. Goldband LP 7770. 1959. Producer for "Puppy Love," "Girl Left Alone": Eddie Shuler. Musicians: Little Billy Earl (Billy Earl Owens), guitar; other personnel unknown. Producer for "It's Sure Gonna Hurt": Jerry Kennedy. Musicians: Harold Bradley, Kelso Herston, Jerry Kennedy, guitar; Buddy Killen, bass; Buddy Harman, drums; Hargus "Pig" Robbins, piano; Ray Stevens, vibes.

Dolly Parton, Faye Tucker. *Hits Made Famous by Country Queens*. Somerset. 1963.

Dolly Parton. *Hello, I'm Dolly*. Monument Records MLP8085. 1967. Producer: Fred Foster. Recording engineer: Mart Thomasson. Technical engineer: Tommy Strong. Musicians: Buddy Harman, drums; Lloyd Green, steel guitar. Producer for "Put It Off until Tomorrow": Owen Bradley. Musicians: Bill Phillips and Dolly Parton, vocals; Harold Bradley, O'Dell Martin, Paul Yandell, guitars; Joe Zinkan, bass; Leo Taylor, drums. Floyd Cramer, piano; Stu Basore, steel guitar (from Decca single originally released in 1965)

Porter Wagoner and Dolly Parton. *Just between You and Me*. RCA Victor LPM-3926. 1968. Producer: Bob Ferguson. Recording engineer: Jim Malloy. Recorded in RCA Victor's "Nashville Sound" Studio, Nashville, Tennessee. Liner notes: Bill Turner, director of *The Porter Wagoner TV Show*.

Dolly Parton. *Just Because I'm a Woman*. RCA. 1968.

Porter Wagoner and Dolly Parton. *Just the Two of Us*. RCA Victor LSP-4039. 1968. Musicians: Fred Carter Jr., George McCormick, Wayne Moss, guitar; Jerry Carrigan, drums; Pete Drake, steel guitar; Hargus "Pig" Robbins, piano; Buck Trent, banjo; Roy Huskey Jr., bass; Mack Magaha, fiddle; Glenn Baxter, Anita Carter, Delores Edgin, vocals.

Dolly Parton. *In the Good Old Days*. RCA. 1968.

Porter Wagoner and Dolly Parton. *Always, Always*. RCA. 1969.

Dolly Parton. *My Blue Ridge Mountain Boy.* RCA Victor LSP-4188. 1969. Producer: Bob Ferguson. Recording engineer: Al Pachucki. Technicians: Roy Shockley, Milt Henderson. Musicians: George McCormick, Wayne Moss, Jerry Reed, Chip Young, guitars; Bobby Dyson, Roy Huskey Jr., bass; Jerry Carrigan, James Isbell, drums; Bob Wilson, Hargus "Pig" Robbins, Larry Butler, piano; Hargus "Pig" Robbins, organ; Pete Drake, Lloyd Green, steel guitar; Buck Trent, banjo; Mack Magaha, fiddle; Joseph Babcock, Delores Edgin, June Page, vocals. "Daddy" recorded September 9, 1968, at RCA Studios in Nashville. "Gypsy, Joe, and Me" recorded May 21, 1969. Liner notes: Bill Owens.

Dolly Parton. *The Fairest of Them All.* RCA. 1970. Recorded October 31, 1969, at RCA Studios, Nashville, Tennessee. Producer: Bob Ferguson. Musicians: Fred Carter Jr., George McCormick, Dale Sellers, guitar; Bobby Dyson, bass; James Isbell, drums; Hargus "Pig" Robbins, piano; Pete Drake, steel guitar; Buck Trent, banjo; Johnny Gimble and Mack Magaha, fiddle; Delores Edgin, June Page, Hurshel Wiginton, vocals. "Down from Dover," recorded September 4, 1968, at RCA Studios, Nashville, Tennessee. Bob Ferguson: producer. Musicians: Fred Carter Jr. and George McCormick, guitar; Bobby Dyson, bass; James Isbell, drums; David Briggs, harpsichord; Pete Drake, steel guitar; Buck Trent, banjo; Mack Magaha, fiddle; Joseph Babcock, Delores Edgin, June Page, vocals). Musicians on *Little Sparrow* cut: Maura O'Connell and Dolly Parton, harmony vocals; Richard Dennison, Chip Davis, Monty Allen, drones; Mark Kelly, guitar; Ciaran Curran, bouzouki; Dermot Byrne, accordion; Ciaran Tourish, low whistle; Stuart Duncan, fiddle; Jerry Douglas, resophonic guitar; Byron House, bass; John Mock, harmonium; Pat McInerney, percussion.

Porter Wagoner and Dolly Parton. *Porter Wayne and Dolly Rebecca.* RCA LSP-4305. 1970. Recorded in RCA's "Nashville Sound" Studio, Nashville, Tennessee. Producer and liner notes: Bob Ferguson. Recording engineer: Al Pachucki. Recording technician: Roy Shockley. Cover photo: Les Leverett. Musicians on "Tomorrow is Forever": George McCormick, Dale Sellers, guitar; Bobby Dyson, bass; Jerry Carrigan, drums; Hargus "Pig Robbins, piano; Pete Drake, steel guitar; Buck Trent, banjo; Johnny Gimble, Mack Magaha, fiddle; Danny Davis, William McElhiney, trumpet; vocalists: Joseph Babcock, Delores Edgin, June Page. Musicians on "Just Someone I Used to Know": George McCormick, Wayne Moss, Chip Young, guitar; Roy Huskey Jr., bass; Jerry Carrigan, drums; Hargus "Pig" Robbins, organ; Lloyd Green, steel guitar; Buck Trent, banjo; Mack Magaha, fiddle; William McElhiney, Glenn Baxter, trumpet; Hurshel Wiginton, Delores Edgin, June Page, vocals.

Dolly Parton. *As Long as I Love.* Monument. 1970.

Dolly Parton. *A Real Live Dolly.* RCA. 1970.

Porter Wagoner and Dolly Parton. *Once More.* RCA Victor LSP-4388. 1970. Recording engineer: Al Pachucki. Recording technician: Roy Shockley. Cover photo by Les Leverett. Liner notes: Louis Owens, manager, Owepar Publishing Company. "Daddy Was an Old Time Preacher Man," recorded April 21, 1970; George McCormick, Dale Sellers, Chip Young, guitar; Bobby Dyson, bass; Jerry Carrigan, drums; Hargus "Pig" Robbins, piano; Pete Drake, steel guitar; Buck Trent, banjo; Johnny Gimble, Mack Magaha, fiddle; Hurshel Wiginton, Delores Edgin, June Page, vocals.

Dolly Parton. *The Best of Dolly Parton.* RCA. 1970.

Porter Wagoner and Dolly Parton. *Two of a Kind.* RCA. 1971.

Dolly Parton. *Golden Streets of Glory.* RCA Victor LSP-4398. 1971. Producer: Bob
Ferguson. Recorded in May 1970 at RCA Studios in Nashville, Tennessee. Musi-
cians: George McCormick, Dale Sellers, Chip Young, guitar; Bobby Dyson, bass;
Jerry Carrigan, drums; Hargus "Pig" Robbins, piano; Jerry Smith, organ; Pete
Drake, steel guitar; Buck Trent, banjo; Joseph Babcock, Delores Edgin, Sonja
Montgomery, June Page, Hurshel Wiginton, vocals.

Dolly Parton. *Joshua.* RCA Victor LSP 4507. 1971. Producer: Bob Ferguson. Liner
notes and bass: Bobby Dyson.

Dolly Parton. *Coat of Many Colors.* RCA Victor LSP-4603. 1971. Producer, Bob
Ferguson. Photograph of cover painting, Les Leverett. Recording engineer, Al
Pachucki. Recording technician, Roy Shockley. Musicians on "My Blue Tears":
Dave Kirby, George McCormick, Jerry Shook, guitar; Bobby Dyson, bass; Jerry
Carrigan, drums; Pete Drake, steel guitar; Mack Magaha, Buddy Spicher, fiddle;
Buck Trent, banjo; David Briggs, Hargus "Pig" Robbins, piano; Joe Babcock,
Dolores Edgin, June Page, vocals.

Porter Wagoner and Dolly Parton. *The Right Combination/Burning the Midnight Oil.*
RCA. 1972.

Dolly Parton. *Touch Your Woman.* RCA. 1972.

Porter Wagoner and Dolly Parton. *Together Always.* RCA. 1972.

Dolly Parton. *Dolly Parton Sings My Favorite Songwriter: Porter Wagoner.* RCA.
1972.

Dolly Parton. *The World of Dolly Parton.* Monument Records. 1972. Cover design:
Bill Barnes. Photography: Lewis Lowens. Liner notes: Mike Frost. (Two-disc
compilation)

Porter Wagoner and Dolly Parton. *We Found It.* RCA. 1973.

Dolly Parton. *My Tennessee Mountain Home.* RCA APL 10033. 1973. Producer: Bob
Ferguson. Musicians: James Colvard, guitar; Dave Kirby, Jerry Stembridge, Bobby
Thompson, rhythm guitar; Pete Drake, Dobro and steel guitar; Bobby Dyson,
bass; Buck Trent, electric banjo; Johnny Gimble, Mack Magaha, fiddle; Charlie
McCoy, James Riddle, harmonica; Ron Oates, Hargus "Pig" Robbins, piano;
Jerry Carrigan, drums; the Nashville Edition, vocals. Recording engineer: Tom
Pick. Recording technician: Roy Shockley. Cover photo by Louis Owens. Back
album photo: Bill Preston. Liner notes: Avie Lee Parton, Robert Lee Parton.

Porter Wagoner and Dolly Parton. *Love and Music.* RCA APL 1-0248 Stereo. 1973.
Producer: Bob Ferguson. Recording engineer: Tom Pick. Recording technician:
Roy Shockley. Cover photo: Les Leverett. Designer: Sandi Bernstein. Art direc-
tor: Lacy Lehman. Liner notes: Carl and Pearl Butler.

Dolly Parton. *Bubbling Over.* RCA. 1973. Photography and design by Les Leverett.

Dolly Parton. *Jolene.* RCA AYL1-3898, previously released as AHL1-0473. 1974.
Producer: Bob Ferguson. Recording engineer: Tom Pick. Recording techni-
cian: Roy Shockley. Cover photo: Hope Powell. Art director: Herb Burnette.
"Jolene" musicians: Fred Carter Jr., Jimmy Colvard, Dave Kirby, guitar; Bobby
Dyson, bass; Kenny Malone, drums; Hargus "Pig" Robbins, piano; Stu Bas-
ore, steel guitar; Johnny Gimble, Mack Magaha, fiddle; June Page, Dolores
Edgin, vocals. Musicians on "I Will Always Love You" (recorded originally on
June 13, 1973): Jimmy Colvard, Dave Kirby, guitar; Bobby Dyson, bass; Larrie
Londin, drums; Hargus "Pig" Robbins, piano; Stu Basore, steel guitar; Bobby
Thompson, Buck Trent, banjo; Hurshel Wiginton, June Page, Dolores Edgin,
Joe Babcock, vocals.

Porter Wagoner and Dolly Parton. *Porter 'N' Dolly*. RCA. 1974.
Dolly Parton. *Love Is Like a Butterfly*. RCA APL1-0712. Producer: Bob Ferguson. Vocal accompaniment by the Lea Jane Singers. Recording engineer: Tom Pick. Recording technician: Roy Shockley. Recorded in RCA's Nashville Sound Studios, Nashville, Tennessee. Cover photo: Hope Powell. Cover illustration: Betty Cherry. Art director: Herb Burnette, Pinwheel Studios.
Dolly Parton. *The Bargain Store*. RCA APL 1-10980. 1975. Producers: Porter Wagoner and Bob Ferguson. Vocal accompaniment by the Lea Jane Singers. Recording engineer: Tom Pick. Recording technician: Roy Shockley. Recorded in RCA's Nashville Sound Studios, Nashville, Tennessee. Cover photo: Hope Powell. Album graphics and art director: Herb Burnette, Pinwheel Art Studios. Musicians on "The Bargain Store" (recorded December 11, 1974): Jimmy Colvard, Dave Kirby, Bruce Osbon, Bobby Thompson, guitar; Bobby Dyson, bass; D. J. Fontana, Larrie Londin, drums; John Hughey, steel guitar; Hargus "Pig" Robbins, Jerry Whitehurst, piano; Mack Magaha, fiddle; the Lea Jane Singers, vocals.
Dolly Parton. *Dolly Parton, in Concert*. RCA. 1975.
Dolly Parton. *Best of Dolly Parton*. RCA. 1975.
Dolly Parton and Porter Wagoner. *Say Forever You'll Be Mine*. RCA. 1975.
Dolly Parton. *Dolly*. RCA Victor APL1-1221. 1975. Producer: Porter Wagoner. Recording engineer: Tom Pick. Recording technician: Roy Shockley. Recorded in RCA's Nashville Sound Studios. Photography: Dennis Carney. Herb Burnette, Art director: Pinwheel Studios. Orchestration: Bill McElhiney. Vocal accompaniment: The Lea Jane Singers, the Nashville Edition. Musicians on "The Seeker": Bill McElhiney, orchestration; Jimmy Colvard, Dave Kirby, Bruce Osborn, Bobby Thompson, guitar; Bobby Dyson, bass; D. J. Fontana, drums; John Hughes, steel guitar; Hargus "Pig" Robbins, piano; Mack Magaha, fiddle; the Lea Jane Singers, vocals.
Dolly Parton. *All I Can Do*. RCA. 1976.
New Harvest . . . First Gathering. RCA Victor APL1-2188. 1977. Producers: Dolly Parton, Gregg Perry. Musicians on "Apple Jack," recorded December 10, 1976, at Creative Workshop, Nashville, Tennessee: Jimmy Colvard, Rod Smarr, guitar; Bobby Dyson, bass; Jerry Kroon, drums; Gregg Perry, piano; Dolly Parton, tambourine; Dolly Parton and Bobby Thompson, banjo; Joe McGuffee, Dobro; Terry McMillan, harmonica; Jimmy Riddle, Jew's harp; Clyde Brooks, Gregg Perry, tambourine; Bob Ferguson, Applejack's voice; Roy Acuff, Kitty Wells, Chet Atkins, Minnie Pearl, Ernest Tubb, Grandpa Jones, Ramona Jones, Carl and Pearl Butler, Wilma Lee, Stoney Cooper, the Willis Brothers, Bashful Brother Oswald, Joe and Rose Lee Maphis, Kirk McGee, Hubert Gregory and the Fruit Jar Drinkers, Johnny Wright, Don Warden, Avie Lee, Lee Parton, vocals. Musicians on "Light of a Clear Blue Morning," recorded August 19, 1976, at the Sound Shop in Nashville, Tennessee: John Pell, Rod Smarr, guitar; Charlie Chappelear, bass; Clyde Brooks, drums; Jimmy Crawford, steel guitar; Greg Perry, piano; Lea Jane Berinati, Richard Dennison, Janie Fricke, Debbie Jo Puckett, vocals.
Dolly Parton. *Here You Come Again*. RCA Victor AFL1-2544. 1977. Producer: Gary Klein, the Entertainment Company. Executive producer: Charles Koppelman. Musicians: Rhythm arranged by Dean Parks. String section and voices arranged by Nick DeCaro. Dean Parks, Dave Wolfert, Ben Benny, Jay Graydon, guitar; Dean Parks, banjo; Al Perkins, pedal steel; David Lindley, slide guitar; David

Hungate, bass; Jim Keltner, percussion; Ed Greene, drums; David Forster, keyboards and synthesizer; synthesizer programmed by Ian Underwood; Nick DeCaro, accordion; Harry Bluestone and Jimmy Getzoff, concertmasters; Dolly Parton, Marti McCall, Myrna Matthews, Jan Gassman, Zedrick Turnbough, Gene Morford, Nick DeCarlo, background vocalists. Music contractor and coordinator: Frank DeCara. Album engineered and remixed by Armin Steiner. Recorded at Sound Labs Inc, Hollywood. Assistant engineer: Linda Tyler. Capitol Recording Studios assistant engineer: Don Henderson. Mastering: Mike Reese, the Mastering Lab, Hollywood. Art direction, photography, and design: Ed Carneff. Lettering: Michael Manoogian.

Dolly Parton. *Heartbreaker*. RCA AFL1-2797. 1978. Producer: Gary Klein, with Dolly Parton for the Entertainment Company. Executive producer: Charles Koppelman. Rhythm arrangements: David Wolfert, Gregg Perry, and Dolly Parton. String arrangements: Nick DeCaro and Gregg Perry. Horn arrangements: Jerry Hey and Larry Williams. Male vocal by Richard Dennison on "We're Through Forever ('til Tomorrow)." Concertmaster: Harry Bluestone. Album coordinator and music contractor: Frank DeCaro. Recorded at Sound Labs, Inc. in Hollywood. Album engineered and remixed by Armin Steiner. Assistant engineer: Linda Tyler. Capitol Recording Studios assistant engineer: Don Henderson. Musicians: Gregg Perry, Michael Omartian, David Foster, David Paich, Mac Rebennack, piano; David Hungate, bass; Jim Keltner, drums and special effects; Paulinho deCosta, congas; Dean Parks, David Wolfert, acoustic and electric guitars; Joe McGuffee, steel guitar; Jeff Baxter, guitar synthesizer; Jerry Hey, Steve Madail, trumpets; Bill Reichenbach, trombone; Larry Williams, tenor sax and flute; Kit Hurchcroft, soprano, tenor, and baritone sax; Anita Ball, Richard Dennison, Jim Gilstrap, Augie Johnson, Myrna Matthews, Stephanie Spruill, Angela Winbush, background vocals. Art direction, photography, and design, Ed Caraeff Studio.

Dolly Parton. *Great Balls of Fire*. RCA Victor APL1-3361. 1979. Producer: Dean Parks and Gregg Perry for the Entertainment Company. Executive producers: Dolly Parton and Charles Koppelman. Engineer: Eric Prestidge. Recorded at Sound Labs Inc., assisted by Linda Tyler, A&M Recordings and Salty Dog, Los Angeles, California. Mixed at Spectrum Studios. Mastering engineer: Gernie Grundmann. Mastered at A&M Recording. Musicians: Abraham Laboriel, bass; Jim Keltner, drums and percussion; Dean Parks, guitars and alto flutes; David Foster, Michael OMartian, Bill Payne, keyboards; Gregg Perry, piano; Joe McGuffee, steel guitar; Lenny Castro, congas; Herb Pedersen, banjo; David Grisman, mandolin; Dean Parks and Gregg Perry, synthesizer; Jim Horn, Quitman Dennis, Gary Herbig, Chuck Findley, horns; Stephanie Sprill, tambourine; Earle Dumler, English horn; Dorothy Remsen, harp; Anita Ball and Richard Dennison, vocals on "Star of the Show," "It's Not My Affair Anymore," and "Do You Think That Time Stands Still;" Carol Carmichael Parks on "Almost in Love," "You're the Only One," "Sweet Summer Lovin'" and "It's Not My Affair Anymore"; Stephanie Spruill, Maxine Waters, Julia Waters, and Roy Galloway on "Star of the Show" and "Down"; Ricky Skaggs and Herb Pedersen on "Help!" Album cover costume by Distorted Reflections. Art direction, photography, and design by Ed Caraeff Studio.

Dolly Parton. *Dolly, Dolly, Dolly*. RCA. 1980

Porter Wagoner and Dolly Parton. *Porter & Dolly*. RCA. 1980.

Dolly Parton. *9 to 5 and Odd Jobs.* RCA AH1-3852. 1980. Produced and arranged by Mike Post. Associate producer: Gregg Perry. Musicians: Eddie Bayers, drums; Leland Sklar, bass; Ron Oates, keyboards; Reggie Young, guitar; Joe McGiffee, steel guitar; Ian Underwood, synthesizers; Sonny Osborne, banjo; Larry Carlton, guitar; John Gouz, slide guitar; Gregg Perry, organ; Mike Post, synthesized flute; Richard Dennison, Anita Ball, Joey Scarbury, vocals; background vocals on "Hush a Bye Hard Times," Sonny and Bobby Osborne. Concertmaster: Sid Sharp. Drill team on "Working Girl": Dolly Parton, Judy Ogle, Eddie Bayers, Reggie Young, Leland Sklar, Mike Post. Recorded at Audio Media, Nashville, Tennessee. Engineer: Marshall Morgan. Second engineer: Pat McMakin. Engineer at Mike's at Smoke Tree Ranch, Chatsworth, California: Doug Parry. Second engineer: Rick Romano. Engineer at Western Recorders, Hollywood, California: Paul Dobbe and Chuck Britz. Engineer at Studio 335, Hollywood, California: Larry Calton. Mastered at Mastering Lab, Hollywood California, by Larry Calton. Mastered at Mastering Lab, Hollywood, California, by Mike Reese. Musicians on "9 to 5": Larry Knechtel, piano; Leonard Castro, percussion; Abraham LaBroel, bass; Richard Schlosser, drums; Jeff Baxter, Martin K. Walsh, guitar; Tom Saviano, saxophone; William Reichenbach, trombone; Kim S. Hutchcroft, Bari sax; Jerry Hey, trumpet; Stephanie Sprull, Anita Ball, Denise Maynelli, vocals. Typewriter: Gregg Perry. Contractor: Frank DeCaro. Recorded at Sound Labs, Hollywood, California. Engineer: Armin Steiner. Mixed at Smoke Tree Ranch, Chatsworth, California, by Doug Parry. Art direction by Tim Bryant and George Corsillo Gribbitt. Album design: George Corsillo. Photography: Ron Slenzak. Props styling: Pie Lombardi and Michelle Elam. Hair styled by Colleen Owens. Clothes designed by Mary Malin. Makeup by Bobbe Joy.

Various Artists (including Dolly Parton). *9 to 5 Original Motion Picture Soundtrack.* 20th Century Fox Record Corporation. 1980. Music composed and original soundtrack recording produced by Charles Fox, except for "9 to 5," produced by Gregg Perry.

Dolly Parton. *Heartbreak Express.* RCA. 1982. Produced and arranged by Dolly Parton and Gregg Perry. Engineer: Doug Parry. Assistant engineer: Rick Romano. Concertmaster: Larry Bluestone. Contractor: Frank DeCaro. Musicians: Michael Severs, Fred Tackett, Jeff Baxter, Albert Lee, Steve Cropper, guitar; Lee Sklar, Nathan East, Abe Laboriel, bass; Eddy Anderson, drums; Ron Oates, Red Young, keyboards; Joe McGuffee, steel guitar; Terry McMillan, harmonica; Buddy Spicher, fiddle; Lenny Castro, congas; Tom Scott, Jim Horn, George Bohanon, Gary Grant, Tom Saviano, Chuck Findley, Slide Hyde, Gary Herbig, horns; Gregg Perry, dulcimer; Richard Dennison, Anita Ball, Jim Salestrom, Stephanie Spruill, Denise Maynelli, Nick DeCaro, Roy Galloway, Alexandra Brown, Willie Greene, Gene Morford, Gregg Perry, background vocals. "Single Women" produced and arranged by Dolly Parton and Gregg Parry. Recorded in 1981. Album recorded and mixed at Smoketree Recording Studio. Additional overdubs: Soundshop Recording Studio with engineer Ernie Winfrey. Warner Brothers Recording Studio engineer: Don Deene. Photography: Herb Ritts. Art direction: Phyllis Chotin and Michele Hart/Media Arts. Design concept: Dolly Parton. Hairstyle: Colleen Owens. Costume coordinators: Shirlee Strahm, Kendall Errair.

Various artists (with Dolly Parton). *The Best Little Whorehouse in Texas* soundtrack. MCA Records. 1982.

Dolly Parton. *Greatest Hits.* RCA. 1982.

Kris Kristofferson, Willie Nelson, Dolly Parton, and Brenda Lee. *The Winning Hand.* Monument. 1982. Producer: Fred Foster. Dolly's vocals are from 1965–67.

Dolly Parton. *Burlap and Satin.* RCA AHL1-4691. 1983. Executive producer: Dolly Parton. Producer and arranger: Gregg Perry. Art direction, photography, design: Ed Caraeff. Photographed at the Baron Margo residence. Recorded at the Sound Shop (Nashville), the Castle (Nashville), and the Record Plant (Los Angeles). Recording engineers: Ernie Winfrey, Phil Jamtaas. Assistant engineers: Fran Overall, Jim Scott. Musicians: Ron Oates, Robbie Buchanan, Mitch Humphries, Gregg Perry, keyboards; Michael Rhodes, Lee Sklar, Tommy Cogbill, bass; Michael Severs, Tom Rutledge, Pete Bordonali, Hugh McCracken, Marty Walsh, guitar; Eddy Anderson, Rick Marotta, drums; Dennis Solee, tenor sax and flute; Joe McGuffee, steel guitar; Ron Oates, synthesizer; Eddy Anderson, percussion; Dewayne Pigg, English horn; Nashville String Machine, strings; Anita Ball, Richard Dennison, Judy Rodman, Donna McElroy, Lea Jane Berinati, Karen Taylor-Good, Lisa Silver, Michael Black, Ray Walker, background vocals; Dolly Parton, Judy Ogle, Anita Ball, Judy Rodman, Ernie Winfrey, hand claps. Makeup: Cassie Seaver. Hair stylists: Colleen Owens, Donna Gilbert.

Dolly Parton. *The Great Pretender.* RCA. 1984.

Dolly Parton. *Rhinestone* soundtrack. RCA. 1984.

Dolly Parton and Kenny Rogers. *Once Upon a Christmas.* RCA. 1984.

Dolly Parton. *Real Love.* RCA. 1985.

Dolly Parton. *Think about Love.* RCA. 1986.

Dolly Parton. *Best of Dolly Parton,* vol. 3. RCA. 1987.

Dolly Parton, Emmylou Harris, and Linda Ronstadt. *Trio.* Warner Brothers 1-25491. 1987. Recorded and produced by George Massenburg. Musical consultant: John Starling. Engineering assistant: Sharon Rice. Production coordinator: Liza Edwards. Art direction and design: Kosh, Ron Larson. Photography: Robert Blakeman. Analog and digital mastering: Doug Sax, the Mastering Lab. Recorded at the Complex, West Los Angeles, January–November 1986. Additional recording: Woodland Studios, Nashville, and Ocean Way Recording, Hollywood. Musicians in addition to Parton and Harris: Albert Lee, acoustic and high strung guitar; Mark O'Connor, viola and fiddle; David Lindley, mandolin, Kona Hawaiian guitar, mandolin, and autoharp; Steve Fishell, pedal steel; Russ Kunkel, drums; Kenny Edwards, Leland Sklar, Ferrington acoustic bass; Ry Cooder, tremolo guitar; John Starling, acoustic guitar; Herb Pedersen, banjo; Bill Payne, acoustic and electric piano, harmonium and Hammond organ; David Campbell, orchestration and conducting; Charles Veal, concertmaster; Herb Pedersen, vocal arrangement on "Telling Me Lies;" Brice Martin, flute; Marty Krystall, clarinet; Ilene "Novi" Novog, viola; Dennis Karmazyn, Jodi Burnett, cello.

Dolly Parton. *Rainbow.* Columbia. 1987.

Dolly Parton. *White Limozeen.* Columbia CK 44384. 1989. Producer: Ricky Skaggs. Musicians on "Why'd You Come in Here Lookin' Like That": Mark Casstevens, Steven A. Gibson, Albert Lee, guitar: Mike Brignardello, bass; Eddie Bayers, drums; Barry Beckett, piano; Jo-El Sonnier, Cajun accordion; Ricky Skaggs, acoustic guitar, mandolin, fiddle, triangle; Curtis Young, Ricky Skaggs, vocals. Musicians on "Yellow Roses": Mark Casstevens, Steven A. Gibson, guitar; Mike Brignardello, bass; Eddie Bayers, drums; Barry Beckett, piano; Lloyd Green, steel guitar; Nashville String Machine, strings; Curtis Young, Lianna Young, Lisa Silver, Richard Dennison, vocals. Arranger: Bergen White.

Dolly Parton. *Home for Christmas.* Columbia. 1990.

Dolly Parton. *Eagle When She Flies*. Columbia CD 46882. 1991. Executive producer: Dolly Parton. Producers: Steve Buckingham, Gary Smith. Musicians on "Rockin' Years" (Dolly Parton with Ricky Van Shelton): Bruce Watkins, Kent Wells, guitar; Steve Turner, drums; Paul Uhrig, bass; Gary Smith, piano, keyboards; Jimmy Mattingly, fiddle, mandolin; Mike Davis, organ; Richard Dennison, Jennifer O'Brian, Howard Smith, vocals.

Dolly Parton. *Straight Talk* soundtrack. Hollywood. 1992.

Dolly Parton. *Slow Dancing with the Moon*. Columbia CD 53100. 1993. Producers: Steve Buckingham and Dolly Parton. Musicians (the Mighty Fine Band): Steve Turner, drums; Paul Uhrig, bass; Bruce Watkins, acoustic guitar; Paul Hollowell, piano; Kent Wells, electric guitar; Michael Davis, keyboards; Jimmy Mattingly, fiddle and mandolin; Richard Dennison, vocal arranger and background vocals; Jennifer O'Brien-Enoch, Howard Smith, Vicki Hampton, background vocals. Additional musicians: Steve Gibson, guitar, mandolin; John Barlow Jarvis, piano; John Hughes, steel guitar; Joey Miskulin, accordion; Terry McMillon, harmonica, percussion; Sonny Garrish, steel guitar; Gove Scrivenor, autoharp; Paul Franklin, steel guitar, pedalbro; Alisa Jones Wall, hammer dulcimer; Mitch Humphries, piano.

Dolly Parton, Loretta Lynn, and Tammy Wynette. *Honky Tonk Angels*. Columbia CK-53414. 1993. Producers: Steve Buckingham and Dolly Parton.

Various artists. *Red Hot and Country*. Mercury 1994. AIDS Fundraiser.

Dolly Parton. *Heartsongs: Live from Home,* Columbia/Blue Eye. 1994.

Dolly Parton. *Something Special*. Columbia, Blue Eye Records. 1995. Producers: Steve Buckingham, Dolly Parton. Musicians: Matt Rollings, Paul Hollowell, piano; Owen Hale, drums; David Hungate, Paul Uhrig, bass; Brent Mason, Brent Rowan, Stuart Smith, Steve Gibson, Don Potter, guitar; Paul Franklin, steel; Terry McMillan, percussion; Reggie Young, electric guitar; Steve Buckingham, acoustic guitar; Steve Turner, drums; Jimmy Mattingly, fiddle; Alison Krauss, Suzanne Cox, Bob Bailey, Louis Nunley, Duawne Starling, Chris Rodriguez, Pam Tillis, Vicki Hampton, Yvonne Hodges, Jennifer O'Brien-Enoch, Carl Jackson, Richard Dennison, Bob Bailey, vocals. Strings arrangement and conductor: Dale Oehler. Concertmaster: Assa Dorori.

Dolly Parton. *The Essential One*. RCA 66533-2. 1995. Compilation producer: Paul Williams. Audio restoration: Bill Lacey. Repertoire selection: Colin Escott. Sequence: Paul Williams. Digital transfers: James P. Nichols, Mike Hartry. Liner notes: Colin Escott. Art direction: Susan Eaddy. Art design: Julie Wanca, Design Solutions. Photography: RCA Records label archives, Country Music Foundation.

Dolly Parton. *I Will Always Love You and Other Greatest Hits*. Columbia. 1996.

Dolly Parton. *Treasures*. Rising Tide, Blue Eye. 1996. Producer: Steve Buckingham. Production assistant: Jennie Carey. Engineers: Gary Paczosa, Toby Seay, Al Schmitt, Marshall Morgan, Chris Tergeson. Assistant engineers: Michelle Shelby, Ed Simonton, Ken Ross, Jeff Demorris, Mel Jones. Mixed by Gary Paczosa. Recorded at Soundstage, 17 Grand, the Doghouse (Nashville), the Hit Factory (New York), Oceanway (Los Angeles). Edited by Don Cobb. Photographer: David LaChapelle. Clothing stylist: Frank Chevalier. Costume designer: Tony Chase. Hair and makeup stylist: David Blair. Art director: Virginia Team. Designer: Jerry Joyner. Musicians: Eddie Bayers, drums; David Hungate, bass, acoustic bass; Dean Parks, acoustic guitar, slide guitar; Reggie Young, electric guitar; Mark Casstevens:

acoustic guitar; Steve Buckingham, acoustic guitar, 12-string electric guitar, baritone guitar, electric guitar, mandolin; Matt Rollings, keyboard, Wurlitzer, B3; Pat McInerney, bodhran; Steve Dorff, string arrangement; Farrell Morris, shaker, marimba, vibes; Pig Robins, piano; Dan Dugmore, lap steel; Joe Spivey, fiddle; Adam Steffey, mandolin; Kim Carnes, Matraca Berg, Crystal Bernard, Andy Landis, Darci Monet, Chris Rodriguez, Louis Nunley, Bob Bailey, Chris Willis, Duawne Starling, Alison Krauss, Dan Tyminski, John Wesley Ryles, Liana Mannis, Darci Monet, Don Potter, Steve Buckingham, Jennifer O'Brien, Vicki Hampton, Richard Dennison, Dennis Wilson, Louis Nunley, vocals.

Various artists (including Dolly Parton). *Annabelle's Wish* soundtrack. Rising Tide, Blue Eye. 1997.

Dolly Parton. *Hungry Again.* Decca, Blue Eye DRND 70071. 1998. Producers: Dolly Parton and Richie Owens. Recording engineers at Train Traxx: Richie Owens, J. Allen Williams Jr. Engineers at the Doghouse: Marshall Morgan, Toby Seay. Engineer at Georgetown Masters: Denny Purcell. Musicians: Richie Owens, Dobro; guitar, autoharp, bouzouki; Gary Davis, banjo; Gary Mackey, mandolin; Eric Ruper, Mark Brooks, bass; Bob Grudner, drums; Al Perkins, steel guitar; Bob Ocker, electric guitar; Rhonda Vincent, Darrin Vincent, Richard Dennison, Jennifer O'Brien, Joy Gardner, Louis Nunley, Richie Owens, Brian Waldschlager, Judy Ogle, Teresa Hughes, Ira Parker, Louis Babaker, Jimmy Boling and the House of Prayer Congregation, David, Bobby, Rachel, Randy, Cassie, Willodeene, Lee, and Dolly Parton, vocals.

Dolly Parton, Emmylou Harris, and Linda Ronstadt. *Trio II.* Asylum, Elektra 62275-2. 1999. Producer: George Massenburg. Associate producer: John Starling. Production assistants: Gail Rosman and Janet Start. Recorded by Massenburg and Nathaniel Kunkel at the Site, in Marin County, California. Mixed by Massenburg and Ronstadt, with additional mixing done at Petewood/Georkel. Recording in Williamson County, Tennessee. Mastered at Doug Sax at the Mastering Lab in Hollywood. Production archivist: John Brenes. Art direction and design by Kosh and Lyn Bradley, with art administration by Michael Hagewood. Musicians: Jim Keltner, road case; Roy Huskey Jr., Leland Sklar, Edgar Meyer, bass; Carl Jackson, Mark Casstevens, acoustic guitar; David Lindley, autoharp; David Grisman, mandolin; Alison Krauss, fiddle; Larry Atamanuik, Jim Keltner, drums; Robby Buchanan, acoustic piano, Rhodes organ; Helen Voices, synthesizers; Dennis James, glass harmonica; string arrangements, Linda Ronstadt; Dean Parks, electric guitar; Ben Keith, steel guitar.

Dolly Parton. *Precious Memories.* Blue Eye. 1999.

Dolly Parton. *The Grass Is Blue.* Sugar Hill, Blue Eye SUG-CD 3900. 1999. Producer: Steve Buckingham. Musicians: Jerry Douglas, Dobro; Stuart Duncan, fiddle; Barry Bales, bass; Sam Bush, mandolin; Bryan Sutton, guitar; Jim Mills, banjo.

Dolly Parton. *Little Sparrow.* Sugar Hill, Blue Eye SUG-CD 3927. 2001. Producer: Steve Buckingham. Musicians: Mike Snider, clawhammer banjo; Jim Mills, banjo; Stuart Duncan, fiddle; Barry Bales, bass; Jerry Douglas, resophonic guitar; Bryan Sutton, Mark Kelly, Daithi Sproule, guitar; Chris Thile, mandolin; Dermot Byrne, accordion; Ciaran Tourish, low whistle; Steve Buckingham, dulcimer, autoharp; John Mock, whistle; Marcia Campbell, Bubba Richardson, Pat McInerney, percussion; Ciaran Curran, bouzouki; Marcia Campbell and Bubba Richardson, clog dancers; Sonya Isaacs, Becky Isaacs Bowman, Rebecca Lynn Howard, Carl Jackson, Alison Krauss, Dan Tyminski, Claire Lynch, Keith Little,

Maura O'Connell, Richard Dennison, Chip Davis, Monty Allen, Mairead NiMh-aonaighi, vocals.

Dolly Parton. *Halos and Horns.* Sugar Hill, Blue Eye SUG-CD 2946. 2002. Producer: Dolly Parton. Assistant producers: Gary Davis and the Blueniques. Musicians (the Blueniques): Jimmy Mattingly, fiddle; Brent Truitt, mandolin; Gary Davis, banjo; Steve Turner, drums, washboard, tambourine; Terry Eldredge, bass; Kent Wells, guitar; Randy Kohrs, resophonic guitar, Weissenborn guitar; Richard Dennison, guitar. Additional musicians: Kent Wells, Robert Hale, guitar; Bob Carlin, clawhammer banjo; Darrell Webb, Brent Truitt, mandolin; David Sutton, harmonica; Steve Turner, Dolly Parton, Richard Dennison, the Kingdom Heirs (Steven French, Arthur Rice, David Sutton, Eric Bennett), Randy Kohrs, Terry Eldredge, Jennifer O'Brien, Vicki Hampton, Beth Stevens, April Stevens, vocals.

Dolly Parton. *Ultimate Dolly Parton.* BMG Heritage. 2003.

Various artists with Dolly Parton. *Just Because I'm a Woman: Songs of Dolly Parton.* Sugar Hill 3980. 2003. Executive producer: Steve Buckingham. Lead vocals: Alison Krauss, Melissa Etheridge, Norah Jones, Joan Osborne, Shelby Lynne, Mindy Smith, Emmylou Harris, Shania Twain with Alison Krauss and Union Station, Kasey Chambers, Sinead O'Connor, Allison Moorer, Me'Shell N'Degeocelo, Dolly Parton.

Dolly Parton. *For God and Country.* Welk Music Group, Blue Eye Records. 2003. Producers: Dolly Parton with Kent Wells and Tony Smith. Musicians: Bruce Watkins, Kent Wells, Robert Hale, guitar; Gary Davis, banjo; Charlie Anderson, Jay Weaver, bass; Randy Kohrs, Dobro; Steve Turner, Billy Thomas, drums and percussion; Jimmy Mattingly, fiddle and mandolin; Darrel Webb, mandolin; Paul Hollowell, Michael Davis, piano and Hammond B-3; Michael Davis, Tony Smith, synthesizer programming. Vocals on "Whispering Hope": The Harding University Concert Choir and Dallas Christian Sound. Vocals on "Peace in the Valley": The Fairfield Four.

Dolly Parton. *Live and Well.* Sugar Hill, Blue Eye SUG-CD-3998. 2004. 2-CD set and DVD. Recorded live at the Celebrity Theater in Dollywood (Pigeon Forge, TN) December 12–13, 2002. Producers: Dolly Parton with Gary Davis and the Blueniques. Musicians: Jimmy Mattingly, fiddle; Brent Truitt, mandolin; Randy Kohrs, Dobro, harmony vocals; Gary Davis, banjo, acoustic guitar; Steve Turner, drums; Jay Weaver, upright bass; Richard Dennison, keyboards, acoustic guitar, harmony vocals; Kent Wells, electric guitar, acoustic guitar, harmony vocals. Production and road manager: Don Warden. Production assistants: Danny Brown, Gary Davis, Teresa Hughes. Hair: Cheryl Riddle. Wardrobe: Judy Ogle. Teleprompter: Janet Humphreys. Production manager at Dollywood: Scott Lawhead. Photography by Dennis Carney. Design by Sue Meyer. Mixed at Southern Sound Studio by Danny Brown. Mastered at Soundcurrent Mastering by Seva.

Dolly Parton. *Those Were the Days.* Blue Eye/Sugar Hill. 2005.

Dolly Parton. *The Acoustic Collection: 1999–2002.* Blue Eye/Sugar Hill. 2006. Compilation of *The Grass Is Blue, Little Sparrow, Halos and Horns.*

Dolly Parton. *Singer Songwriter and Legendary Performer Dolly Parton.* Dolly Records. 2007. Distributed free in London newspaper to promote European tour.

Dolly Parton. *The Very Best of Dolly Parton.* Sony BMG. 2007.

Dolly Parton. *Dolly Parton: 16 Biggest Hits.* Sony BMG. 2007.

Dolly Parton. *Backwoods Barbie.* Dolly Records. 2008. Producers: Kent Wells and Dolly Parton. All tracks except "Only Dreamin'" and 'Shinola" recorded at

Blackbird Studio A by Patrick Murphy, assisted by Allen Ditto, Kyle Dickinson, and Ben "Snake" Schmitt. "Only Dreamin'" recorded at Kent Wells productions by Ben "Snake" Schmitt and Kyle Dickinson. "Only Dreamin'" strings recorded at Sound Kitchen by Patrick Murphy, assisted by Kyle Dickinson and Ben "Snake" Schmitt. "Shinola" recorded at Emerald Studio A by Patrick Murphy, assisted by Kyle Dickinson and Ben "Snake" Schmitt. Mixed by Justin Niebaunk, assisted by Drew Bollman. Editing by Patrick Murphy, Kyle Dickinson, Ben "Snake" Schmitt, and Brian Willis. Mastered by Jim DeMain and Alex McCullough at Yes Master. Production assistant: Christine Winslow. Art direction and photos: Kii Arens. Conceptual assistants: Steve Summers and Stephen Shareaux. Lighting: Trever Gens. Photo assistant: Pat Blewett. Makeup: Valorie W. Cole. Costume design: Robert Behar. Hair: Cheryl Riddle. Musicians: Paul Hollowell, piano, organ, B3, Yamaha Motif; Jerry McPherson, Kent Wells, electric guitar; Bryan Sutton, Kent Wells, acoustic guitar; Steve Mackey, bass; Jimmy Mattingly, fiddle, mandolin; David Talbot, banjo; Lonnie Wilson, drums, percussion; Paul Franklin, Terry Crisp, steel guitar; Tom Bukovac, electric guitar; Biff Watson, acoustic guitar; Mike Brignardello, bass; Steve Turner, drums, percussion; Aubrey Haynie, mandolin; Lloyd Green, steel guitar; Lonnie Wilson, drums, percussion; Kristen Wilkinson, string arrangement; Craig Nelson; percussion, Sam Bacco; tin whistle, bodhran, harmonium: John Mock; Sonya Isaacs, Rebecca Isaacs Bowman, Richard Dennison, Vicki Hampton, Jennifer O'Brien, Dolly Parton, Carl Jackson, Alecia Nugent, Terry Eldredge, Jamie Johnson, Rhonda Vincent, Darrin Vincent, Christine Winslow, Billy Davis, Marty Slayton, vocals. Orchestral music preparation: Stephen Lamb.

Dolly Parton. *Playlist: The Very Best Of Dolly Parton*. Sony BMG. 2008.

Dolly Parton. *Sha-Kon-O-Hey! Land of Blue Smoke*. Dolly Records. 2009.

Dolly Parton. *Dolly*. RCA Nashville/Legacy Recordings. 2009. 99-song boxed set. Compilation producer: Rob Santos. Mastered by Vic Anesini at Battery Studios and Sony Music Studios, New York Legacy A&R, by Steve Berkowitz. "Everything Is Beautiful (in Its Own Way)," "God's Coloring Book," "Eugene Oregon," "What Will Baby Be" mixed by Steve Rosenthal at the Magic Shop, New York. Assistant engineer: Ted Young. Projection direction: Gretchen Brennison. Project marketing: Iris Maenza and Mandy Eidgah. Art direction and design: Frank Harkins. Photo research: Jessica Connelly and Elizabeth McShea. Introduction: Laura Cantrell. Liner notes and testimonials: Holly George-Warren.

Dolly Parton. *Dolly: Live From London*. Dolly Records. 2009.

Dolly Parton. *Letter to Heaven: Songs of Faith and Inspiration*. RCA Nashville, Legacy. 2010. Material originally recorded in 1970 and 1971. Deborah Evans Price, liner notes. Photographers: Les Leverett, Michael Ochs Archives/Getty Images, Raeanne Rubenstein, Michael A. Norcia/Globe Photos Inc.

DISCOGRAPHY NOTE SOURCES: Duane Gordon, www.dollymania. net; Sugar Hill Records; www.dollypartonmusic.net; liner notes on various albums.

Notes

INTRODUCTION

1. Duane Gordon, www.dollymania.net.

CHAPTER 1

1. Holly George-Warren, liner notes to *Dolly*, RCA Nashville/Legacy, 2009, 11.

2. Ibid. (quote from Dolly Parton, *Dolly: My Life and Other Unfinished Business* [New York: Harper Collins, 1994]).

3. "The Songwriter's Craft," exhibit, Country Music Hall of Fame and Museum, Nashville, Tennessee.

4. Ibid.

5. "Biography," official website of Dolly Parton, www.DollyPartonMusic.com.

6. "The Songwriter's Craft."

7. Alanna Nash, *Dolly, The Biography* (New York: Cooper Square Press, 2002), 38–39, quoting from a 1977 article written by Chet Flippo for *Rolling Stone* magazine.

8. Nash, *Dolly, The Biography*, 29.

9. George-Warren, liner notes, 11.

10. Nash, *Dolly, The Biography*, 38–39.

11. Eddie Shuler, liner notes to *Dolly Parton and Friends at Goldband*, Goldband LP 7770, 1959.

12. Edd Hurt, "Dolly Parton, Queen of the Backwoods," *American Songwriter*, January/February 2008, 70.

13. Fred Foster, interview by Nancy Cardwell, January 2010, Nashville, Tennessee.

14. Fred Foster, liner notes from *Hello, I'm Dolly*, Monument MLP8085, 1967.

15. Nash, *Dolly, The Biography*, 1.

16. Ibid., 25.

17. "The Songwriter's Craft."

18. Ibid.

CHAPTER 2

1. Marvin Kaye, "Country Music's Royal Couple," Show-Biz Spotlight, *Grit*, March 19, 1973.

2. Jack Hurst, "Dolly Parton: Blonde Bombshell of Great Smokies," *Nashville Tennessean*, September 27, 1970, 4.

3. Ibid.

4. Ibid.

5. Buck Trent, interview by author, Branson, Missouri, April 3, 2010.

6. Buck Trent, *Buck Trent, Entertaining You for Over 50 Years* (Banjo Enterprises, Inc., www.bucktrent.com).

7. Les Leverett, interview by author, Nashville, Tennessee, December 29, 2009.

8. Porter Wagoner, interview by Rob Simbeck for *American Music Legends* (Lebanon, TN: Cumberland Records, 2005), 98.

9. Ray Waddell, "The Importance of Being Dolly," *Billboard*, April 26, 2008.

10. Tom T. and Dixie Hall, interview by author, Franklin, Tennessee, September 2010.

11. "The Songwriter's Craft," exhibit, Country Music Hall of Fame and Museum, Nashville, Tennessee.

12. Ibid.

13. *Anderson (Indiana) Herald*, February 18, 1975.

CHAPTER 3

1. Robert Christgau, "Robert Christgau, Dean of American Rock Critics," www.robertchristgau.com. Quote also appears in Edd Hurt, "Dolly Parton, Queen of the Backwoods," *American Songwriter*, January/February 2008, 69.

CHAPTER 4

1. Alanna Nash, *Dolly, The Biography* (New York: Cooper Square Press, 2002), 20–21.

2. Jack Hurst, "Dolly Parton: Blonde Bombshell of Great Smokies," *Nashville Tennessean*, September 27, 1970, 4.

3. Nash, *Dolly, The Biography*, 18.

4. Duane Gordon, www.dollymania.net.

5. Nash, *Dolly, The Biography*, 20–21.

6. Ibid., 21.

7. Ibid., 20–21.

CHAPTER 5

1. Keith Herrell, "Tour Is Step in Dolly's Quest," *Evansville (Indiana) Press*, January 18, 1975.

2. Ibid.

3. Duane Gordon, "Frequently Asked Questions," www.dollymania.net.

4. Fred Vail, interview with Nancy Cardwell, February 20, 2010, Nashville, Tennessee.

CHAPTER 6

1. John Starling, telephone interview with Nancy Cardwell, February 20, 2010.

CHAPTER 7

1. Duane Gordon, "Frequently Asked Questions," www.dollymania.net.

2. Laura Bly, "Hooray for Dollywood: Tennessee Theme Park Celebrates 25th Anniversary," www.usa.com, May 25, 2010.

3. Pat Gallager, "Dolly Parton's '9 to 5: The Musical' Opens in Nashville," AOL The Boot, www.theboot.com, September 17, 2010.

4. Fiona Soltes, "Parton Right at Home Writing Musical, Just as '9 to 5' is at Home at TPAC," *The Tennessean*, September 19, 2010.

5. Ibid.

CHAPTER 8

1. Alanna Nash, review of *Hungry Again*, Amazon.com. Based on 1997 interview.

2. Steve Buckingham, interview by Nancy Cardwell, April 6, 2010, Nashville, Tennessee.

3. Bill Conger, "In Session with Stuart Duncan," *Bluegrass Unlimited*, October 2008, 43.

CHAPTER 9

1. Edd Hurt, "Queen of the Backwoods," *American Songwriter*, January/February 2008, 68.

2. Ray Wadell, "The Importance of Being Dolly, *Billboard*, April 26, 2008, 32.

3. Ibid., 31.

4. Ibid., 32.

5. Hurt, "Queen of the Backwoods," 73.

6. Meg Grant, "How Dolly Does It," *AARP*, May 2009, www.aarp.com.

7. Ibid.

8. Ibid.

9. Hurt, "Queen of the Backwoods," 72.

10. Michael McCall, "A Hefty New Collection Reflects the Many Facets of Dolly Parton's Talent," *Nashville Scene*, October 20, 2009.

11. Duncan Mansfield, "Call Her Dr. Dolly," *The Tennessean*, May 9, 2009, 3A.

12. Dolly Parton, *I Am a Rainbow* (New York: Putnam, 2009),

13. Jamie Johnson (The Grascals), interview by Nancy Cardwell, June 25, 2010, Nashville, Tennessee.

14. Terry Smith (The Grascals), interview by Nancy Cardwell, June 26, 2010, Nashville, Tennessee.

15. Marty Stuart, liner notes from *Dolly*, RCA Nashville/Legacy, 2009.

Bibliography

Anderson (Indiana) Herald, February 18, 1975.

Bly, Laura. "Hooray for Dollywood: Tennessee Theme Park Celebrates 25th Anniversary." *USA Today*. May 25, 2010. www.usa.com.

Christgau, Robert. "Robert Christgau, Dean of American Rock Critics." www.robertchristgau.com.

Conger, Bill. "In Session with Stuart Duncan." *Bluegrass Unlimited*, October 2008, 43.

Flippo, Chet. "Dolly Parton." *Rolling Stone*, August 15, 1977, 32–38.

Gallager, Pat. "Dolly Parton's '9 to 5: The Musical' Opens in Nashville. AOL The Boot. www.theboot.com, September 17, 2010.

Gordon, Duane. www.dollymania.net

Grant, Meg. "How Dolly Does It." *AARP*, May 2009.

Herrell, Keith. "Tour Is Step in Dolly's Quest." *The Evansville Press*, January 18, 1975.

Hurst, Jack. "Dolly Parton: Blonde Bombshell of Great Smokies." *The Nashville Tennessean*, September 27, 1970.

Hurt, Edd. "Dolly Parton, Queen of the Backwoods." *American Songwriter*, January/February 2008, 66–73.

Kaye, Marvin. "Country Music's Royal Couple." Show-Biz Spotlight. *Grit*, March 19, 1973.

Mansfield, Duncan. "Call Her Dr. Dolly." *The Tennessean*, May 9, 2009.

McCall, Michael. "A Hefty New Collection Reflects the Many Facets of Dolly Parton's Talent." *The Nashville Scene*, October 20, 2009.

Nash, Alanna. *Dolly, The Biography*. Los Angeles: Reed Books, 1978.

Nash, Alanna. *Dolly, The Biography*. New York: Cooper Square Press, 2002.

Parton, Dolly. *Dolly: My Life and Other Unfinished Business*. New York: Harper Collins, 1994.

Parton, Dolly. Biography. www.DollyPartonMusic.com.

Parton, Dolly. *I Am a Rainbow.* New York: Putnam, 2009.

Simbeck, Rob. "Porter Wagoner." *American Music Legends* (Lebanon, TN: Cumberland Records, 2005.

Soltes, Fiona. "Parton Right at Home Writing Musical, Just as '9 to 5' Is at Home at TPAC." *The Tennessean,* September 19, 2010.

Trent, Buck. *Buck Trent, Entertaining You for Over 50 Years.* DVD. Branson, MO: Banjo Enterprises, Inc.

Wadell, Ray. "The Importance of Being Dolly." *Billboard,* April 26, 2008.

Index

About the Author

NANCY CARDWELL edits publications and manages professional development and leadership programs for the International Bluegrass Music Association. She also freelances as a musician, songwriter, and journalist in Nashville. Originally from the Missouri Ozarks, Cardwell grew up in an old-time/bluegrass family band and has worked previously as a teacher and a professional Girl Scout. She is the 2006 recipient of the Charles Lamb Award for Excellence in Country Music Journalism from the International Country Music Academic Conference and a graduate of both Leadership Music and Leadership Bluegrass. She holds a BS in education from Northwest Missouri State University (English, Spanish), and she has been writing professionally about music since 1980.